Searching the Soul of *Ally McBeal*

Searching the Soul of *Ally McBeal*

Critical Essays

EDITED BY ELWOOD WATSON

McFarland & Company, Inc., Publishers
Jefferson, North Carolina, and London

LIBRARY OF CONGRESS CATALOGUING-IN-PUBLICATION DATA

Searching the soul of *Ally McBeal* : critical essays / edited by
    Elwood Watson.
        p.   cm.
    Includes bibliographical references and index.

    ISBN-13: 978-0-7864-2527-3
    ISBN-10: 0-7864-2527-X (softcover : 50# alkaline paper) ∞

    1. Ally McBeal (Television program)   2. Sex role on
television.   I. Watson, Elwood.
PN1992.77.A533S43   2006
791.45'72 — dc22   2006017649

British Library cataloguing data are available

On the cover: Calista Flockhart as Fox Television's Ally McBeal (Photofest)

Manufactured in the United States of America

McFarland & Company, Inc., Publishers
    Box 611, Jefferson, North Carolina 28640
    www.mcfarlandpub.com

To my fellow contributors,
for their patience and
dedication to this project

Table of Contents

Preface

> "I am Human. I am Temperamental. I am Guilty."
> — Ally McBeal

Surreal comedy, occasional gut-wrenching drama, dancing babies, gaspy quirkiness, and babes, hunks and average Joes behaving badly at times. These were just a few situations that were a part of *Ally McBeal.* The immensely popular television series by producer David E. Kelley that ran on Fox from 1997 to 2002 was both groundbreaking and controversial in many ways. The mostly atypical and largely dysfunctional law firm of Cage and Fish was the setting where more than a half dozen Generation X attorneys and a few youngish baby boomers would support, antagonize, ridicule and argue with one another about the high and low points of their lives. It was a place where anything could happen and many things did. After all, on how many other shows could you be subjected to topics including genital size, dancing babies, cappuccino foam, unisex bathrooms and micro miniskirts?[1]

After only a few episodes, the program became a lightning rod for discussion in various quarters. Single women, feminist groups, single men, attorneys, academics, media critics and Generation Xers were all touched by and talking about the show. It seemed that more than a few people had an opinion about Ally McBeal, either the character or the series. The program spawned a plethora of op-ed pieces, panel discussions, college seminars, avant-garde chat rooms, ad hoc *Ally McBeal* debating societies and *Ally McBeal* bar nights,[2] all-female dinners and slumber parties as well as a late 20th century renaissance of the status of professional career women. The show was a perennial topic in young female adult magazines as well as in psychology magazines and journals. In 1998, *Time* magazine ran a cover story with photos of Susan B. Anthony; Betty Friedan, author of the groundbreaking 1963 classic, *The Feminine Mystique*[3]; Gloria Steinem; and Calista Flockhart (AKA Ally McBeal). It was headlined "Is Feminism

1

Dead?"[4] The ensuing controversy managed to help *Ally McBeal* become the most talked about popular hit of the 1997–1998 television season.

To a number of critics, *Ally McBeal* was a hybrid dramedy constructed from many previous television programs which showcased single women, such as the pensive Donna Reed and the cheerful, optimistic Ann Marie of *That Girl* of the late 1960s, the feminine career women Mary Tyler Moore and Rhoda Morgenstern of the 1970s and the divorced Molly Dodd of the 1980s.[5] The truth is that Ally was a little bit of all these women. At times, she was the reserved and dutiful Donna Reed, the frantic yet humorous Mary Tyler Moore, the independent, no-nonsense strident feminist Rhoda Morgenstern and the unpredictable Molly Dodd, although, many times, she appeared to yearn for the life of June Cleaver, the doting, loving suburban wife of the 1950s with two perfect kids and a strong, confident, virile husband. June Cleaver always seemed to be content within the domestic sphere of motherhood and the comfort of a man who provided handsomely for her and her family.

It was this perceived image of desperation, coupled with Ally's (and her female co-workers') constant, wanton pursuit of "Mr. Right," that prompted many women's groups to label the show "anti-feminist." Moreover, Flockhart's increasingly wafer-thin image coupled with her subsequent passing out on the set during the show's second season further charged some Ally critics to argue that she was complicit in promoting dangerously unhealthy images for young women.[6]

Not since *All in the Family,* which premiered on CBS in January 1971, can I recall a television show that from its infancy was so controversial. *Ally McBeal* explored the conflicts and contradictions about women's roles in post-feminist Western culture the way *All in the Family* explored bigotry and the generation gap during a prior time of social change. *Ally McBeal* garnered more criticism for its presentation of feminist issues than any other program. One journalist went so far as to as to argue, *"Ally McBeal,* even more than the other shows, has been embraced as a canonical statement of post feminist exhilaration."[7] Other journalists argued that the show undoubtedly connected with more than a few professional, twentysomething women of all races and ethnicities who harbored conflicting emotions of satisfaction and anxiety about the choices that were provided for them due to the feminist movement.[8] Indeed, as a man who considers himself a feminist, I found myself arguing with fellow feminists (mostly women) about the often ambiguous messages the show espoused at times.

More than a few lawyers as well as aspiring attorneys made their opinions about the show known. Interviews conducted with a number of groups involved in the legal profession indicated that while a large majority found the show amusing and entertaining, they were concerned that it gave many law students and others aspiring to a legal career a misguided impression of what working in a law firm is like, particularly for young, newly minted junior associates fresh out of law school. There is no doubt that the often 60-plus hour weeks researching through dusty old legal records and taking on tedious legal cases were a far cry from the enticing situations, dramatic adventures and frequent sexual banter that the associates at Cage and Fish found themselves engaged in.

While there have been a number of law programs, such as *L.A. Law, Law and Order, The District, Courthouse,* and *The Practice* to name a few, the fact is that *Ally McBeal* was distinct from many of them in that its principal character was a woman. Moreover, it was also unique in the fact that it was the first legal "dramedy."[9] Despite these differences, it was similar to its predecessors in that it frequently worked several cogent themes of the human condition into its program — happiness, sorrow, uncertainty, insecurity, sexuality and intimacy, and so on. As a young, single, Generation X college professor beginning my first teaching job the same year *Ally McBeal* premiered, I identified with many of the challenges that the character faced even though the series was far-fetched and, at times, seemed to venture into the "twilight zone." The program often became the focus of e-mail and telephone conversations with friends of both genders. Most of the conversations were amusing, but some episodes left us pondering serious questions about what we believed our personal *and* professional futures held for us. I then found out that several of my graduate students, almost as many males as females, were fans, and we watched a few episodes together.

Due to the program's success, many critics thought that there would be a number of *Ally* clones populating television screens the following season. As a matter of fact, there were hardly any. There are probably several reasons for this, one being that the show was so original that it was hard to emulate. The chemistry between the cast members was fabulous and the themes of the show always teetered on the brink. Perhaps this is why the program ranked among the top three programs with the 18–34 demographic.[10] The show received an Emmy award for outstanding comedy series during the 1998–1999 television season. It was also one of the few shows to win a prestigious Peabody award.

Ally McBeal was also unique in the way it used music and the way it presented relationships, sexuality and physical disabilities. From the soulful R&B crooning of Barry White and Al Green, to the gospel sounds of Jennifer Holiday, to the intellectual, deeply engaging music of rock legend Sting, to the sentimental, deeply heartfelt lyrics of perennial guest Vonda Shepard, *Ally McBeal* employed music like no other program to date with the exception of the short-lived ABC program *Cop Rock.*[11] The program presented gender issues, including cross-dressing, violently aggressive women, hopelessly timid men, transgender issues and women's biological clocks, to name a few. Health issues such as obesity, Tourette's syndrome and aging were given attention, even though outlandishly at times.

Another aspect of the program that accounted for its immense popularity in its earlier seasons was that it so cleverly employed and analyzed many symbols and mores of everyday human life, even if some of them were considered taboo. The program's treatment of racial issues was particularly noteworthy.

Due to its racially diverse ensemble, *Ally McBeal* escaped the NAACP's 1998–1999 report of programs that lacked sufficient diversity.[12] Racial tension seemed to be absent from the program. Ally's roommate was sexy, voluptuous, African American Generation X district attorney Renee Raddick, played by Lisa Nicole Carson. During season two, a new cast member, Ling Woo, played by Asian American actress Lucy Liu, joined the cast. It was also during this season that Ally became involved with a black doctor named Greg Butters, played by *Law and Order* actor Jesse L. Martin.

In a society where people are still often segregated along racial lines, interracial mixing and dating seemed to be nothing out of the ordinary for this group of young people. In spite of this image of a racial utopia, the show, whether intentionally or not, managed to promote long-standing historical racial and gender stereotypes. Among them: the sassy, strong, trash talking, "take no stuff" black woman; the dragon-like, aggressive, cold and aloof Asian woman; the supposedly well-endowed African American man as the sexy buck; the icy, self-centered blonde; the neurotic short man; the sexist, insecure single man; the sexist, dominating married man; the big-breasted, promiscuous woman; and the occasional interlopers, usually above-average looking men, who frequently became involved with one of the female lawyers much to the chagrin of the male lawyers.

The program ended its first two years to critical acclaim and a host of awards. By season three, there were critics who began to argue that the show had lost its original luster. Some went so far as to call the third and fifth seasons "disastrous."[13] Despite its increasing number of critics, the show still managed to have a loyal core of fans that stayed until the end. Robert Downey, Jr.,'s appearance during season four garnered him a Golden Globe award and temporarily silenced the critics who forecasted the slow demise of a once groundbreaking show. By its fifth and final season, ratings had dropped 24 percent among the coveted 18–49-year-old demographic and the program ran its last episode on May 20, 2002.[14]

During its five-year run, the show firmly established its place as one of the most innovative and critiqued in history. To paraphrase one critic:

• The show spawned countless debates about the state of contemporary feminism and the state of marriage.

• Viewers could count on seeing a colorful array of entertainers such as Sting, Al Green, Christina Ricci, Dame Edna, Dyan Cannon, Vanessa Williams, Robert Downey, Jr., Jon Bon Jovi, Taye Diggs and Bernadette Peters. Several of these stars appeared in the same episode. Very few, if any, other shows have pulled off such innovative casting.

• Ally's boss, Richard Fish, introduced us to the wattle (see page 192), causing us to look at older women — and particularly at attorney general Janet Reno— in a remarkable new way.

• The dancing baby, Baby Cha-Cha, created by software company Kinetix, was brought into the mainstream by *Ally McBeal.* Imitators such as Rasta Baby and drunken baby soon hit the market.[15]

Ally McBeal was intelligent and smart.

She was cautious.
She was foolish.

She was responsible.
She was careless.

She was strong-willed.
She was flexible.

She was indecisive.
She was precise.

She was self-absorbed.
She was sympathetic.

She was poised.
She was neurotic.

She was good and she was bad.

Whether one loved, hated or was ambivalent toward the show, there is no doubt that Ally McBeal was one of the most memorable television characters to hit the television screen in some time. As the essays in this anthology prove, the highly innovative program that introduced her to us will be talked about for generations to come.

—*Elwood Watson*, June 2006

Notes

1. Benjamin Svetkey, "Everything You Love or Hate About *Ally McBeal,*" *Entertainment Weekly,* January 30, 1998.

2. Tim Appelo, *Ally McBeal: The Official Guide* (New York: HarperCollins, 1999).

3. Betty Friedan, *The Feminine Mystique* (New York: W.W. Norton, 1963).

4. Gina Bellafante, "Feminism. It's All About Me!" *Time,* June 29, 1998, 54–61.

5. Many critics have referred to *The Days and Nights of Molly Dodd,* which ran on *Lifetime* television from 1987 to 1991 and starred Blair Brown, as the 1980s version of *Ally McBeal.*

6. A number of news organizations and magazines reported and speculated on Calista Flockhart's weight and subsequent passing out on the set of *Ally McBeal.*

7. Ruth Shalit, "Cagney and Lacy: Betrayal of post feminism in TV portrayals of women," *The New Republic,* April 6, 1998, p. 27–33.

8. Veronica Chambers, "How Would Ally do it?" *Newsweek,* March 2, 1998, pp. 58–61.

9. The term "dramedy" defines a television program that is both comedic and dramatic in its scope.

10. During four of the five seasons that it ran on Fox television, *Ally McBeal* managed to secure such high ratings.

11. *Cop Rock* was a show that was created by producer Stephen Bochco and ran on ABC during the fall of 1990.

12. In the fall of 1998, former NAACP president Kweisi Mfume held a press conference decrying the fact that none of the new fall programs had an African American, Hispanic or Asian character in any leading or supporting role. He further admonished the networks, stating that they were either "clueless, careless or both."

13. Robert Bianco, "'Ally' exit is more proof of Kelley's excesses," *USA Today,* May 20, 2002, p. 2D.

14. Nicolas Fonseca, "Court Adjourned: How *Ally McBeal* struck a nerve before getting FOX's gavel," *Entertainment Weekly,* May 3, 2002, p. 35.

15. Ibid.

Introduction

David Payson

David E. Kelley's *Ally McBeal* attracted a tidal wave of popular attention during its five-year run on the Fox television network, and will attract scholarly attention for years to come. The program's controversial address to feminism embodied by a title character who is simultaneously a well-educated, competent professional, and a neurotic, love-starved, provocatively dressed and strikingly thin woman drew great attention from the popular press and media critics in the United States and abroad. Perhaps the most powerful sign of the series' prominence in American media is that its title character was featured on the June 29, 1998, cover of *Time* magazine in the company of three historical figures in the feminist movement, underscored by the headline "Is Feminism Dead?" The series also garnered press attention in many countries around the world. In Finland, for example, there was heated discussion in the press about the assault upon the ideal of Finnish womanhood manifest in the character of *Ally McBeal*. The series' presentation of the character of Ally, and indeed the program's entire cast, has placed *Ally McBeal* in the epicenter of the ever-expanding international debate over feminism and roles of women in modern society. This television series' role as the ignition point of such lively and widespread debate is reason enough to dedicate critical scholarly attention to it.

While *Ally McBeal*'s challenging presentation of issues regarding gender roles and gender politics places the program in that small rank of Prime Time American television series that have broken with convention to wrestle with controversial, timely issues of social concern, this is not the only attribute of the program that will make it stand out in the history of American television programming. *Ally McBeal*'s narrative structure is as controversial as its content. Prime Time television is built upon a foundation of strict adherence to generic formulas. Change comes infrequently to net-

7

work television, most often with the introduction of a new generic formula. Reality programming is the most recent example of this. It is very rare for a program that mixes formulas to succeed. Producer David E. Kelley has successfully mixed generic elements taken from the now-established television dramedy form with elements of surrealist magical reality taken from literature and elements of the Hollywood musical in *Ally McBeal*. One need only consider the very conservative history of commercial television programming in the United States to appreciate the significance and potential consequences of Kelley's achievement here.

The three national radio networks — ABC, NBC, and CBS — that had the most to do with bringing television to the public planned to use it as they did radio, as a means of generating profit by attracting the largest possible audiences to advertising associated with programming. The networks did this in part by directly transplanting successful genres of radio programming, and in many cases particular programs, including dramas, melodramas, comedies, game shows, and variety shows, into this new medium. The strength of the conservative impulse in commercial television with regard to generic form is confirmed by the fact that these program genres imported from radio are still dominant forces in American television.

The networks' marketing philosophy of appealing to the most and offending the least, a part of the bid for the largest possible audience, was also imported from radio to television. To the extent possible networks kept programming content safely within the uncontroversial mainstream. Some programming from the first Golden Age of television, exemplified by such live dramas as *Twelve Angry Men* and *Marty*, broke with this conservative stance. This type of program was born in some part out of the networks' inexperience with and willingness to experiment with the new medium, but in larger part out of desperation to fill television schedules in a time before the development of the highly efficient three-camera studio recording technique and in the face of the film industry's unwillingness to provide product for television. Two key events helped bring the first Golden Age of television to an end. One was the development of the three film-camera studio shooting technique that was developed in the production of *I Love Lucy*, which became a part of standard situation comedy production practice. This technique provided a relatively quick and efficient way to produce prerecorded television programs. The second was a change of heart within the film industry, inspired perhaps by the inevitability of television's success and recognition of the medium as a source of profit for film studios. Hollywood dropped its resistance to producing for television to become a bountiful source of television series drama. These changes allowed the networks to replace the technically and sometimes thematically challenging live programming of television's first Golden Age with a continuing stream of programs with predictable styles in established genres which presented audiences with familiar, uncontroversial content.

From the end of television's first Golden Age significant changes in the form and content of television have often come from the imaginations of powerful producers. Many of these influential producers have used their power to introduce controversial contemporary issues into the discourse of the television programs they produce. Sheldon Leonard's insistence, in the face of great network pressure, that Bill Cosby play a co-starring role in the 1965 dramatic series *I Spy* provided a radically different portrayal of interracial relations in American television programming and paved the way for the 1968 program *Julia,* the first American drama in which an African American stood alone as the lead actor in a series. In 1970 the cumulative power of the three principal producers involved in MTM convinced CBS to broadcast a program that broke from the industry practice of restricting narrative themes in situation comedies to light presentations of the trivial, the adolescent and the absurd, and seriously addressed the then controversial theme of the life of a single professional woman. This first MTM offering, *The Mary Tyler Moore Show,* established the idea that a situation comedy that presented a more realistic worldview could succeed, and according to many critics, launched the second Golden Age of Television. While *The Mary Tyler Moore Show* did introduce controversy to the situation comedy, it did so in a subtle and polite manner.

In 1971 Norman Lear's *All in the Family* took the idea of controversial social commentary in entertainment programming a giant step further, and demonstrated that the American audience would accept a comedy grounded in nakedly confrontational and impolite ideological conflict. The work of Sheldon Leonard, Norman Lear and the producers at MTM broke the conservative conventions of network programming and made significant and enduring changes in the nature of Prime Time television entertainment television in the United States. Their efforts enabled programming to deliver a broader range of socially significant messages in new and compelling ways. David E. Kelley's choice of the controversial content of *Ally McBeal* may have been fostered by his experience as a second generation student in the MTM programming school, having worked as a writer on Steve Bochco's *L.A. Law.* His choice of such a generically mixed narrative structure for the program does not have such a strong hint of historical origins, but by its groundbreaking nature it may be of greater significance with regard to the program's contribution to growth within the paradigm of Prime Time television. It is too early to tell whether Kelley's work in *Ally McBeal* will foster permanent change in the nature of Prime Time as

Leonard's, Lear's and the MTM team's have. But the relative longevity of *Ally McBeal*, given its unique combination of form and content, does suggest that the program may have opened the door to a new style of socially relevant storytelling in television.

Whether *Ally McBeal* marks the beginning of a new generic freedom in Prime Time television programming or stands as an isolated anomaly in the conservative flow of the programming stream, the international popular attention the program has garnered from the controversial nature of its form and content mark it as a program worthy of serious scholarly attention. The essays in this anthology explore a wide range of the contributions that David E. Kelley's *Ally McBeal* makes to the discourse in Prime Time about the nature of both Prime Time television in America and the nature of the society it addresses. That range includes: consideration of the definition of feminism in the early twenty-first century; the challenges that women's interests in sexuality and heterosexual romance present to feminism and feminist thought regarding women in the workplace; bisexuality; the struggle for an understanding of masculinity in light of the growing power of feminism to challenge patriarchy; the participation of entertainment programming in the maintenance of national identity in a time of crisis; and the reconfiguration of the generic conventions of Prime Time television to present controversial ideas in a new narrative style. The essays selected for this anthology provide insights into both the stories told by and the discourse of the series from media scholars representing a variety of disciplines including literature, American studies, film studies, philosophy, sociology, and the law. Contributions included in the anthology come from the United States, Canada, Great Britain, Australia and Switzerland.

The presentation of women's behaviors, desires and images in *Ally McBeal* has received more attention from the popular press, media critics and the general public than any other aspect of the program. Questions about the program's discourse regarding feminism, sexuality in and beyond the workplace, romantic desire, the lead character's adolescent behavior and flights of fantasy, and the leading actress's weight have all been energetically debated in the public sphere. The public attention and concern that the series has attracted demonstrate a popular awareness on some level of the cultural studies perspective that the media participates in the construction of culture and cultural values, a perspective grounded in part in Louis Althuseur's recognition of the commercial media as an ideological state apparatus. If Althuseur is correct that the media is an important player in shaping cultural values and beliefs, and scholars with such divergent backgrounds as Stuart Hall and George Gerbner believe he is, then the contribution of any television program to its culture should be worthy of consideration. Given the public and critical attention it has garnered, *Ally McBeal* is not just any television program. *Ally McBeal* stands as a quintessential example of John Fiske and John Hartley's conception of the television program as cultural bard, calling an audience together and placing important issues of the day before it for consideration.

One of the outstanding qualities of *Ally McBeal* is the way the series fulfills its bardic function. The series' narratives consistently challenge the tidy conventions of social reality that insist that issues and people are either-or, fish or fowl, one or the other, that meanings are contained in simple, established, mutually exclusive categories that support a clear and stable worldview. This kind of strict binary epistemology is a central tenet of the police and lawyers genres (the latter of which *Ally McBeal* arguably belongs in) that are currently overrunning the Prime Time television schedule. The narrative in *Ally McBeal* is stubbornly resistant in the face of this dominant paradigm, arguing for a vision of people and the issues they are involved with that is unresolvably bipolar. The series consistently refutes the ideology of either-or with narrative threads that begin and end with an unmediated both-and or ambiguous liminality that call for recognition of the complexity of contemporary social life in the modern West and question the dominant vision of social reality. Among the most significant challenges that the larger narrative of *Ally McBeal* brings to the dominant ideological meaning structure are the issues of women's images, desires, and roles in society. A number of the essays in this collection explore the presentation of these issues in *Ally McBeal*.

Perhaps the greatest public uproar about the series involves the position of the series' presentation of women in relation to feminist thought. There has been considerable public discussion about whether or not *Ally McBeal* is a feminist text. Patricia Leavy argues (in chapter 1) that Ally's character is what S. Paige Baty would call a "representative character," a site through which large, emergent sociological questions may be raised and social reality altered. Two issues that are always raised in the discussion about *Ally McBeal* are the presentation of the title character and the actress who portrays her. Media critics of all stripes have commented on the juxtaposition of Ally's professional role as an attorney with her adolescent appearance and personal behavior, and her surreal personal experience of the world, and what this juxtaposition might mean with regard to feminism. One of the interesting aspects of the series is the way its producer has acknowledged and responded to criticism of the series through the series' narrative. Leavy's essay examines the way Ally is presented as both a professional attorney and the primary resident of a magical reality, the mass mediated reaction to this dichotomous presentation of her character, and the ways the series has responded to this reaction in program narratives.

Jessica Lyn Van Slooten and Susan E. McKenna (chapters 2 and 3) explore ways that the series addresses issues of sex and romantic love. Van Slooten's study responds to Barbara Ryan's observation that heterosexual love does not carry the political and politically correct weight to receive sufficient attention within the universe of feminist issues, and Ann Snitnow's argument that the popularity of the romance genre across a range of media including books, film and television identifies romance as a primary category of the female imagination that is either overlooked or trivialized by critics, and Tania Modleski's assertion that the conflicts between feminist ideology and romantic love must be addressed to understand the full complexity of women's relation to culture. Van Slooten postulates that the series' exploration of this ignored but important conflict accounts in part for the attention it has received, that the conflict between feminist ideology and romantic love played out in the series' narratives through Ally and supporting regular characters is one of the compelling reasons for the popularity of the series and the controversy over it. Van Slooten ties her study of *Ally McBeal* to another popular narrative that has been distributed through the media and addresses the same conflict, *Bridget Jones's Diary*. Van Slooten examines the way both texts self-consciously critique the conflicts between the mythic and revolutionary roles of women in contemporary society, between feminist ideology and romantic love, within the context of the romantic genre.

Susan E. McKenna (chapter 3) explores the messages that *Ally McBeal* delivers regarding female sexuality, demonstrating that while the series confirms a heterosexual male perspective of sexuality that seems to reinforce female heterosexuality, narrative threads within the series contradict this perspective, questioning the validity not only of the dominant heterosexual paradigm, but also the idea that there are clear sexual categories, that characters are either-or. Her analysis of sexual encounters between female characters who appear in the series reveals a picture of women as secretly attracted to other women, but almost always in the tradition of — and subjugated to — their attraction to men. McKenna finds conflicting messages in *Ally McBeal*, simultaneously homophobic and gay-positive, reinforcing cultural stereotypes of lesbian, bisexual and heterosexual women and subverting them. As with other elements in the series, the overarching statement the series makes about women's sexuality is, in McKenna's analysis, ambiguous. The series acknowledges distinctions between lesbian, bisexual, and heterosexual orientations, but argues that most women are heteroflexible.

Michele Hammers (chapter 4) identifies the clown-like persona of the title character in *Ally McBeal* as an important mechanism through which the series presents its discourse regarding post-feminist politics, female professionalism, the feminine, and the importance of the female body as a site of identity formation. Using Kenneth Burke's theory that social reality is constructed through perception of acceptance and rejection frames, Hammers investigates the series' portrayal of Ally to determine whether she appears more as a "comic clown" who steps out of the social mainstream, serves society as a relief valve by exposing imperfections in the social order and then is redeemed by and readmitted into society, or a "burlesque clown" whose exposure of society's flaws is rewarded with banishment in the hope that utter rejection of the messenger will dismiss the problem. Hammers' examination of *Ally McBeal*, like those of the other authors in this anthology who consider the meanings the series carries regarding women's identity and roles in society, is focused on ambiguity in the series' text, on the unresolved conflicts in the series universe of meanings.

The *Time* magazine cover from June 29, 1998, that featured portraits of a trio of famous feminists and Calista Flockhart, and asked, "Is feminism dead?" is perhaps the best known example of the flood of the popular and critical attention directed at *Ally McBeal* that speculates about the seemingly contradictory messages the series presents regarding women and their roles in society. In feminist theory, the body is often perceived as a foundation for agency, pleasure, desire and voice. Producer David E. Kelley's casting of an actress with an adolescent physical appearance in the role of the series' feminist heroine and dressing her in clothing more appropriate to the upper class dating scene than the courtroom presents her as disempowered from the traditional feminist perspective. Kelley's portrayal of Ally's romantic struggles suggests that she cannot be happy without a man. Amanda Rees argues in *Feminist* that "lack of a partner for the *Ally McBeal*'s of this world doesn't just imply the absence of masculine attention, but the presence of a very real emotional turmoil and self-doubt; having a husband or boyfriend, it would seem, is a real mark of success."

Kristyn Gorton's essay (chapter 5) provides a close reading of the texts of the series in an attempt to resolve the ambiguity regarding whether Kelley is arguing in *Ally McBeal* for a new understanding of feminism or that feminism is dead. In their analysis of the program, Laurie Ouellette and Susan E. McKenna together (chapter 6) examine how during its tenure on television *Ally McBeal* entered the public consciousness as a "statement" about feminism, post-feminism, and women. Ouellette further argues that by combining the iconography of the presumably achieved feminist revolution with new manifestation of the antipathy and doubt frequently ascribed to postfeminist media representations, *Ally McBeal* provided an important cultural reference point for understanding what might be termed the discourse of "post-victimization" femininity.

The last essay in this collection that directly addresses *Ally McBeal's* engagement with feminism seeks to turn the general public perception of the series on its head by challenging the raft of popular and scholarly critics who have identified the series as anti-feminist. Amanda D. Lotz (chapter 7) argues that rather than marking the death of feminism, as the *Time* magazine cover suggested, *Ally McBeal* is a positive feminist text from the perspective of post-feminist theory. Lotz's essay explores the limitations of criticism that characterizes the series and its leading character as anti-feminist, and the inadequacy of applying previous standards of feminist television criticism to late 1990s American television, through a thorough critical examination of popular and academic discussions of *Ally McBeal* within the context of post-feminist theory. The essay argues that early criticism of the series perpetuated outdated and limiting standards of belief and behavior for women instead of engaging the innovation that provides the series' true contribution to the cultural debate regarding women's circumstances, participation, and challenges in modern society, and that the series offers a new positive perspective on female identity.

While the great wave of public attention directed at *Ally McBeal* has focused on the values and meanings the series may carry that address feminism, the series is also noteworthy for its groundbreaking narrative structure, and other issues that it brings to its audience as a part of its bardic function. The program blends generic forms in a unique way: dramedy flavored with the magical realism that was previously the exclusive realm of sitcoms including *Bewitched* and *My Mother the Car*, legal drama and melodrama with roots in such programs as *Perry Mason* and *L.A. Law*, and the Hollywood musical which has no established generic history in Prime Time series television, with the possible exception of the short-lived *Cop Rock*. The coexistence of these disparate narrative forms in one program creates tensions within the series texts, and in great probability within the minds of viewers who have become accustomed to the distinct, uncomplicated generic narrative forms that dominate the Prime Time landscape. Three essays in this collection explore elements of the series' narrative structure that help create an overarching sense of connectedness within individual episodes and across the series. Other essays look at the critique *Ally McBeal* makes of society and the law in the early 21st century, the series' presentation of the politics of masculinity, and the way *Ally McBeal* demonstrates the potential for fictional entertainment programming to participate in national discourse at a time of crisis.

One of the aspects of *Ally McBeal* that has been largely overlooked in both the public and critical responses to the program is the discourse of the series as a legal drama. Legal dramas have maintained a consistent presence in Prime Time from the time of *Perry Mason*, providing a platform for examining the flaws in contemporary society and the ability of our legal system to secure justice. The presentation of lawyers in these series has provided models of appropriate and inappropriate individual belief and behavior within contemporary society. Legal dramas thereby contribute an important voice to the ideological debate regarding the nature of society and appropriate behavior in it. Ally McBeal follows both the general form of the legal drama and the tradition of Prime Time female lawyers, who are either good at their jobs, or good at their relationships, but not both. Several essays address this topic in various forms.

Another aspect of the series that has not received sufficient attention from either the popular media or media scholars is the series' traditional historical treatment of its ethnic minority characters. It is understandable, given the tidal wave of interest that the series' address to feminism has provoked, that these aspects of the series have not been the focus of critical examination. Jennifer Harris' essay (chapter 8) investigates the ways *Ally McBeal* contributes to the American cultural discourse regarding race and sexuality, and the ways the culture of white corporate masculinity prevalent in *Ally McBeal* participates in and reproduces certain stereotypes of ethnic sexuality, while simultaneously appropriating elements of deeply ingrained stereotypes to construct a model of white masculinity. Harris explores the uses of black characters, particularly Jackson Duper played by Taye Diggs, Renee Raddick played by Lisa Nicole Carson, and Dr. Greg Butters played by Jesse L. Martin, in addition to Asian-American character Ling Woo played by Lucy Liu, to advance particular plots in the series' narrative, develop the series' presentation of a politics of minority sexuality, and serve as sites of humor either in juxtaposition with white bodies or as sexualized objects. She also offers an analysis of the meanings inherent in the appropriation of the music and persona of the late R&B singer Barry White by white characters.

One of the distinguishing qualities of *Ally McBeal* is that so much in the series refuses easy, singular categorization. In the universe of conformist, predictable Prime Time entertainment programming, *Ally McBeal's* ambiguity is unavoidably recognizable. This ambiguity is most evident in the series' discourse regarding sex and gender roles, the series' narrative style, and its representation of "reality" within the context of the program. In chapter 9 Twyla Gibson examines Ally McBeal in terms of how the series represents classical and contemporary sex and gender issues, both at home and in the workplace. In particular, Gibson's essay looks at the ways the character of Richard Fish produces meaning and bridges ambiguities within the series. The essay explores the ambiguity of Fish's role in the series: that

he is sophist and statesman, charlatan and wise man, adversary and advocate. Gibson identifies two important contributions Fish's character makes
to the body of meanings made available through the series' narrative content. One contribution comes from Fish's embodiment of "the angler." Plato
identifies "the angler," a longstanding character in Western oral tradition,
in the *Sophist* as an embodiment of thoughts and feelings that lurk below
consciousness and polite society. The other contribution is as a characterization of masculine bewilderment in the face of changing sex and gender
roles in American society. Gibson also argues for an understanding of Fish's
role in the series' narrative structure, observing that his character bridges
the gap between the trials on a professional level and the trials on a personal level in episodes, and that it is through the juxtaposition of these personal and professional trials that the series achieves its emotional impact.

Music has been an uncontroversial dramatic element seamlessly incorporated into television programs' generic structures from the inception of
the medium, distinguishing individual programs from the programming
flow with theme songs and underscoring significant narrative moments with
subtly introduced nondiegetic scores. Music is used quite differently in *Ally
McBeal,* in ways that contribute to the air of ambiguity that surrounds the
program. The generic structure of the series as a legal drama is consistently
interrupted by song and dance routines in the unisex bathroom of the law
firm of Cage and Fish PC, and the program always ends with a musical coda
delivered through the performance of an extradiegetic character, singer-
songwriter Vonda Shepard, in nightclub scenes that include members of
the series' cast. Diana Sandars' essay (chapter 10) explores the musical anom-
alies in *Ally McBeal,* the ways the series integrates the stylistic and formal
elements of the classical Hollywood musical and music video with the realist narrative of a television dramedy to provide a context through which
competing ideological constructs in the different genres can be assessed
simultaneously. Sandars observes that the tenets of the primary ideologies
presented in the series, romantic love and postmodern feminism, may each
be viewed from the context of the other genre and that the ironic distance
created through *Ally McBeal*'s hybrid generic structure creates a viewing
position through which both classical romance ideologies and the social
forces that construct and perpetuate socially condoned models of femininity can be re-examined.

Ally McBeal's hybrid generic structure also creates problems for audience members trying to follow the stories told in the series. Conventional
television series and serials rely on the audience's unconscious understanding
of established sets of narrative conventions to follow characters and stories
from one episode to another and one season to another. *Ally McBeal* violates

narrative convention and confounds audience expectation by presenting a program structure that combines dramatic television series and melodramatic television serial formats, legal drama and romantic comedy genres, and protagonist driven and ensemble narrative. The mixed narrative structure of *Ally McBeal,* its generic hybridization, challenges the series with problems of how to resolve segmentation into narrative flow and establish narrative perspective for its audience. Ursula Ganz-Blaettler and Thomas Christen's essay (chapter 11) explores the ways that the series addresses these challenges through a variety of narrative elements to help audience members engage in long-term relationships with the program. Ganz-Blaettler and Christen pay particular attention to the ways dramaturgical strategies applied in episode and season beginnings and endings, voiceover, and the introductory and final moments of the series knit disparate narrative elements together to create a unique sense of narrative continuity for the audience.

The development of a broader range of outlets for television programming through the expansion of cable and satellite delivery systems has unquestionably increased the diversity of programming content available to the viewing public in the United States. But with the possible exception of "reality shows" these programs are largely conventional in content and form. The essays collected in the following pages explore the ways that *Ally McBeal* breaks from the conservative conventions of American commercial television with regard to both form and content. The popularity of the series demonstrates that this unconventional approach can succeed. It is too early to tell whether *Ally McBeal* will serve as the progenitor of a new wave of alternatively structured television programs, or be remembered like *Rowan & Martin's Laugh-In,* as an exceptional moment in the mundane flow of programming. Either way the series merits serious study for the insights it offers into the nature and roles of television in contemporary society. The essays in this anthology contribute to that process.

1

Ally McBeal as a Site of Postmodern Bodily Boundaries and Struggles Over Cultural Interpretation: The Hysteric as a Site of Feminist Resistance

Patricia Leavy

Introduction

"Herman's Head *meets* My So-Called Life *meets* Dream On *meets* Molly Dodd *meets* Nine-to-Five ... *you get the idea.*"
— Lynne Harris, *New York Daily News,*
as quoted by Kathy Mitchell, p. 9

In this essay I analyze Ally McBeal as a "representative character" through whom to address larger emergent sociological questions pertaining to gendered symbolism within the mass media. Interestingly, critical analysis shows that the character Ally McBeal has been used in a similar way within the social world — as a vehicle through which a range of cultural narratives about gender have been written and resisted. This, in fact, constitutes the very reason why the show beckons scholarly interrogation.

The television series *Ally McBeal* was accompanied, if not overshadowed, by a systematic and complex media frenzy starting with its initial airing. The media craze signifies social struggles over creating cultural meaning in a mass-mediated society. The spectacle has primarily centered on the title character and lead actress who portrayed her. Further complicating the varied cultural "uses" of Ally is that the line between the character and actress (Calista Flockhart) was ritualistically blurred almost beyond (re)cognition. However, the *nature* of the media's strong response to the Ally character is relatively simple to discern. Ally McBeal was rapidly and repeatedly constructed into a cultural symbol transforming her from a mere television character into a vessel for groups aiming to create a host of cultural meanings. In this essay I show that the main elements of her social construction into competing media symbols are gender related. In other words, the abundant production of cultural narratives centering on Ally is primarily related to larger cultural ideas about gender within American society. Ally has been used as a vehicle for (re)enforcing and challenging dominant gendered power, particularly in relation to conceptions regarding the state of contemporary feminism and female body ideals. Congruent with the complexities of the postmodern media age, the bodily site for these struggles over gendered symbolism was, it seems, a fictitious character. Categorizing Ally McBeal as a "representative character" allows me, methodologically, to sociologically address these theoretical points.

My conception of "representative character" is based on the work of S. Paige Baty who analyzed Marilyn Monroe as a "representative character" in her book *American Monroe: The Making of a Body Politic.* Drawing upon Donna Haraway's theory of the hybrid subject and Roland Barthes' analysis of "Myth Today," Baty states:

> a representative character through whom to approach the political cultural condition of our time. Remembered as a product or story or some hybrid of the two, the representative character operates as a site on which American political culture is written and exchanged. The mass mediated representative character operates as a figure through whom multiple meanings, references, and roles are remembered ... [Baty, p. 10–11].

Using Baty's conception of "representative character" Ally McBeal can be viewed as a site on which other cultural narratives are written and resisted. Through the character of Ally, stories about gender have been written, rewritten, and challenged within our society. Under this conception, Ally McBeal acts as an organizing mechanism for the culture to create cultural meanings— meanings relating to feminism and female body image. She is the symbol through which symbolisms are created. But being a cultural symbol is not a natural phenomenon, it is rather a social construction. How did the mass media construct and reconstruct Ally McBeal into a vehicle for telling the culture larger stories about gender? And what were the specific stories about gender that were mediated through this fictional character?

The Media Responds to Ally McBeal: Ally *is* Imaged *as Icon*

"Should this miniskirted neurotic be a role model?"
— London's *Daily Mail* as quoted by Kathy Mitchell

On June 29, 1998, *Time* magazine labeled Ally McBeal "the postergirl for post(modern) feminism." Placing a color shot of Ally alongside black and white photos of Susan B. Anthony, Betty Friedan and Gloria Steinem, the cover of *Time* magazine then asked: "IS FEMINISM DEAD?" This served as the impetus for a mega multi-media and public response to the show and lead character. Referring to this issue of *Time* magazine, show story lines, and the character of Ally McBeal, Ally has repeatedly been represented as the quintessential post- or postmodern feminist. A fictitious character came to represent *the symbol* of contemporary feminism. Accordingly, story lines "relating to gender" were vehemently critiqued and Ally ritualistically scrutinized, particularly representations of her struggle to balance desires for autonomy with yearnings for an all-consuming romantic relationship. The media, scholars, and public engaged in a debate centering on the question: is Ally McBeal a feminist role model? Is she a feminist icon? Is she Generation X's answer to the feminist dilemma?

But my question is: isn't Ally a fictitious character? Further, what does it mean to compare her to "real" self-identified feminists? Isn't feminism an achievement based on standpoint, experience and choice? What or whose purpose is served by constructing her as the current feminist ideal? How does all of this affect real-world feminism? And finally, why was her headshot on the cover of *Time* in color when the "real" women were *imaged* in black and white? In order to unravel the social significance of the media's repeated imaging of Ally as feminist icon, we must situate these acts within the larger time-space context in which they have occurred and then analyze the gendered social power manifested by the appropriation of the Ally McBeal character.

The comparison of a fictitious character to real human beings, such as *Time* magazine offered, is representative of the larger cultural landscape in which this text is (re)produced, distributed, and consumed. In this historical time and space, the real and the imaged-imaginary are blurred to such an extent that any distinctive voice of authentic origin is near silenced. The fictitious, the color photograph literally (re)places the real, the earned, into black and white. The real and the imagined are no longer (re)presented as distinct. *Time* magazine's cover choice made Ally McBeal the symbol for "post(modern) feminism" while simultaneously the cover itself symbolizes the postmodern dilemma in which the magazine is produced. Scholar Jean Baudrillard speaks to this issue as follows:

> It is the generation by models of a real without origin or reality: a hyperreal ... the era of simulation is inaugurated by a liquidation of all referentials—worse: with their artificial resurrection in the systems of signs, a material more malleable then meaning, in that it lends itself to all systems of equivalences, to all binary oppositions, to all combinatory algebra. It is no longer a question of

limitation, nor duplication, nor even parody. It is a question of substituting the signs of the real for the real ... [Baudrillard, p. 1–2].

Perhaps beyond all else what does simulation do? "Simulation threatens the difference between the 'true' and the 'false,' the 'real' and the 'imaginary'" (Baudrillard, p. 3). Ally McBeal is a cultural product, as is *Time* magazine. They both bear traces of themes particular to the era in which they are produced. The June 29, 1998, cover exemplified that the American postmodern context is a space of simulation where "the difference between the 'true' and the 'false,' the 'real' and the 'imaginary'" is no longer relevant in the traditional sense. This is a hyperreality where a color headshot of Ally McBeal without an organic link to feminism is used to denote a new feminist icon.

Ally McBeal was not only compared to real human women on the cover elucidating the world of simulation in which she and we "live," but Ally was compared to feminists and labeled a "post(modern) feminist" which naturally beckoned the question: "Is feminism dead?" This phenomenon is sociologically significant and in need of exploration. The mass media needs to be conceptualized as a semiological system in order to understand how it is a space where social meaning is constructed. In other words, within the mass media cultural meanings are created. Emphasis here is on the social *production* of meaning. When analyzing a semiological system, or a system designed to produce meanings, our analytical attention is called to the *appearance* of naturalness, although there is nothing "natural" about this phenomenon; it is a cultural process. Roland Barthes explains this phenomenon in his analysis of myth. He explains that myth is a system where meaning is produced with the appearance of being natural. Barthes cautions that all myths are at their core "political prepositions" (p. 116) and must be critically interrogated. So when thinking about the imaging of Ally McBeal as a feminist symbol it is important to apply a semiological perspective. In this light, by placing the picture of Ally McBeal, a fictional character, on the cover of *Time* as a symbol of feminism, it would only make sense to then ask: Is Feminism Dead? The signifier, the picture of Ally, conjures up the question as if it were natural. The signifier seems to have an organic relationship to the signified (post-feminism). Simply by placing the Ally photograph next to images of other well-known feminists, the association between Ally and feminism is made. The association appears natural when in fact it was actually artificially produced. Questioning, or even attacking, this association is inevitable once the association has been made to appear natural. But it is the placement of the Ally photo itself, the constructed association between the fictional character and feminism, between the character and the real-life feminists that must be interrogated. Imaging Ally

McBeal as a symbol of feminism is a form of mythification and as myth is a "political preposition" (Barthes, p. 116), even if under the guise of being "natural," then what are the gendered political ramifications of imaging Ally in this way?

While the mass media barely responded to the blurring of fiction and the "real" as evidenced in *Time,* the response to Ally being labeled a feminist symbol was swift and overwhelming. The reaction was wholly in the form of fierce criticism. Two examples follow:

> *Ally McBeal* is a slap in the face of the real-life working girl, a weekly insult to the woman who wants sexual freedom and gender equality, who can date and litigate in the same week without collapsing in a Vagisil heap [Ruth Shalit, the *New Republic* as quoted by Kathy Mitchell, p. 12].

> The one thing that I don't buy about *Ally McBeal's* breakout success is that people are watching it because *Ally* herself is a postfeminist role model. *Ally McBeal,* stripped to its essentials, is a program about a young woman with an interesting job who can't quite get her life together. Yet the Naked Truth, Suddenly Susan, and Caroline in the City all focus on beautiful, talented young women who can't quite get their lives together. And nobody's talking about them [John Queenan, *TV Guide,* as quoted by Kathy Mitchell, p. 8].

So while on October 19, 1998, Ally McBeal caused a media frenzy when she went to prison for refusing to wear longer skirts in court, does this compare to Susan B. Anthony going to jail in pursuit of women's suffrage? Moreover, why was this link ever made? Does the show or character embody real feminist themes that are in fact stifled through this nonsensical comparison?

> Comparing *Ally McBeal* to Susan B. Anthony is ludicrous [Janelle Brown, *Salon,* as quoted by Kathy Mitchell, p. 11].

But why was comparing Ally McBeal to noted feminists necessarily inappropriate? Is it because she did not adequately represent feminist ideals, as most critics focus upon, or, because she was a fictitious character — a model without origin that was somehow equated with feminism?

Beyond questions of simulations this imaging of Ally as feminist icon raises questions about the relationship between feminism and the commercial media. Why was Ally labeled a feminist? Actress Calista Flockhart responded as follows:

> What I find fascinating is that there can be TV shows featuring men, all kinds of men, and they are just characters. The moment a woman is on TV as a lead character, she is expected to be a role model, but we never said "That is what women are like." We said that is what *Ally* is like.

This response raises a crucial point. In our political-cultural context gender can act as a metalanguage that subsumes all other personal attributes.

The media, being located within the discourse of the broader historical time and space, replicated this practice and thus labeled Ally McBeal a "feminist." An award-winning, highly rated show that primarily revolves around a female lead draws media and public attention, as other top programs, but the attention-attraction is towards Ally *because she is a woman.* Ally was expected to (re)present all women whereas Seinfeld was just one man. That says less about Ally McBeal's possible feminism than it reveals about how gender serves as a metalanguage within the larger postmodern context. The media and public then respond to Ally McBeal, the myth, as if she is "supposed to" represent all women, and not surprisingly, this response involves severe scrutiny.

Postmodern Feminism and Ally

Despite all of this, not all female lead characters on highly rated shows are placed on the cover of *Time* magazine as the symbol of feminism even when they address gender-related issues on their programs. Was this show or character *actually* "feminist," and ironically the media attention has had the effect of *overshadowing that feminism?* If so, what kind of feminist was Ally? Did she threaten more conventional and controllable notions of feminism?

Sexual harassment cases regularly made their way through the show's law firm starting with Ally's own arrival at the firm in the first episode. The firm also represented a character, played by former *Charlie's Angels* star Kate Jackson, who was fired from her job as a television anchorwoman for being "too old" (meaning no longer pretty enough for the viewers' taste). Guest star John Ritter portrayed a character that was fired as editor from *La Femme* magazine (a feminist publication) when it was discovered that he was a Baptist. Ally was his attorney. The show also explored gender-related themes as Ally struggled between her desire to marry and have a family, which she claimed "society did to her and all women," versus her intellectual need for career and independence. In these, and many other ways the show and character addressed issues that have historically been related to feminism. But does all of this necessarily make Ally McBeal a feminist show and Ally a feminist role model?

The media's response to Ally as a feminist symbol primarily focused on Ally's personal life while *systematically* ignoring the issues raised on the show via the law firm. This is a diversionary tactic that serves only to contain the show's *possible* feminism. A similar phenomenon occurred regarding the show *Designing Women.* While both the show and characters addressed feminist concerns weekly in their workspace (the primary site of action in the show), the media focused on the characters' and stars' romantic lives. Author Patricia Mellencamp analyzed the media's fierce reaction to *Designing Women* in the following way:

> Paradoxically, the publicity about the show and the stars ... runs counter to the self-sufficiency of the program's characters, as if to contain the show's feminism —featuring the actresses' heterosexual qualities and relationships by focusing on the importance of men and romance [Mellencamp, p. 198].

I offer this as a comparative case of a female dominated show whose characters and story lines explicitly dealt with feminist themes. Here, a critical definition of television is helpful.

> a system of deterrence, in which the distinction between the passive and the active is abolished ... one enters into simulation, and thus into absolute manipulation — not into passivity, but into the *indifferentiation of the active and the passive* [Baudrillard, p. 29–31].

If we view television, the medium which circulates Ally McBeal, as a system of deterrence we can then start to develop an analysis of the nature of this "deterrence" by returning to the *Ally McBeal–Designing Women* parallel. In both instances, after the media labeled the lead characters as symbols of "feminism," the mass media and politicians repeatedly responded to this label by criticizing the characters' personal lives and struggles. These directed attacks on possible feminism centered solely on the characters' lives in the private sphere while completely discounting the actions of these characters in their fictional public spheres. This is significant. Historically feminism developed in order to help women participate in all aspects of the public sector (which is how they would help gain rights in the private sphere) while anti-feminist actions have focused on entirely relegating women to the private sphere. This binary separation would diminish women's ability to attain self-sufficiency and participate in political resistance. In the cases of both *Ally McBeal* and *Designing Women* the mass media contained the shows' possible feminism by falsely using the private sphere as its point of departure, when, in fact, it is in the fictional public spheres that possible feminism can be most readily located.

Calista Is Imaged as Beauty Ideal Calista-Ally — Calista Is Imaged as Ghostly Body

Calista is Greek for "most beautiful."

Seemingly concurrent with Ally's imaging as feminist icon, Calista Flockhart was imaged as the nation's beauty ideal. In the fall of 1998 Calista's image was reproduced on the covers of more American magazines than any one model (in addition to foreign fashion publications). Calista's image did not challenge existing beauty ideals, but rather reproduced the normative American female ideal including the following physical characteristics which are enmeshed in a complex web of gendered and racialized social power: tall, white, hyper-thin, chiseled facial features, large eyes. Interestingly, many of these photographs contained postmodern captions such as the one on the cover of *Harper's Bazaar*: "The Real *Ally McBeal*: Calista Flockhart." Again a blurring between fiction and the "real" is evidenced. In fact, at the time the phrase "The Real McBeal" became typical in both fashion and entertainment magazines. Where does Calista end and Ally begin? Is it even possible that there is a "Real Ally McBeal?"

In another magazine Calista posed in Armani clothing and the accompanying caption read: "Feminine Mystique." Is the reference to the book that solidified Betty Friedan as a feminist pioneer intentionally placed alongside of a photograph of Calista Flockhart who shares a face and body with the character Ally McBeal? Does this message reinforce unconscious associations between the faces of Betty Friedan and Ally McBeal further solidifying the mass-produced conception of Ally as feminist icon? If so, why use Calista's image and not Ally's? Who is the "post(modern) feminist" symbol? As images are "murders of the real" (Baudrillard, p. 5), a distinction can barely be drawn in a society that engages in the mass production of imagery that is detached from any referential while simultaneously referencing histories— in this case, Betty Friedan's achieved status as feminist. Here we can see how Ally McBeal's construction as a feminist persona was co-opted as actress Calista Flockhart was transformed into a symbol of female beauty.

Shortly after Calista became a symbol for the body beautiful, rumors of an eating disorder besieged the star and the mass media that had constructed her as both a feminist and beauty icon now linked her image to captions such as "horrifying." It began when Calista appeared at the 50th annual Emmy Awards wearing a sleeveless and backless gown that exaggerated her thin frame. Calista's photographic image from that evening was splattered across the covers of every major tabloid for weeks to come, all reporting that her appearance at the Emmys showed that she suffered from anorexia nervosa. Soon, newspapers were also "reporting" on the subject. A point that did not make its way into the media's discourse surrounding this subject is that all of the photographs published in conjunction with rumors of an eating disorder were taken from a specific vantage point. These photographs show her with her back facing the camera and her head turned towards the camera. At that moment her body was positioned in such a way that her backbones are particularly apparent as her muscles contracted. This specific photograph created a media scandal yet no one discussed the specifics of the image: an image being reproduced in multiple texts connected to the message "gruesome." The processes of production are completely abstracted from the resulting image and meaning is created via connotation through linking the visual image to textual claims of an illness. Just as the media constructed Ally as the feminist ideal and Calista as the beauty ideal, they too started rumors of an illness that plagued both Calista and Ally for years. What does this gossip express about the larger context in which it occurs?

> Gossip is, as Foucault might argue, about power/knowledge, a productive network of daily exclusions and inclusions, a machinery no one sees, a productive network of pleasure, of evasion and containment [Mellencamp, p. 168].

Was this productive network trying to contain Ally's feminism by associating Calista with a gender-related illness? The common sense knowledge about the Ally McBeal character that was constructed by the media is enmeshed within a complex web of power relations and thus the result of both inclusions and exclusions. This exemplifies the hegemonic power of the mass media to construct images for mass consumption while maintaining authority over how those images are distributed and subsequently consumed. When discussing the work of scholar Ulf Hannerz, Patricia Mellencamp writes:

> He discovers that gossip operates because of the discrepancies between "impression" and "reality" ... keeping up the appearance is not only costly; the manufactured and/or fascinating image becomes a target for investigation [p. 194].

Calista-Ally's image *was* manufactured as icon and correspondingly became a site of fascination — a target for scrutiny. Up until this point the discrepancies between "impression" and "reality" had been tremendous as a result of the blurring of "real" and "imaginary" boundaries. This fueled the fire for later attacks on Calista's appearance, which again, focused on her as female first. I was unable to determine who the media was claiming to be ill, Calista or Ally, when sayings such as "Meals for McBeals" became normalized in entertainment television programs. A 1996 film titled "The Secret Life of Mary-Margaret: Portrait of a Bulimic," starring Calista Flockhart, suddenly became the topic of media scrutiny. *Was fiction imitating life?* This is an ironic question given the fusion of Ally-Calista in the media.

One of the most interesting aspects of the imaging of Calista as anorexic was the *People* magazine anomaly. Calista Flockhart is one of the celebrities featured on the cover of *People*'s September 28, 1998, Emmys edition published immediately after the award show *but prior to* the rumors that Calista had an eating disorder. No negative mention of her appearance is made. In fact, both on the cover and inside of the magazine photographs of Calista at the Emmys are shown to be representative of Hollywood glamour. The November 9, 1998, edition of *People* magazine used photographs of Calista at the Emmys on both the cover and inside of the magazine as a vehicle for addressing the rumors of an eating disorder. This time, *People* did not use these photographs to represent glamour, but rather to exploit her "horrifying" appearance. The contradiction between how these same photographs were used at different moments in time as representative of binary opposites did not make its way into public discourse. This discrepancy does however illustrate the effects of mass-mediated constructions within our culture. The mass media retains the power to construct personas, out of real or fictitious material, into vehicles for symbolism and sites of cultural interpretation. As they create the baseline narratives that spark public discourse, their initial interpretations mediate the public's vision. As John Berger explains, and this contradiction illustrates, "The way we see things is affected by what we know or what we believe" (Berger, p. 8). When we believe Calista to be beautiful we see her as such. When we believe her to be "gruesome" we know her as such. When we see Calista's image and associate it with Ally, we normalize phrases such as "Meals for McBeals."

On one day Calista was held as the nation's beauty ideal, and literally a day later she was demonized as a bodily nightmare. Did she lose weight overnight? It doesn't matter if she did because the fact is that the same photographs were used to denote both the body beautiful and the anorexic. So what does that say about our culture's female beauty ideal? As feminist scholars (Hesse-Biber, 1996) in the area of body image explain, American mainstream beauty standards for females correspond to a body easily equated with anorexia.

It is worth noting that Calista Flockhart reported that she felt very special the night of the Emmys and was hurt to hear people refer to her appearance as "horrifying." In addition, she could not understand why her physical body was the focus of so much attention.

Ally's Postmodern Response to Her Mass Imaging: Acts of Cultural Resistance

"Somewhere every culture has an imaginary zone for what it excludes, and it is that zone we must try to remember today."
— Cixous and Clement, p. 6

Calista Flockhart was interviewed numerous times as one of the top celebrities of 1998 and 1999, making her way into every "year end" top entertainer category, at which point she vehemently denied having an eating disorder and responded to her character's comparison to Susan B. Anthony as "ridiculous." How did Ally McBeal respond to the cultural uses of her image? How did she use the medium of television in order to reclaim authority over her own representation?

Ally's response to the media frenzy regarding her image began during a Christmas episode. And I must disclose that as an avid viewer I was stunned. In the opening scene of the show Ally bumps into a character from *The Practice* (a show which converged with *Ally McBeal* on several occasions as both were written by David E. Kelley) played by actress Lara Flynn Boyle. The tabloid rumors regarding Calista Flockhart's alleged eating disorder had served as the impetus to the public scrutiny of the thin bodies of other celebrities. Lara Flynn Boyle was featured in many of these magazines and criticized for appearing anorexic. The media's intense campaign against a selected few female celebrities with similar body types resulted in the pop cultural phrase "lollypop people," indicating that the heads of these women appeared disproportionately large atop their stick-thin bodies. So in this Christmas episode of *Ally McBeal* these characters (who were adversarial) meet and Lara's character slowly looks Ally up and down. When Ally asked: "Is something wrong?" Lara's character responded, "I like your outfit but you look a bit thin. Maybe you should eat a cookie." Ally then responded, "Maybe we could share it."

While Calista Flockhart had publicly stated that she hated being mistaken for her character, Ally, she responded to public attacks on her body *through* the character of Ally McBeal. Again, Ally McBeal blurred the distinction between "fiction" and "reality" in new ways. Also significant is that she, Ally-Calista, utilized the very vehicle that exploited her image, in response to that assault: the voice of hegemonic authority — the mass media. Is this a form of resistance? I posit that this is a way Calista and show producers were able to create tensions within a hegemonically situated domain, thereby altering the fields of power through which it operates. In Luce Irigaray's terms, this was a very direct method of "jamming the theoretical machinery itself" (Irigaray, p. 78), not to explicitly construct new meaning, but rather to expose the system of power and othering on which the system operates. In other words, Ally's response helped to reveal the power-laden system of knowledge production the media engages in. Such a public unraveling of this typically invisible and ritualized process is a method of transforming the knowledge produced within the system.

Ally's response did not end there. In the January 18, 1999, episode, Ally dreamt that a famous women's organization nominated her as role model of the year. When Ally, in her dream, promptly responded that she didn't want to be a role model, she was immediately told that it was not her decision to make. She was then informed that she needed to stop wearing miniskirts, gain weight because they don't want her "glamorizing that thin thing," lose that "emotional void without a man thing" and finally, "be exactly who we want you to be." Ally said, "I crave some kind of dependency and that makes me feel like a failure as a woman." She awoke terrified and the next morning told her confidant John Cage that she had a nightmare that *Time* magazine put her on their cover "as the face of feminism ... imagine that."

Again, Ally and Calista blur the realm of the "real" and of the "imaginary" by using the same cultural vehicle which makes such distinctions fluid. Whose feelings were expressed in that scene, Ally or Calista's? Well, does Ally have any feelings? What about David E. Kelley who created the show and character? Remember, Ally is actually written through the I and eyes of a man. When looking at this phenomenon we must ask why Ally-Calista is held accountable for the words of this character when her words are written by a man. This attack on Calista presents an illusion of strong female power within the media when in this particular case men are actually controlling these words; however, we are deterred from analyzing that part of the process of production. Just as with the visual images used to associate Ally with beauty ideals or fears, the process of how visual and textual narratives are produced is totally abstracted from the resulting symbolic association.

This is not the first time a media-labeled feminist female lead character has been attacked in the media and subsequently responded *in character*. During George Bush's presidency, Vice President Dan Quayle attacked the television character Murphy Brown for choosing not to marry the father of the child she was carrying. The Republican Party used this character as a vehicle through which to attack unmarried mothers. The fictitious character Murphy Brown responded through a parallel storyline on the television series in which her character was attacked by the vice president for this very reason. The show even used real footage of Quayle speaking about Murphy Brown. Again, a "feminist" character is attacked and responds through that very character. This is a new phenomenon of sociological import.

The negative politics circulated through the bodies of fictional female characters serve to reinforce modes of gendered social power that have historically oppressed women, particularly women's participation in the public sphere. The only pertinent differences between attacking Ally McBeal and Murphy Brown rather than Susan B. Anthony and Elizabeth Cady Stanton is that a fictitious feminist: (1) may or may *not* embody feminist intentions as they have only been *ascribed* to her and are not an achieved status, and (2) can't speak back (or at least not in real time). As far as the latter point, following in the footsteps of Murphy Brown, Ally McBeal (the show and character) actively challenged this notion of silence by using the medium which constructed her into a false icon in order to expose, resist and transform mass-mediated conceptions about feminism and gender. Like Murphy, Ally joined the discussion, thereby *contributing* to its narrative, by using the voice of her character. This act, a form of cultural resistance, is what makes Ally an interesting and lasting pop-political figure.

While up until this point I have addressed many of the ways Ally was portrayed in the media, I have not discussed who Ally was. So who was Ally McBeal and what was it about the writing of her character that prompted so much fear in the media?

Ally McBeal as Hysteric

"When '*The Repressed*' of their culture and their society come back, it is an explosive return, which is *absolutely* shattering, staggering, overturning, with a force never let loose before."
— Cixous and Clement, p. ix

Ally McBeal has "visions" where she sees things that others do not see. Ally hears music in her head that at times causes her to dance without full awareness of her bodily movements. When feeling overwhelmed Ally visualizes herself swimming underwater. When desirous of having children Ally sees a high-tech computer-generated "dancing baby" with whom she dances (and argues). Ally sees unicorns that aren't illusions, but are "real" to her. Ally believes in the imaginary to the extent that she said, "Sometimes I get attached to things that aren't there."

Ally McBeal breaks down dichotomies within patriarchal culture as she moves between the public and private spheres. But Ally is not unique in this regard. Similar situations exist on most female-lead comedies where audiences see the lead move between her work life and private life. It is Ally's fluid movement between the "real" and "imaginary" realms, an utter rejection of the rational-emotional dichotomy which anchors patriarchal social orders, that makes her a unique character as well as a target for criticism. Rejecting the rational-emotional dichotomy is a common feminist practice advocated by scholars who aim to challenge the patriarchal paradigm (Jaggar, 1989; Sprague & Zimmerman, 1993). In this context, it becomes clear that the potential "feminist" elements of the Ally McBeal character that truly challenge patriarchal modes of power have not been the locus of her media attention. Let's look at some examples of how this character blurs the traditionally dichotomous realms of the "real" and the "imaginary."

On January 11, 1999, Ally fought for an elderly woman to be induced into a permanent state of sleep because the woman, Bria, was happier in her "dreamworld" than in "this world." Ally believes that the quality of life Bria experiences in her dreamworld may in fact be better than in the "rational" world and thus she should be allowed to "live" there. When a priest tells Ally that this request is unnatural her response is, "If we both agree that there's a better world waiting for us, maybe some of it's locked up in her dreams." This character explicitly calls into question relations between the imaginary and the real while simultaneously exposing the realm of unconsciousness as an active place of tension repressed by reason-based patriarchal culture. Ally wants to expose that space and uses one of the most patriarchal-rational institutions to do so: the legal system.

As stated by colleague and former lover Billy, Ally "completely rejects the world of absolutes and at the same time dies by it." So, who is Ally McBeal? The Hysteric. Hysteria has traditionally been classified as a female "malady" and accordingly recruited participants in hysteria studies have been female. The term "hysterical" is still popularly applied to women much like the term "neurotic." This is a method of undermining women's unique viewpoints. The label "hysteric" is thus used in the execution of gendered social power — it is used to culturally oppress women. Ally McBeal made visible the repressed female hysteric and the hegemonic order contained within the commercial media subsequently attacked her by constructing her as a feminist role model, only to then publicly brand her a neurotic, which she is. But it is only in a reason-driven social order that a neurotic is, by basis of a tautology, unfit for "feminine role model" status.

> The Hysteric, whose body is transformed into a theater for forgotten scenes, relives the past, bearing witness to a lost childhood that survives in suffering. This feminine role ... of hysterics, is ambiguous, antiestablishment, and conservative at the same time. Antiestablishment because the symptoms — the attacks — revolt and shake up the public, the group, the men, the others whom they are exhibited ... because they touched the roots of a certain symbolic structure, these women are so threatened that they have to disappear [Cixous and Clement, p. 5].

While Ally McBeal has been publicly branded a feminist icon, historically hysteria has also been strongly identified with the feminist movement (Showalter, p. 143). Many of the women who served as case studies in hysteria later became active participants in the women's movement creating an interesting link between the external label "hysteric," characteristics defined as "hysterical," and feminism. Visual representations that appear as iconographic rememberings have been a crucial component in the study of hysteria (Showalter, p. 149). As in Charcot's well-known work, hysterics were historically photographed repeatedly (Showalter, p. 152). In fact, one hysteria patient, "Augustine," was photographed so many times that she began to see in black and white which was then noted as a hysterical symptom (Showalter, p. 154). Let's recall how Ally's headshot on the infamous *Time* magazine cover appeared in color while the other faces were imaged in black and white. Furthermore, hysterics have historically become celebrities which corresponds with the Ally McBeal character receiving celebrity status or icon status in her own right.

Joseph Breuer, who together with Sigmund Freud conducted case studies on hysteria, was "Anna O's" therapist. This famous case study bears many similarities with my analysis of Ally McBeal. Anna O., who eventually became a feminist activist (like Calista Flockhart, who fought against the rape of Bosnian women), often found herself in a world of daydreams which Breuer labeled "hallucinations." Additionally, she suffered from anorexia nervosa and speech disorders yet was clearly intelligent and creative, easily shifting from the realm of "reality" into the realm of "imaginary." A similar description would easily suit the character Ally McBeal.

In terms of the relationship between anorexia and hysteria, why does Ally McBeal *appear* anorexic in seasons two and three of the series given the ability to use make-up artists, hair stylists, wardrobe and lighting experts? I could not help but notice the decline in her physical appearance including dark circles under her eyes, dry hair and an apparent reduction in breast size. Despite these blatant differences in her appearance, concurrent with the public scrutiny of "her" *body,* Ally-Calista continued to lighten her hair and wear tight clothing. In a context where padded "push-up" bras are common, Ally did not seem to wear them. Rather then attempting to combat perceived changes in her physical appearance, the shows' producers seemed to be *actively* allowing her physical transformations to be broadcast.

When shifting from different realms of consciousness and the imaginary versus "real" Ally's hearing and speech was affected. Ally, like Anna O., suffered from "not hearing" due to "absences." Breuer stated the following as amidst signs of Anna O's "not hearing":

> Not hearing, that someone entered while in a state of distraction. Not hearing, when alone, when she was directly addressed. Becoming deaf in deep absences. Becoming deaf through long listening, so that when she was then addressed she could not hear [Freud and Breuer, p. 24].

Ally McBeal repeatedly exhibited these same "signs of hysteria" and was often deemed "crazy" by other characters on the show, making a cultural attack of her feminist construction very simple. These characteristics caused her to be labeled "neurotic" by the mass media thereby deterring people from the possible feminism *embedded within the neurotic.*

Was Ally McBeal rejecting patriarchy when "words fail her" (Showalter, p. 157) as Breuer asserted Anna O. was? Is that why Ally was so vehemently criticized by the mass media?

It is my central hypothesis that Ally McBeal was not a weekly slap in the face to women, but rather to rational and patriarchal culture. Ally McBeal embodied a form of feminism that publicly rejects "the world of absolutes." That realm *reactively* attacked her. Ally McBeal created a public spectacle out of the silenced hysteric which created a space where the ritualized execution of gendered social power could be subversively resisted. Ally McBeal was not a neurotic in the popular negative sense but rather she challenged normative conceptions of what a "together woman" is. By embracing and physically embodying the role of "hysteric" Ally McBeal served as a bodily site of resistance to dominant methods available for interpreting cultural notions about autonomous women.

Concluding Thoughts

"The pleasure of the text is that moment when my body pursues its own ideas—for my body does not have the same ideas I do." — Barthes, p. 17

I loved the television show *Ally McBeal.* This show and character challenged patriarchal-rational discourse in provocative ways which perhaps accounts for my personal but shared feeling that Ally was somehow very real. While she was unable to represent all that has been repressed by gendered social power, a part of what our culture has shadowed was exposed weekly through the body of Ally. Perhaps it is not despite the tensions contained within this show which are most acutely manifested through this character, but rather *because of these tensions* that, for me and many others, intellectual reckonings subside and Ally just resonated as embodying (postmodern) truth. At the very least, this character prompted cultural struggles over meaning and was repeatedly chosen to actively participate in resisting dominant power in one way or another. In these ways she ultimately seemed, ironically, to earn the symbolic value bestowed upon her as she helped make the cultural landscape fertile for change.

Acknowledgments

My heartfelt thanks to Dr. Stephen Pfohl for serving as my advisor on the master's research at Boston College upon which this essay is based.

References

Barthes, R. (1998). "Myth Today." In Susan Sontag (ed.), *A Barthes Reader* (pp. 93–149). New York: Hill and Wang.

_____. (1998). *The Pleasure of the Text*. Translated by Richard Miller. New York: Hill and Wang.

Baty, S. P. (1995). *American Monroe: The Making of a Body Politic*. Berkeley: University of California Press.

Baudrillard, J. (1999). *Simulacra and Simulation*. Translated by Sheila Faria. Glaser: University of Michigan Press.

Berger, J. (1977). *Ways of Seeing*. New York: Penguin Books.

Cixous, H., and Clement C. (1996). *The Newly Born Woman*. Translated by Betsy Wing and Introduction by Sandra M. Gilbert. Minneapolis: University of Minnesota Press.

Freud, S., and Breuer, J. (1950). *Studies in Hysteria*. Translated and with Introduction by A. A. Brill. New York: Nervous and Mental Disease Monographs.

Hesse-Biber, S. (1996). *Am I Thin Enough Yet? The Cult of Thinness and the Commercialization of Identity*. Oxford: Oxford University Press.

Irigaray, L. (1996). *This Sex Which Is Not One*. Translated by Catherine Porter. Ithaca, NY: Cornell University Press.

Jaggar, A. (1989). "Love and Knowledge: Emotion in Feminist Epistemology." *Inquiry* (32), pp. 151–172.

Mellencamp, P. (1992). *High Anxiety: Catastrophe, Scandal, Age, & Comedy*. Bloomington: Indiana University Press.

Mitchell, K. (1998). *Ally McBeal: The Totally Unauthorized Guide*. New York: Warner Books.

Showalter, E. (1985). "Feminism and Hysteria." In *The Female Malady: Women, Madness and English Culture, 1830–1980* (pp. 145–164). New York: Pantheon.

Sprague, J., and Zimmerman, M. (1993). "Overcoming Dualisms: A Feminist Agenda for Sociological Method." In P. England (ed.), *Theory on Gender/Feminism on Theory*. New York: Aldine DeGruyter.

2

A Truth Universally (Un)Acknowledged: *Ally McBeal, Bridget Jones's Diary* and the Conflict between Romantic Love and Feminism

Jessica Lyn Van Slooten

"Feminist writers seem presently in conflict (not to say confusion) about the meaning and impact of romantic love as a subject that is not simply theoretical, but affects the lives of women everywhere in their everyday relations with men."
— Susan Ostrov Weisser, *Women and Romance: A Reader*

I used to watch *Ally McBeal* with glee. Here was a show that featured a young, professional woman whose romantic struggles were depicted with honesty and over-the-top hilarity. I would call my friends outside the academy and we would laugh at how our own searches for romantic love were not that different from Ally's. Talking about the show with my female colleagues in the English Department, I met with a vastly different response: "I can't believe you like that show—it's so anti-feminist." I started approaching the show and my own life with a great deal of skepticism, because, after all, I wanted to be a "good feminist." My viewing of *Ally McBeal* waxed and waned along with my ambivalence about the issues of feminism and romantic love. I feared that the two were not compatible after all. I had a similar experience when I first read Helen Fielding's novels *Bridget Jones's Diary* and *Bridget Jones: The Edge of Reason* and later saw the film adaptation. I realized that there was a greater issue at stake than my apparent affinity for pop-feminist texts. My personal conflict regarding

Ally McBeal and *Bridget Jones's Diary* illustrates the conflict between heterosexual romantic love and feminism present in both works. Both *Ally McBeal* and *Bridget Jones's Diary* are self-consciously aware of this conflict, and Ally's and Bridget's primary struggle, besides finding Mr. Right, is navigating the conflicts between the myths of both romantic love and feminism. As romance texts, *Ally McBeal* and *Bridget Jones's Diary* self-consciously critique and question the mythic and revolutionary place of romance in contemporary women's lives, ultimately proving that romance and feminism need not be mutually exclusive.

In this essay, I situate *Ally McBeal* and *Bridget Jones's Diary* within the conflict between romantic love and feminism. The first half of the paper will clearly delineate this conflict by considering the texts' relationships to the romance genre and feminism. The second half of the paper will concentrate on the texts themselves as productive sites of inquiry, looking more closely at the conflicts raging within Ally and Bridget, followed by a vision of "marriage" between romance and feminism. Following Modleski's suggestion that the cultural analyst needs to include herself to provide "a place for the feminist textual critic who recognizes her commonality with other women," I draw on my own relationship to *Ally McBeal* and *Bridget Jones's Diary* throughout the essay (345).

True Love Awaits: The Romance Genre

I have always been drawn to romantic novels, movies, and television programs. From *Wuthering Heights* to *When Harry Met Sally*, romantic texts stir my imagination and heart. In writing this essay I realized that during graduate school, I developed an academic skepticism of romance, and especially popular romantic texts. Having been told on several occasions that I am too sentimental, too soft, I cultivated a critical exterior that scoffed at romance. Yet I remained a sentimental romantic on the inside. My experience with *Ally McBeal* and *Bridget Jones's Diary,* as well as my reading in feminist criticism pushed me to explore the conflicts between these outer and inner attitudes both within myself and within these texts. Ally and Bridget are my comrades, as they too search for romantic heterosexual love in a culture with a barrage of conflicting messages. We are romantics in the various senses of that word — imaginative, hopeful, dreamy, and wistful. And we are critics too — comparing our worldly experience with our ideals, and reacting accordingly.

Both *Ally McBeal* and the *Bridget Jones's Diary* texts can be located in the romance genre. Like many of the romances that pioneering romance scholars Janice Radway and Ann Snitow studied, both works are part of a "series." One of the benefits of the series convention is the continuation of the story over a period of time; we can witness the characters' continued escapades, and watch them evolve. Also, the series format provides glimpses of the dailiness of Ally's and Bridget's lives. This is achieved through both formats—the weekly television series of *Ally McBeal* and the diary structure of *Bridget Jones's Diary*. Moreover, the overarching plot structure of *Bridget Jones's Diary* echoes that of Jane Austen's classic novel *Pride and Prejudice*, which many consider the quintessential romance. Beyond structure, both *Ally McBeal* and *Bridget Jones's Diary* are romances because the search for romantic love suffuses the texts.

While Radway and Snitow studied romance novels in the 1980s, serious feminist criticism has tended to shift away from romance as a genre. As Barbara Ryan has noted, heterosexual romantic love does not bear the political and politically correct weight of other feminist issues (465). For many women, the romance genre best articulates their private everyday desires and anxieties. Much of the highly publicized attention that *Ally McBeal*, and to a lesser extent, *Bridget Jones's Diary* has received trivialized the texts, focusing on Ally's short skirts, Calista Flockhart's weight, Bridget's incompetencies, and actress Renée Zellweger's weight gain for the role of Bridget rather than engaging with the real conflicts the show was addressing, or failing to realize that these issues were inextricably linked to the larger issues the texts explore.[1] To fully uncover the texts' significance, these conflicts or contradictions (in the romance genre) "*must* be brought to bear in any attempt to understand the full complexity of women's relation to culture" (Modleski "Feminism without Women," 344).

Scholars debate the validity of romance, alternately proposing romance as a mythic construction or as a biological need. According to Willard Gaylin and Ethel Person, romance flourished with the increasing popularity of the novel during the nineteenth century into a "sentimental love religion" (xii). However, Susan Ostrov Weisser notes that "some anthropologists and other social scientists argue [that romance] is possibly a cultural universal or part of our biological inheritance" (4). While the origins of romance remain debatable, the results of romance are clear. Weisser rightly states that "romance bears a good deal of weight, some of it laden with tangles of meaning difficult to separate and see clearly" (3). In creating ideal worlds, relationships, and characters, romance has the potential to transform the world as we know it, or at least the lives of the women who read or watch its texts. On the other hand, the escapist quality of the genre remains one of its most attractive features. These works promise to deliver a world where a happy ending is of utmost importance, a world we can escape into. Radway explains:

Despite such internal variation within the genre, however, all popular romantic fiction originates in the failure of patriarchal culture to satisfy its female members. Consequently, the romance functions always as a utopian wish-fulfillment fantasy through which women try to imagine themselves as they often are not in day-to-day existence, that is, as happy and content [*Reading the Romance*, 151].

Romance will necessarily never fully reflect reality; instead, it lies somewhere between fantasy and reality.

The popular press seems torn about whether Ally and Bridget bespeak realism or fantasy. Characters like Ally and Bridget are realistic in their embodiment of the struggles, anxieties, desires, and ambitions of "real life" women. Yet they remain fictional creations of David E. Kelley and Helen Fielding. As such, they are not bound by the same reality as real life women. Hence, the characters can experience alternate world and extreme adventures, experiences not bound by reality. The fictional characters embody the range of fantasies and nightmares of real life women; readers and viewers can then safely play out their own conflicts through these fictional characters. To critique Ally and Bridget for being unrealistic is to simply overlook this complex relationship between reality and fantasy at the heart of the romance genre.

Radway sees romances as "compensatory fiction because the act of reading them fulfills certain basic psychological needs for women that have been induced by the culture and its social structures but that often remain unmet in day-to-day existence as the result of concomitant restrictions on female activity" (*Reading the Romance*, 112–113). Romance, then, would seem to exist because current social systems do not meet women's needs. Ironically, however, this very system also creates those needs, if one follows Radway's reasoning, making romance a cultural construct. The cross-cultural proliferation of romance suggests that the romantic impulse is part of the human desire for the connection and validation that come through love. Romance is the stylized trappings of that deeper need for love. And when those needs are unmet, romance texts offer consolation. They can also be a way for women temporarily to meet those needs while not settling for a love less than what they truly desire. Ally and Bridget would attest to this fact. Both women have rich imaginations, where they create scenarios or visions to express their unmet yearnings. The infamous dancing baby of *Ally McBeal* and Bridget's daydreams about her wedding to Daniel Cleaver are two key examples. Both women also turn to other outlets to fulfill their needs. For part of the show, Ally sleeps with an inflatable doll; Bridget turns briefly to vodka and Chaka Khan in the face of her break-up with Daniel Cleaver. While these may not be the most psychologically healthy avenues,

Ally and Bridget are adept at using their romantic energy to assuage their feelings of loneliness.

The search for romance motivates Ally and Bridget. Both already have careers, friends, and successful lives by conventional standards, yet they seem particularly troubled in the arena of love. Veronica Chambers writes that "like Ally, many of the women who watch the show find that romance is much more elusive than professional success." With their professional lives more or less in control, both women then focus their attention on romantic relationships. However, Ally and Bridget both, despite their various romantic entanglements, want more out of a committed relationship than what is offered by most of the men they encounter. Ally's numerous but brief relationships attest to this fact, as does Bridget's final conversation with Daniel Cleaver in the film:

> DANIEL: If I can't make it with you, I can't make it with anyone.
>
> BRIDGET: That's not a good enough offer for me. [She pauses.] I'm not willing to gamble my whole life on someone who's well, not quite sure. It's like you said, I'm still looking for something more extraordinary than that.

Both Ally and Bridget want an extraordinary man who will be their equal and their "top person." Despite dating numerous men and even pursuing relationships with them, Ally and Bridget ultimately refuse to settle for men who do not embody the right characteristics. Ally's attractions to the man she rear ends at a stoplight, a new young, attractive co-worker, and even her closest and equally eccentric friend John Cage don't last because these men's quirks do not match Ally's and ultimately, the spark of attraction dissipates. Women of my generation, like Ally and Bridget, have been raised to demand equality and exceptionality, and some of us refuse to settle until we find our Mr. Darcy.

"Independent Women": Feminist Critiques of Romantic Love

As a Generation X feminist, I find myself, in Kathleen Newman's assessment: "Torn between the more radical, bra-burning feminism of our mothers' generation and the sassy 'girl power' rebellion of our younger sisters, we are faced with the problem of reclaiming feminism for ourselves" (320). I take my feminism personally and seriously, and want my choices to match my philosophy. Yet when that philosophy is confused by contradictory messages and desires, my personal life becomes as chaotic and messy as Ally's and Bridget's lives. I find myself carefully weighing my decisions (both romantic and otherwise) against the various "isms" I identify with. This becomes particularly volatile in the arena of romance. As a self-avowed romantic, am I betraying feminism's key goals every time I daydream about my elusive Mr. Darcy?

One significant problem in many feminist responses to romance is the disjunction between academic feminism's ideology and the lived realities of most women. In the 1970s while feminists like Kate Millet, Ti-Grace Atkinson, and Shulamith Firestone strongly critiqued heterosexual love and romance, the romance novel business was booming, according to romance critics Radway and Modleski. This disjunction between the academic and popular response to romance persisted and became particularly heated with the debut of *Ally McBeal* in 1997. The June 29, 1998, *Time* cover story on the death of feminism featured a photo of Calista Flockhart–Ally McBeal alongside feminist icons Gloria Steinem, Susan B. Anthony, and Betty Friedan, implicating Ally in feminism's purported demise. The media uproar was focused on whether or not Ally McBeal's particular brand of "feminine appeal" symbolized the transformation of a feminism concerned with the oppression of women into an apolitical and frivolous movement.[2] In one of the accompanying articles, a transcribed discussion between academic feminist Phyllis Chesler and journalist Gina Bellafante typifies a hostile attitude towards the show:

> BELLAFANTE: I think feminism worked long and hard to erase stereotypes of women as neurotic incompetents unconcerned with matters of public life, Ally McBeal, in my humble opinion, is helping undue that work.
>
> CHESLER: I agree.... And I would say that if Monica Lewinsky goes to law school and continues to behave in the same fashion, she will turn into Ally McBeal — obsessed with men and sex and love and short skirts, and not with children being beaten to death in their own homes and not with women losing child support. These are not Ally McBeal's fantasy concerns.

Chesler and Bellafante's conversation illustrates a prevailing critique of *Ally McBeal,* which dismisses the show, basically for being a romantic comedy and not a serious legal drama series. Moreover, Chesler and Bellafante suggest that women's fantasy concerns should be serious political matters to be considered feminist. This discussion also connects to the contemporary political question of women like Monica Lewinsky using their sex appeal to connect with powerful men, as well as powerful men's use of their political influence to engage women sexually. *Ally McBeal* and *Bridget Jones's Diary* arguably touch on these "deeper" political issues via the world of comic fantasy, urging readers to think of the greater implications of short skirts in the workplace.

Academic feminism, of course, continued to flourish despite the media's pronouncements of its demise.[3] The 1990s saw the publication of a string of texts that discussed the "betrayals" of feminism and the creation of a culture where academic feminisms were being challenged by popular, conservative texts that sought to prove the emptiness of feminism's promises. In *Backlash,* Susan Faludi dispels these popular myths: "These so-called female crises have had their origins not in the actual conditions of women's lives but rather in a closed system that starts and ends in the media, popular culture, and advertising — an endless feedback loop that perpetuates and exaggerates its own false images of womanhood" (xv). Faludi sees the messages in popular texts as promoting myths that undermine and blame feminism for women's ailments when in fact these symptoms are fabricated by alarmists. The popular media undermines feminism by preying on women's fears and uncertainties about love, marriage, and independence. Yet, as Heywood suggests, feminist criticisms, like Faludi's, can also backfire, creating their own backlash: "[Feminist criticisms] may even exasperate Ally's fans so much that they create a kind of antifeminist backlash" (B9). Because so many women identify with Ally's and Bridget's anxieties, the failure to take these fictional characters seriously is a failure to take real women's similar anxieties seriously.

Despite the validity of Faludi's powerful critique of the popular media, she fails to take into account the reality of these fears for many women. Women do face conflict when cultural expectations clash with feminist ideologies, and the media often does insidiously exploit these fears. Popular texts like *Ally McBeal* and *Bridget Jones's Diary* provide dialogue between cultural myths and expectations and feminist ideologies. They also illustrate the effects of these often contradictory messages on women. Fielding even alludes to *Backlash* in the novel *Bridget Jones's Diary,* in the first awkward conversation between Bridget and Mark Darcy:

> "I. Um. Are you reading any, ah ... Have you read any good books lately?" he said....
> I racked my brain frantically to think when I last read a proper book.... I'm halfway through *Men Are from Mars, Women Are from Venus,* which Jude lent me, but I didn't think Mark Darcy, though clearly odd, was ready to accept himself as a Martian quite yet. Then I had a brainwave.
> "*Backlash,* actually, by Susan Faludi," I said triumphantly. Hah! I haven't exactly read it as such, but feel I have as Sharon has been ranting about it so much. Anyway, completely safe option as no way a diamond-pattern-jumpered goody-goody would have read five-hundred-page feminist treatise.
> "Ah. Really?" he said. "I read that when it first came out. Didn't you find there was rather a lot of special pleading?" [13].

This self-referentiality to a key feminist text like *Backlash* clearly places the novel in dialogue with feminism's ideas. It also illustrates several significant points: first, that Mark Darcy is well-read, open to feminist ideas, and would make a suitable boyfriend for Bridget because he is ostensibly not misogynistic; and second, Mark's critique of the Faludi text allows Fielding to include her own subtle critique of Faludi's message. Ironically, Bridget hasn't read *Backlash,* because doing so would invalidate or trivialize many of her concerns about love, marriage, and companionship. Reading this text might help Bridget dispel her neuroses, and channel her energy into the meaningful tasks at work. However, Faludi's text could just as well alienate a woman like Bridget, whose concerns are, to her at least, immensely valid. Instead, Bridget reads John Gray's problematic bestseller, which will confirm her fears but also give her outdated, stereotypical, prescriptive relationship advice that will eventually lead her astray. This interchange between Bridget and Mark may seem to undermine feminism's goals; however, Fielding engages the conflicting messages about gender and romance via a humorous and realistic situation. Fielding subtly takes feminism (Faludi) to task for dismissing Bridget's concerns and driving her towards a seemingly sympathetic but ultimately anti-feminist alternative (Gray).

Both David E. Kelley and Helen Fielding, answering accusations that their protagonists are either pre- or postfeminist throwbacks, have stressed that Ally and Bridget are fictional characters. Fielding says: "It is v. [sic] funny to think of people in the book being ultimate representations of anything, as they were just meant to be funny. But maybe, it is quite end-of-this-century to be confused about life, really trying to get it right, but not exactly sure what 'it' is."[4] While the creators of these characters claim no specific agenda, cultural critics rightly argue that mass cultural texts are both a creation *of* culture, and *create* culture. *Ally McBeal* and *Bridget Jones's Diary* concern feminist critics precisely because of their cultural influence.

Such critics dismiss the sense of identification viewers and readers share with the text. Dismissing the texts, one dismisses the viewers and further alienates them from the feminist movement. Snitow astutely assesses the role of Harlequin romances in the 1970s: "The ubiquity of the books indicates a central truth: romance is a primary category of the female imagination. The women's movement has left this fact of female consciousness largely untouched. While most serious women *novelists* treat romance with irony and cynicism, most women do not" (321). This comment could easily be redirected at some feminist critics, like Elaine Showalter, who dismisses the film version of *Bridget Jones's Diary* as "a charming and frothy fairy tale with no feminist consciousness whatsoever." I am among the numerous women who do not dismiss the film so easily. As a good friend of mine states: "Bridget is us," meaning that she is single, professional, independent, struggling with issues of romance, and self-image. She wants to have it all. Women like Bridget are concerned with feminist politics;

however, for most women, these issues play out in their everyday lives of working with and relating to others in our residual patriarchal society. Seemingly trivial matters like fashion, diet, and romantic love are significant arenas of women's daily struggle. Navigating the conflicting messages from feminisms and patriarchy can make many women feel as incompetent as Ally and Bridget feel.

Many of the mass media reviews of *Ally McBeal* and *Bridget Jones's Diary* label the texts as post-feminist, a troublesome concept that indicates the death of feminism. Tara Zahra reads this post-mortem of feminism as a problem of definition: "What the right is doing its best to bury belongs not to feminism but to a caricature of it created by both the media and the right's own propaganda machine." The standards for defining feminism are not generated by feminists themselves, but by the media who oversimplifies the feminist project. The conservative media, in Zahra's view, tells us that "Women's enthusiasm for 'postfeminist' fictional characters such as Ally McBeal and Bridget Jones is supposed to represent feminism's bankruptcy, the selling out of feminist elders by all young women." Yet the conservative media are not the only ones involved in this line of criticism — so too are academic feminists like Showalter and Chesler. The "rightist" media and feminist critics both need to heed Zahra's reminder that the primary goal of feminism is "to expand choices and opportunities for large numbers of women." The plurality of feminist voices and experiences will continue to create heated debate and, ultimately, attest to the strength of feminism. As Zahra explains: "No matter how much the pundits would like us to think otherwise ... Ally's popular success does not contradict well-documented majority support for essentially feminist views on equal rights, child care provisioning, welfare, education, and abortion." Ultimately, then, women's engagement with "serious" political issues and popular concerns should not be seen as a contradictory impulse, but instead as representing the plurality of concerns faced by contemporary women.

Wanting It All: Ally and Bridget Navigate Romance and Feminism

In clarifying what I find so appealing about *Ally McBeal* and *Bridget Jones's Diary* I have discovered that the characters' ability to examine and laugh at their own flaws keeps me connected. Ally and Bridget are dedicated to self-improvement and self-awareness, and both remain optimistic despite the dire warnings about declining fertility, decreasing desirability, and inevitable aging in a youth obsessed culture. This emphasis on self-improvement and introspection also makes *Ally McBeal* and *Bridget Jones's*

Diary powerful sites for exploring the intersections of romantic love and feminism. Ally has a series of therapists and "visions" to help her puzzle through her life, and Bridget has a trusted diary and friends to aid her process of self-awareness. Self-improvement remains an elusive goal because of the barrage of contradictions the women face. Rosemary Johnson-Kurek suggests that these contradictions are a byproduct of the feminist movement:

> The women's liberation movement and the sexual revolution left confusion in their wake. Models of gender roles are still evolving and the issues — expectations in employment, relationships, marriage, and reproduction — re being worked out in contemporary romances by authors, some of whom were not yet born and some of whom were teens and young women in the early sixties, when these movements began [142].

Certainly David E. Kelley and Helen Fielding are playing with the tensions that thirtysomethings face as their generation comes of age.

One of the biggest tensions professional single, thirtysomething women face is whether to accept their independence as "Singletons" or to continue searching for a fulfilling romantic relationship. Despite their successful careers, both Ally and Bridget desire the companionship of a relationship to enhance their lives. Both are aware that they *could* survive as independent single women. As Bridget says to her mother: "But if you're a feminist you shouldn't need a —" (Fielding, *Bridget Jones: The Edge of Reason*, 299). Yet, both characters earnestly desire to combine romantic love with a successful career, and they represent many women who want the entire package. Ally and Bridget embody the conflict between wanting to "form functional relationship[s] with responsible adult[s]" and "sulk about having no boyfriend, but develop inner poise and authority and sense of self as woman of substance, complete *without* boyfriend, as best way to obtain boyfriend" (Fielding, *Bridget Jones's Diary*, 3, 2). Bridget succinctly clarifies the crux of the conflict: developing a strong sense of self complete without a romantic relationship and continuing to desire a romantic relationship. Although seemingly flippant, her assessment that the route of inner poise will be the best way to obtain a boyfriend matches much contemporary thought about ideal relationships. Ironically, Bridget's continual lack of inner poise defines her, and it is this less-than-perfect woman who Mark Darcy falls in love with. Ultimately, Bridget learns that simply being her own conflicted self is the best way to obtain a boyfriend, dispelling the pressure created by "*Cosmopolitan* culture," which has convinced Bridget "that neither [her] personality nor [her] body is up to it if left to its own devices" (Fielding, *Bridget Jones's Diary*, 52). Bridget need not be a supermodel with cellulite-free thighs to win the heart of Mark

Darcy. Ally too discovers that a blatant honesty about her neuroses ultimately connects her with Larry, the man with whom she experiences a serious relationship in season four. Both women discover that being themselves garners the love they desire.

One key difference between *Ally McBeal* and *Bridget Jones's Diary* is that Ally's quest for marriage dominates the series, whereas Bridget is more skeptical of becoming a "smug married" and would be content with a committed boyfriend. While all romantic relationships can be fraught with anxiety, marriage continues to be the primary site of conflict between romantic love and feminism because of its deep traditions, symbols, and cultural weight. That marriage permanently eludes Ally indicates her inability to successfully wed her desires for romance and feminism. Bridget has much more success in her relationship with Mark Darcy, although their relationship is strained by a series of misunderstandings.

Yet many popular reviewers of both texts believe that the contradictory and neurotic tics of these characters undermine feminist consciousness. Rick Marin and Veronica Chambers describe Ally as "beautiful, smart, successful ... [an] emotional train wreck." Another tactic is to speak of Ally and Bridget as teenagers— thirtysomething embodiments of the "not a girl, not yet a woman" status of which pop diva Britney Spears croons. Alyssa Katz describes *Ally McBeal* as a "lite dramedy about the self-destructive neuroses, childish foibles and desperate romantic needs of a female character who appears to be fully grown, even if she does weigh about 100 pounds. In her many wistful moments, McBeal appears to be channeling 15-year-old Angela Chase from *My So-Called Life*." Jane Rosenzweig explains: "American pop culture has become preoccupied with our collective inability to grow up. People are staying single longer, and the beauty industry is constantly coaxing us to make ourselves look younger if we want to stay in the romantic business." She suggests that "the packaging of female adulthood as an extended adolescence" is in direct contrast to shows like *Buffy the Vampire Slayer* that showcase "more assertive, more independent" teenagers. The infantilization of adult women is, to Rosenzweig, a function of the relentless, biological clock driven search for a mate. The younger television characters like Buffy simply are not concerned with such matters, and are, according to Rosenzweig, more realistic, more self-possessed, and more feminist than the older women.

According to such critiques, thirtysomething women should be mature, self-possessed, focused on their careers, and not primarily concerned with settling down. Or, as Rosenzweig states: "Television's message: only when they're not worrying about their biological clocks can women have fully developed characters." Such a statement trivializes Ally's and

Bridget's desire for fully developed lives containing careers and romantic love. This modern conundrum causes the neuroses and tics of Ally and Bridget to reach a fever pitch. They are products of their culture, a culture which on one hand tells them that having a career and being independent is the path to true success in a male-dominated professional world. On the other hand, they are constantly reminded that youth, beauty, and the "tick-tock" of the biological clock work against them. Ally and Bridget's over-the-top scrapes and anxieties are directly linked to these contradictory messages about their ages.

The final season of *Ally McBeal* is particularly pertinent to this discussion because, as Sarah Blustain states, "One thing we know is that in the last season, Ally grew up." Ally achieves ultimate professional and personal success when she makes partner in the law firm, buys a house, is surprised by a 10 year old daughter she didn't know she had, and finds a house "husband" in handyman Victor. Blustain links this evolving plot with the eventual demise of Ally — the viewers gave up on her because, for one reason, "the old Ally and the issues that engaged her were simply more interesting — more true to our lives — than the new, improved version." Ally's struggle to "get it together" was more entertaining and also, according to Blustain "more engaged in questions of feminist politics than the I've-got-it-together reincarnation, who makes being a single working mom look like a piece of birthday cake." The new Ally has succeeded by feminist standards, but this flawless success diminishes the opportunity for real dialogue about the professional and personal issues that contemporary women must face. The neat resolution of the series in a fantasy of the woman who has it all ultimately fails to resonate with the audience, who recognizes this as a myth.

Bridget Jones remains in that tumultuous, messy, "adolescent" world and remains conflicted throughout the novels. Awash in a sea of self-help books like the ubiquitous *Men Are from Mars, Women Are from Venus,* Bridget attempts to understand the complicated relationships between the sexes in order to succeed with her unreconstructed and blatantly misogynistic boss Daniel Cleaver. While some critics would chalk this relationship up to Bridget's own unreconstructed feminist consciousness, readers know that her infatuation will not last. Daniel Cleaver obviously epitomizes all of the qualities Bridget despises in men, summed up by the concept of "fuckwittage" — the emotional gameplaying and manipulation often employed by members of both sexes. Bridget rebounds from Daniel's betrayal by finding a television job at quirky *Sit Up Britain,* and successfully escapes the awkwardness of continuing to work with Daniel. More importantly, Bridget's new job better suits her personality and allows her to focus more seriously on her career. Bridget temporarily concentrates on her career: "It is great when you start thinking about your career instead of worrying about trivial things—men and relationships" (Fielding, *Bridget Jones's Diary*, 193). We know, as does Bridget, that this singular focus will not last because she is committed to a well-rounded life, and does not really believe that men and relationships are trivial matters.

Significantly, both the Bridget Jones novels and films and *Ally McBeal* include a significant amount of direct commentary on the conflict between feminist ideology and romantic love. Sometimes the conflict gives women increased options. Mrs. Jones, for example, realizes that she was "like the grasshopper who sang all summer" and needed to do something for herself like Germaine Greer, the feminist icon of her generation, would suggest. Feminist ideology, as often spouted by Bridget's outspoken friend Shazzer, strengthens Bridget's resolve to stay away from misogynistic Daniel Cleaver, who is much more demeaning and despicable in the book than the lovable cad played by Hugh Grant in the film version. The film, however, removes some of the tension Bridget faces in the book and replaces it with a less complex and clearer plot.

Ally McBeal, as Heywood astutely notes, "has a refutation of all the standard feminist critiques built right into its script. It has anticipated our arguments before we can even make them" (B9). From the infamous unisex bathroom to Richard Fish's misogynistic "fishisms," and the bizarre legal cases of love and loss, *Ally McBeal* constantly engages in gender politics. Ally and her colleagues at Cage and Fish often disagree about issues of gender and romance in their law cases, providing a space for open debate within the context of the show, and also in the culture at large. Richard Fish's notorious ogling of women and skewed logic allows the other characters to create opposing positions. Ally's enduring search for love, the overarching theme of the series, includes an active critique of romantic relationships in contemporary society, delivered with postmodern comedic twists. While *Ally McBeal* does not always engage in the deeper complexities of the issues, it nevertheless does important cultural work by introducing these issues to a large audience.

Finally, Ally and Bridget demonstrate a resiliency and determination to pursue romantic love, professional success, and sustaining friendships despite the grim struggle and dizzying conflicts. While both characters have indeed "bought into" the dream of romantic love, they do not sacrifice other aspects of their lives to that dream. Both characters attempt to create balanced lives of love, friendship, and work, arguably what most individuals desire. Their failures, flaws, and goofiness make them all the more human, endearing, if sometimes aggravating.

"Made for Each Other": Towards a Happy Marriage between Romance and Feminism

Ultimately, the endings of works in the romance genre illustrate the level of feminist consciousness. Many films and books end neatly, with all the loose ends resolved with only the promised ring of gold. In such endings, the women relinquish a key aspect of their independence. This capitulation to the happy ending can be a major stumbling block for me. In the recent film *Kate and Leopold,* for example, the heroine Kate (played by romantic comedy darling Meg Ryan) literally walks away from a significant career promotion to time travel to 1876 to reunite with her beloved Leopold (played by the dashing Hugh Jackman). Such a "romantic" ending asks the female protagonist to abandon her success in the career world in exchange for the perfect romantic relationship. Such a choice reflects an either-or choice that is not satisfactory to most women, who don't want to relinquish either one for the other.

The traditional romantic text ends with a marriage, which many feminists read as a patriarchal ending. As Modleski notes in "Feminism without Women: Culture and Criticism in a 'Postfeminist' Age": "For feminist criticism has, of course, rejected the ideology—purveyed in romance and many other forms of popular and high art—that holds marital commitments to be women's chief goal and greatest desire" (47). Yet neither Ally nor Bridget stands at the altar herself at the conclusion of their texts. The heroines' more ambiguous endings suggest that marriage does not always ensue from contemporary romance texts. While both women desire marriage, it is not their ultimate goal, as they discover along the way. And even if both texts emphasize the protagonists' search for love, it is because this quest proves most difficult.

The material conditions to ending a television series like *Ally McBeal* make analyzing this ending difficult; the storyline must account for the ending of the series itself. *Ally McBeal*'s series finale "Bygones" addresses several key concerns for both romance and feminism. First, love and marriage triumph, albeit between the misogynistic Richard Fish and the postfeminist Liza Bump. This ultimate love revelation is all the more powerful because it is made between two people who are, as Richard states in his wedding vows: "Outwardly dismissive of [love] but inside just as desperate for it." Furthermore, Richard credits Ally with his increasing capacity to love, as she was always committed to this ideal. However, Ally's imminent departure to New York, a move precipitated by daughter Maddie's emotional problems, necessitates the ending of the show. The Ally who once confessed that her problems were more important than everyone else's because they were hers leaves a successful career and an "urban family" out of concern for her daughter. Admittedly, the sudden move jars viewers and seems, dare I say it, rather forced. This ending moves Ally in a different direction — one in which the ultimate fulfilling relationship is between mother and daughter.[5] Ally, as to be expected, follows her heart. The ending is problematic because it leaves Ally's future outside of Maddie ambiguous. Ally says "there are law firms in New York," but she makes no concrete professional plans. I was pleased that the series didn't magically marry Ally off to one of her departed loves even though Kelley does include a typical Ally daydream about her own marriage to "Billy, Larry, Victor, whoever" during Richard and Liza's wedding. Yet I was disappointed that her life seemed similarly skewed in another *single* direction — her role as a mother.

The conclusion of *Bridget Jones's Diary* is more satisfactory to me because Bridget emerges triumphant in both her career and her relationship. Both novels end with her reunited with Mark Darcy, and with her positive career goals intact. Although in the second novel she is planning on traveling to Thailand with Mark, her career as a freelance journalist allows her mobility and continued professional evolution. The film version concludes, interestingly enough, with Mark Darcy capitulating a job offer in America in order to return to London and pursue a relationship with Bridget and presumably stay on with his old firm in London. The conclusion of the *Bridget Jones's Diary* texts are also more satisfying to me than the conclusion to *Ally McBeal,* because the texts assure me that despite my contradictions, my insecurities, and incompetencies, I can maintain a successful career and be in a relationship with someone who loves me for those very flaws. In the film *Bridget Jones's Diary,* Mark's declaration of love includes a list of Bridget's "flaws"—which he then follows up with, "I like you — just as you are." In this romance, the protagonist is loved simply for being herself. And Bridget in turn loves Mark just as he is— even with his too long sideburns. Also, notably in the film, Mark buys Bridget a new diary for their fresh start, after reading a few entries in the old one that described him as "dull" and stiff. Mark recognizes the importance of this self-aware, independent space where Bridget writes herself.

When I began writing this essay, I was admittedly trying to justify my affinity for popular romance texts like *Ally McBeal* and *Bridget Jones's Diary;* since I was looking for a justification, it is safe to assume I myself thought of *Ally McBeal* and *Bridget Jones's Diary* as suspect texts. That suspicion is a byproduct of being part of the academic system, and the suspicion of romantic love is more specifically a byproduct of being an academic feminist. Suspicion or skepticism can serve us well, and can contribute to a more nuanced understanding of culture and texts. But part of me wants to stop justifying these texts, wants to stop being suspicious of every deployment of romantic heterosexual love. Some evenings I want to curl up on the couch and pop in a tape of *Ally McBeal* and *Bridget Jones's Diary,* or dive into one of Fielding's novels and feel connected to the emotional lives of these women. I want to put suspicion aside and laugh as Ally throws an elegant leather pump at some man's head, or laugh when Bridget tells Daniel Cleaver that she would "rather have a job wiping Saddam Hussein's ass" than work with him any longer. I want to cheer as Ally finds love with Victor, and Bridget finally kisses her Mr. Darcy. Yes, the texts are contradictory, and these protagonists often bumbling through their days. But in their verisimilitude to my own experience, they bring me a great deal of laughter and comfort, and give me ways to explore my own thoughts and expectations about my life, in and out of love.

Following the model of Radway's study of Harlequin Romance readers in the late 1970s, questioning how real women relate to these texts would provide greater insight into the feminist consciousness and concerns of this constituency. As Radway writes in 1994, "The romance is now, and has been at least for the last 15 years, a principle site for the struggle over feminine subjectivity and sexuality and, I would argue, over feminism as well" ("Romance and the Work of Fantasy," 395). Taking the texts more seriously, we could then ascertain whether or not these women see feminism as obsolete, or if their definition of feminism renders it inapplicable to their own lives. If romantic love is seen to be antifeminist, then certainly a great percentage of these women will be hesitant to be part of the movement. Also, although many women might not label themselves as feminists, their values and behaviors might be decidedly feminist. Academic feminists should ultimately make a place for critical discussions of romantic heterosexual love, the texts that explore this issue, and the real women who are affected by it.

Additionally, much of the available criticism of romance as a literary genre is dated; while the scholarship establishes a foundation for studying the romance genre, the works fail to address the concerns of contemporary romances like *Ally McBeal* and *Bridget Jones's Diary.* "Chick Lit," an ever-expanding genre, exposes new twists on age-old questions of romance, sex, and power and poses many new questions for scholars to explore. While some scholars critique the romance genre for perpetuating the necessity of marriage and compulsory heterosexuality, many texts explore more non-traditional and contemporary arrangements. *Ally McBeal* in particular has presented a variety of alternative relationships for a mass audience —from the recurring character of Claire played by Dame Edna, to the transgen-dered relationship between Mark and Cindy, to power virgin Kimmy, to interracial and intergeneration relationships. While these relationships are treated comically in some aspect — what on the show is not? — the variety of romantic love speaks to our more progressive times, and *Ally McBeal* successfully brought these alternative versions of romance to mass audiences. Romance itself is in a state of transformation, as the heirs of *Ally McBeal* and *Bridget Jones's Diary* suggest.

As I conclude this essay in 2005, Ally and Bridget's heirs are numerous, and they provide new twists on this conflict between romance and feminism. Television heroines like the character Elliot on *Scrubs* display a quirky mixture of vulnerability and tenacity, while agent Sidney Bristow on *Alias* uses her sexuality as yet another tool in her arsenal of toughness. Now, Ally and Bridget seem quaint in comparison to the much analyzed foursome on *Sex and the City*. Novels like *Jemima J.* by British journalist Jane Green follow in Fielding's footsteps, introducing readers to "flawed" women they can identify with. Even Harlequin is following Fielding's success; published under the Red Dress Ink label, Harlequin's newest series features novels with young urban professional women who search for romance to complement their professional lives.[6] *Flyover States,* a novel in this line, humorously depicts young women navigating romantic and academic pursuits in an English literature graduate program. This novel, in particular, illustrates the ability of these "chick lit" texts to be smart, asking those tough feminist questions while also displaying a concern with the trappings of modern romance, strappy sandals and all. *Ally McBeal* and *Bridget Jones's Diary* helped create the climate for such incarnations by showcasing women of my generation struggling with their choices as women, and the role of romance in their lives. In the words of Bridget Jones, I hope that "the wilderness years are over" and "Singletons" like Ally, Bridget, myself, and numerous other women will find a place where romance and feminism will be happily married.

Notes

1. Indeed, all of these examples embody conflicts about women's roles, particularly women's embodiment. However, most of the criticism seizes on these obvious cues to simplify the texts, instead of engaging them in a sustained critique.

2. It is important to note that academic feminism is in no way a monolithic movement. One of the major critiques of the feminist movement over the years has been its tendency to subsume all women under its category, overlooking key differences in class, race, and sexual orientation. Current academic feminism resonates with a plurality of voices, and should be referred to as feminisms. Despite this plurality, "popular feminism" is still suspect. Yet I believe it should be another valid voice within the larger umbrella of feminisms, to be taken as seriously as the other voices.

3. I use the plural feminisms pointedly, as feminism is an increasingly pluralistic movement.

4. This interview was included in the online *Time* Web site that featured the Ally McBeal cover stories; such pairings are not uncommon in later reviews of both *Ally McBeal* and *Bridget Jones's Diary.*

5. In *Reading from the Heart: Women, Literature, and the Search for True Love,* Suzanne Juhasz explores the connection between the mother-daughter relationship and romance novels, which would provide another way to "read" the series finale of *Ally McBeal.*

6. Information about this new Harlequin line can be found at http://www.eharlequin.com.

Works Cited

Blustain, Sarah. "Washington Diarist: Split End." *The New Republic,* 6 May 2002: 58. Infotrac. Auburn University Library, Auburn, AL. 15 July 2002. <http://www.gale-group.com>

Bridget Jones's Diary. Directed by Sharon Maguire. Screenplay by Helen Fielding, Andrew Davies, and Richard Curtis. Miramax, 2001.

"Bygones." *Ally McBeal.* Fox. 20 May 2002.

Chambers, Veronica. "How Would Ally Do It?" *Newsweek,* 2 March 1998: 58 (3). Infotrac. Auburn University Library, Auburn, AL. 15 July 2002. <http://www.galegroup.com>

Chesler, Phyllis, and Gina Bellafante. Transcribed Discussion. *Time.* Accessed 15 July 2002. <http://www.time.com/time/magazine/1998/dom/980629/cover1.htm>

Faludi, Susan. *Backlash: The Undeclared War Against American Women.* New York: Crown, 1991.

Fielding, Helen. *Bridget Jones's Diary.* New York: Viking, 1998.

_____. *Bridget Jones: The Edge of Reason.* New York: Viking, 1999.

_____. Online Interview. *Time.* Accessed 15 July 2002. <http://www.time.com/time/magazine/1998/dom/980629/cover1.html>

Gaylin, Willard, and Ethel Person. "Introduction: Thinking about Love." *Passionate Attachments.* Willard Gaylin and Ethel Person, eds. New York: The Free Press, 1988. ix–xiii.

Gray, John. *Men Are from Mars, Women Are from Venus: A Practical Guide for Improving Communication and Getting What You Want in Your Relationships.* New York: HarperCollins, 1992.

Green, Jane. *Jemima J.* New York: Broadway Books, 1999.

Heywood, Leslie. "Hitting a Cultural Nerve: Another Season of *Ally McBeal.*" *The Chronicle of Higher Education,* 4 Sept. 1998: B9.

Johnson-Kurek, Rosemary. "Leading us into Temptation: The Language of Sex and the Power of Love." *Romantic Conventions.* Anne K. Kaler and Rosemary Johnson-Kurek, eds. Bowling Green, OH: Bowling Green State University Press, 1999. 113–148.

Juhasz, Suzanne. *Reading from the Heart: Women, Literature, and the Search for True Love.* New York: Viking, 1994.

Kate and Leopold. Directed by James Mangold. Miramax, 2001.

Katz, Alyssa. "Ally McBeal." *The Nation,* 15 Dec. 1997: 36 (3). Infotrac. Auburn University Library, Auburn, AL. 15 July 2002. <http://www.galegroup.com>

Kelley, David. E., producer. *Ally McBeal.* Fox. Sept. 1997-May 2002.

Marin, Rick, and Veronica Chambers. "Ally McBeal." *Newsweek,* 13 Oct. 1997: 71 (1). Infotrac. Auburn University Library, Auburn, AL. 15 July 2002. <http://www.gale-group.com>

Modleski, Tania. "Feminism without Women: Culture and Criticism in a 'Postfeminist' Age." *Women and Romance: A Reader.* Edited by Susan Ostrov Weisser. New York: New York University Press, 2001, 342–346.

_____. *Loving with a Vengeance: Mass-Produced Fantasies for Women.* Hamden, CT: Archon, 1982.

Newman, Kathleen. "The Problem That Has a Name: *Ally McBeal* and the Future of Feminism." *The Colby Quarterly 36 (4):319–24.*

Radway, Janice. *Reading the Romance: Women, Patriarchy, and Popular Literature.* Chapel Hill: University of North Carolina Press, 1984.

_____. "Romance and the Work of Fantasy: Struggles over Feminine Sexuality and Subjectivity at Century's End." *Feminism and Cultural Studies.* Edited by Marag Shiach. Oxford: Oxford University Press, 1999. 395–416.

Rosenzweig, Jane. "Ally McBeal's Younger Sisters." *The American Prospect,* 23 Nov. 1999:62. Infotrac. Auburn University Library, Auburn, AL. 15 July 2002. <http://www.galegroup.com>

Ryan, Barbara. "Beyond Embarrassment: Feminism and Adult Heterosexual Love." *Women and Romance: A Reader.* Edited by Susan Ostrov Weisser. New York: New York University Press, 2001, 464–473.

Showalter, Elaine. "Sex Goddess." *The American Prospect,* 21 May 2001: 38. Infotrac. Auburn University Library, Auburn, AL. 15 July 2002. <http://www.galegroup.com>

Snitow, Ann. "Mass Market Romance: Pornography for Women Is Different." *Women and Romance: A Reader.* Edited by Susan Ostrov Weisser. New York: New York University Press, 2001, 307–322.

Weisser, Susan Ostrov. Introduction. *Women and Romance: A Reader.* Edited by Susan Ostrov Weisser. New York: New York UP, 2001, 1–6.

Zahra, Tara. "The Feminism Gap." *The American Prospect,* January 1999: 20 (1). Infotrac. Auburn University Library, Auburn, AL. 15 July 2002. <http://www.galegroup.com>

3

Cultural Occupancy, Television Reception, and Multiple Identifications in *Ally McBeal*

Susan E. McKenna

This study examines how differentiated viewers constructed televisual identifications through a series of trajectories: sexual, gender, race, and political. I conducted a series of in-depth interviews asking questions about the television program *Ally McBeal* and changing models of lesbian identity. Through exploring the discursive interactions between previous models of postfeminist television and critical analyses of the 1990s phenomenon of lesbian chic, I suggest that this historical juncture opens up new possibilities for viewer identifications. The postfeminist-lesbian chic intersection speaks to broader discourses about the gender and sexual politics of contemporary feminism, and in turn, to an expanded understanding of lesbian identity. Ultimately, I propose that the act of self-identifying can be a form of cultural occupancy that moves beyond previous models of narrative recuperation and audience reception.

The current status of lesbian visibility in popular culture — often designated as *lesbian chic*— is marked by an intersection with the discourses of contemporary postfeminism. Lesbian chic and postfeminism each typifies what Suzanna Danuta Walters (1995) defines as "a cultural 'moment'—a convergence of various discourses ... that produce a particular sensibility or ethos" (pp. 116–117). The widespread public circulation of the lesbian chic-postfeminist cultural moments converges with the narrative limitations and consumer constraints of popular television. These dynamics are exemplified in the Fox network series *Ally McBeal*. Widely touted as geared towards the highly desirable female audience (with a crossover to male fans), the program's "symptomatic" status (Walters, p.

6) is a cultural territory that is shared with and shaped by the lesbian fans for whom the playful sexual liminality of the female characters carries a cultural currency and an experiential resonance.

Following a feminist cultural studies approach, I have conducted a series of interviews asking lesbian fans about *Ally McBeal*.[1] The *McBeal* interviews were engendered from a larger study about how changes in lesbian visibility might impact upon understandings of interpretive communities, viewing strategies, and audience identifications. The line between researcher and my own *Ally* fandom blurred when *Ally McBeal* began to disrupt and intrude upon the interviews of the larger study with what I came to characterize as a *queer insistence*. Some lesbian respondents discussed watching the program together as a special ritualistic event, while others reported making arrangements to exchange copies of *Ally* episodes that had lesbian content. Participants described the overt lesbian visibility of *Ally McBeal*—long lingering looks and hot sexy kisses exchanged between female characters—as an excessive and campy representational acknowledgement of the lesbian audience. These social and self-conscious ruminations raised questions about previous understandings of lesbian identifications as subcultural and homogeneous.[2]

Ally McBeal has become synonymous with postfeminism (Bellafante, 1998), and because I was exploring lesbian chic as a component of postfeminism, the queer insistence of *Ally McBeal* was compelling. The *Ally*-postfeminist association was frequently expressed through the critical rejection of the program's reification of negative sexual and gender hegemonies (see Shalit, 1998). Although the program might appear to close down the potential for viewer resistance, I began to wonder if *Ally McBeal*'s flirtation with lesbian chic might speak to changes in lesbian positionings in broader cultural contexts, and, in turn, if these changes might open up new possibilities for viewer identifications.

The queer insistence of *Ally McBeal* was inserting itself into my social life as well. At parties, in stores, and in restaurants, women talked about what the *Ally* characters looked like, how they behaved, and whether or not they were "real lesbians." The *Ally McBeal* iconography included a range of female characters of differing race, body, and age categories, and I overheard heated discussions of these portrayals that suggested a nuanced reconfiguration of viewer identifications. By *queer insistence,* I mean that the queerness of *Ally McBeal* was entering into the lesbian communal lexicon with a recurring perseverance. Even women who were ambivalent about the homophobic and sexist limitations were watching the program in order to keep up. The multiplicity and subtlety of these identifications suggested that *Ally McBeal*'s queer insistence reflected a broader cultural fragmentation of lesbian identity.[3]

Queer has a dual meaning: It functions as an umbrella term for sexual identities, but to queer also means a queering, or a fragmenting, of categories and dichotomies.[4] Criticisms of changes in lesbian visibility maintain that lesbian chic perpetuates a widespread cultural dichotomy: The good apolitical lesbian who is a gorgeous, sexual adventurer for whom the accouterments of an urban upper middle class life-style are central, versus the bad political lesbian who is a man-hating, unfashionable, anti-sex espouser of feminist tenets (see Hamer and Budge, 1994). The good-bad lesbian dichotomy has great utility for discussing the interrelationships of lesbian chic and postfeminism. Lesbian chic and postfeminism are typically framed in similar ways by critics who decry an equality that hinges upon a sexualized appearance constructed through consumer ideals and an erasure of difference; this equality — which is argued to be comprised — is sustained through a depoliticizing individualism. The good-bad lesbian dichotomy highlights these criticisms, and was a viable presence in lesbian fan discussions of the queer insistence of *Ally McBeal.*

This paper complicates an easy rejection of *Ally McBeal* (and by extension of lesbian chic and postfeminism), and instead asks questions about how lesbian viewers might queer, through their engagements with, the good-bad lesbian dichotomy, and in turn, negotiate shifts in the lesbian cultural lexicon. In this essay, I will use the good-bad lesbian dichotomy, as disseminated through *Ally McBeal,* to examine viewer responses to themes that have been significant to feminist cultural studies: first, through questions about beauty standards and consumer culture, and relatedly, sexual objectification and the male gaze; and, second, through questions about representations and erasures of difference.

Postfeminism and Lesbian Chic

In 1987, Judith Stacey defined postfeminism as "the simultaneous incorporation, revision, and depoliticization of many of the central goals of second-wave feminism" (qtd. in Dow, 1996, p. 87). The popular[5] positioning of postfeminism reflects these contradictory negotiations of feminist principles. These have manifested in a conservative "backlash" that portrays a failed feminist movement whose legacy is a responsibility for contemporary gender problems (Faludi, 1991). At the nexus of this media-constructed postfeminism is the antithetical belief that gender equality has already been achieved and, as a 1998 *Time Magazine* cover heralded, that "Feminism Is Dead."

The contradictory reworkings of feminism are illustrated in television programming of the 1980s and 1990s (for summaries, see Dow, 1996; and

Press, 1991). Aspects of feminism such as economic parity and professional access are incorporated into plot and character development, yet professional success is attributed to individual initiative rather than to any collective action. When gender issues are included, they are resolved as personal problems and not through a reconfiguration of the system. Furthermore, there is no critique of gender roles, sexual norms, or family relations (Press and Strathman, 1993), and no recognition of race, sex, or class differences (Dow, 1996). The depolitical, individualistic, and homogenous televisual revisions of feminism are regulated through postfeminist symbols that resonate through the cultural imaginary, and, as we shall see, work hand in hand with the good-bad lesbian dichotomy: the increasingly sexualized professional female, the family oriented "new traditionalist," the frustrated unstable single career woman, and the masculinized angry feminist. These symbols reflect a tension between femininity and feminism that has a dialectical relationship with the good-bad lesbian dichotomy.

On postfeminist television, the emphasis on the individual in gender equality is sustained through the traditional feminine appearance and behavior of the female characters. The oppositional negotiation of femininity and feminism embodied in the symbol of the successful, yet attractive career woman appeals to advertisers who incorporate messages of female empowerment into ads geared toward the highly desirable female demographic. Feminist cultural studies have been concerned with how television constructs female consumer pleasures through the appeal of lifestyle aesthetics (see Spigel and Mann, 1992, for an overview). Numerous critics have linked the postfeminist backlash to this consumer driven commercial lib that simultaneously stresses highly sexualized beauty ideals and increasingly unrealistic body norms (Faludi, 1991; Douglas, 1995; and Kilbourne, 1995). As Press (1991) writes, "Because of the mass media's commercial packaging, whatever thin slices of feminism might survive in the finished product are sandwiched between thicker slices of commercial femininity" (p. 39).

The contradiction between feminist principles such as professional gender equality and the individualizing emphasis on feminine looks and sexualized beauty also relates to questions about sexual objectification and the male gaze. As Susan Douglas (1995) has noted, popular portrayals of successful independent female professionals are made more palatable when the characters are overly focused on how they appear to the male characters. The feminized self-surveillance reifies the postfeminist positioning of successful female characters as sexualized objects of the male gaze. This televisual positioning is in correspondence with the sexualized chicness of the good-bad lesbian dichotomy. The alliance of gender equality with sexualized femininity, and therefore, with lesbian chic, is most fruitful when hetero-sexual female characters temporarily play with lesbianism through conventions that are traditionally constructed in pornography for the imaginary male spectator. These conventions— exemplified by the chic feminized style of the hyper-sexed participants— reaffirm the normative heterosexuality of the characters, and in turn, their temporary sexual mobility is attributed to their upwardly mobile class currency.[6] Thus, sexual agency is situated and valorized as an aesthetic choice, devoid of political implications. Additionally, on postfeminist television, the commercial conflation of traditional femininity with individual female empowerment is articulated with discourses about the family and the symbol of the new traditionalist, which locates the home as women's natural province (Probyn, 1990). This further maintains the parameters of femininity, and the boundaries of heterosexuality, through the correlation of female chicness with traditional roles and behaviors.

The sexualized professional and the new traditionalist are organizing principles of femininity versus feminism, and, as will be developed, of the good-bad lesbian dichotomy. These symbols are positioned alongside the trope of the frustrated single career woman who "in wanting it all" has ended up lonely and alone in a manifestation of the popular positioning of a bankrupt feminism that is simultaneously to blame for gendered dissatisfactions. The lines between femininity and feminism are likewise delineated through the extension of the frustrated single professional into the angry and threatening career woman, sometimes depicted as masculinized, but always as disturbed. The out-of-control career woman is regularly associated with feminism by narrative structures and visual conventions, and feminist critiques and principles are further diminished through this affiliation. Through this recurring cultural trope, Probyn (1990) stresses, the validating portrayal of "women's issues" in the workplace or home is sustained through not only the subversion of feminist principles, but also the positioning of feminism as the "other" (p. 128). The angry career woman resonates through the popular imaginary as the postfeminist embodiment of feminism, and, like the sexualized professional, the new traditionalist, and the frustrated single female, this symbol has a correspondence in the good-bad lesbian lexicon. Moreover, when the angry career woman is masculinized, the commercial compromise between femininity and feminism metamorphizes into the good-bad lesbian dichotomy.

It is important to note that on television (as in society at large) feminist is frequently equated with lesbian, and this equation is maintained by the emphatic situating of female characters as normative heterosexuals.[7] As Bonnie Dow stresses, "The still powerful romanticization of heterosexuality, the nuclear family, and motherhood" is central to postfeminism (1996, p. 91). The lesbian-feminist conflation looms large in the genealogy of popular euphemisms, and produces and regulates long-standing media and social stereotypes. Through this discursive collapse, Douglas (1995) writes, "the result is we all know what feminists [and, lesbians] are. They are shrill, overly aggressive, man-hating, ball-busting, selfish, hairy, extremist, deliberately unattractive women with absolutely no sense of humor who see sexism at every turn" (7). The depiction of feminists, and by association lesbians, as undesirable and unattractive, and as angry and militant, works in concert with and serves to mollify the contradiction that women can be equal and successful on television only if they are sexualized. In other words, as Douglas argues, strong, successful, and sexually attractive women cannot be feminists. And by extension, especially when portrayed in opposition to the new traditionalist, feminists cannot be sexually attractive. Thus, the conjoining of lesbian and feminist is not only a central subtext of postfeminism, where it works as an appeasing mediator, but also a cornerstone of the good-bad lesbian dichotomy. This is well evidenced in recent changes in lesbian visibility — in lesbian chic.[8] Lesbians may be in style, but the proliferation of suggested lesbian subject positions is clearly delineated through the good-bad lesbian dichotomy. To further evoke the postfeminist connection, some have even termed the good-bad lesbian dichotomy the lesbian chic backlash.

Both academics and activists critique the image bank of contemporary lesbian visibility — the good-bad lesbian dichotomy — and share a concern that the emphases on fashion, celebrity, and consumption are incompatible with political goals and erase a long history of political struggle (Clark, 1993; Hamer and Budge 1994; Moritz, 1995; Cottingham, 1996; Inness, 1997; Walters, 2001). Many activists believe that the apolitical emphasis on individualism will result in a loss of gay and lesbian culture and community (Harris, 1997). Danae Clark argues that lesbianism, in this glamorous "good" version, "is treated as merely a sexual style that can be chosen — or not chosen — just as one chooses a particular mode of fashion for self expression" (193). Like the depoliticizing of feminism in postfeminist television, the lesbian chic promises of assimilation and equality are constituted only through individual consumer lifestyles with no acknowledgement of history, community, or politics. Furthermore, the recent formations of lesbian visibility engender other forms of invisibilities such as the erasure of race and class differences. Lesbian chic does not represent a full range of lesbian lives; images of sexuality, class, age, and race might be left out or normalized through the good-bad lesbian dichotomy.

Others maintain that new renderings of lesbian visibility are just different formations of symbolic annihilation, stressing that so-called positive images of hip, stylish, and affluent lesbians are recycled versions of previous cultural stereotypes. The good-bad lesbian dichotomy is not new; it is historically positioned. Lesbian portrayals have been viewed previously as either pathologically present or epistemologically absent — as deviant presences constructed through stereotypes such as the man-hating butch, the neurotic, embittered spinster, and the oversexed femme-fatale (Sheldon, 1999); and as apparitional presences (Castle, 1993) meant to be read as *lesbian* through codes such as female violence (Rich, 1996) or female friendship (Straayer, 1995a). These depictions of lesbianism have permutated into the recycled images of the good-bad lesbian dichotomy, which is in a co-extensive relationship with the symbols of postfeminism. These images are replayed through characters such as the masculinized career woman and the angry feminist; and through the aesthetics of privileged career women playing with temporary lesbianism,[9] for the imaginary male spectator. In brief, both lesbian chic and postfeminism are regulated through a traditional, yet highly sexualized, feminine appearance and behavior that is constructed through consumer ideals, an erasure of difference, and by the oppositional positioning of unattractive and militant feminists. This commercially compromised equality is sustained through a depoliticizing emphasis on individual solutions to complex structural and institutional problems.

Postfeminism, Lesbian Chic, and Ally McBeal

The legal dramedy of *Ally McBeal* speaks to the contradictions of postfeminism through the litigation of cases involving matrimonial law, date rape, sexual harassment, and gender discrimination.[10] Interoffice romances are rampant and the legal narratives are self-reflexively intermingled with the personal lives of the lawyers at the prestigious Boston firm of Cage and Fish. An excess of sight gags reveals the inner emotional states of the successful, affluent, and above all, stylish, and attractive characters who perform song and dance numbers that veer into a gendered camp.[11] Although the recurring female characters evoke feminist principles in their courtroom arguments, none identify as feminist, and they take their individual success for granted while simultaneously distancing themselves from feminism.

Ally McBeal is predicated upon a distancing from feminism, which is partially maintained by the sexualized yet traditional femininity of the upwardly mobile *Ally* women. These markers evoke previous televisual incarnations of postfeminism and are well illustrated in the character of

Ally McBeal (Calista Flockhart). A self-admitted neurotic whose personal problems frequently intrude upon her professional life, the Harvard educated McBeal's success is attributed to her flirtatious skills, toned body, and short skirts. In a fragmented mirroring of the new traditionalist and the unhappy single career woman, Ally yearns for marriage and children, yet she is an aggressive litigator and a liberated sexual adventurer. Like all of the female characters, McBeal is depicted through a sexualized femininity, which is accentuated by the extensive media documentation of the glamorous Hollywood style of the actresses who play them. Flockhart's child-like appearance and increasingly thinner body are extratextually articulated to debates over commercially driven beauty ideals and body norms, while simultaneously diminished, in various *McBeal* plotlines, by refutations of feminist stances on sexual objectification, and through, as we will see, the visual othering of feminists.

Lesbianism is regularly the subject matter of the self-reflexive plot devices and humorous sensory excess on *Ally McBeal*. Chris Straayer (1995a) writes that the eroticization of codes such as female looking and female bonding "has stood in for lesbian content" (p. 57), and the *Ally* women recurringly flirt with lesbian codes through an overt representational acknowledgment that can only be called a lesbian camp. They longingly gaze into each other's eyes and constantly talk about lesbian sex. Ally and her best friend and roommate, Renée Radick (Lisa Nicole Carson), an African American attorney, are depicted cuddling in bed in their jammies and eyeing one another's reflection in the bathroom mirror. Two of the *Ally* women are partnered at a swing contest with the lead dancer, Ling Woo (Lucy Liu), a Chinese American partner at the firm, attired in the male drag of a thirties zoot suit and snazzy fedora. In one episode, Ally demonstrates to a female colleague how to savor a morning cappuccino through orgasmic ecstasy; in another she kisses a woman to scare away an unwanted male suitor. The movement of the subcultural codes of lesbianism into the manifest *Ally* arena reflects the cultural queering of lesbian identity. Furthermore, the regular guesting of celebrity lesbian icons such as Rosie O'Donnell and Anne Heche augments the overt lesbian acknowledgement.

Ally McBeal's flirtations with lesbianism are a subset of postfeminist sexualized gender equality: the unhappy single career woman vents her frustration through flirting with lesbianism; lesbianism becomes part of the repertoire of the sexualized professional, while still maintaining the boundaries of the heterosexuality of the new traditionalist. Despite the well-publicized flirtations with lesbian chic on *Ally McBeal*, there are no regular *out* characters. Lesbianism is presented as a temporary adventure for the decidedly heterosexual characters, and as an individual lifestyle that can be chosen devoid of community, politics, or discrimination. Moreover, temporary lesbianism on *Ally McBeal* is related to the othering of feminism that regulates the good-bad lesbian dichotomy.

The program pits the lesbian chic of the *Ally* women against the demonized, political feminist as part of the repetitive *Ally* iconography. In opposition to the tight, bright clothing and disheveled hairstyles of the *Ally* women, outside female attorneys are attired in dour, plain clothing, frequently wearing glasses with their hair cut short or restrained in tight buns; their bodies are draped in shapeless clothing and dark suits or portrayed as dowdy or overweight; their physical appearances evoke the frustrated career woman, the masculinized female professional, and the angry feminist. On *Ally McBeal*, we see the postfeminist symbols personified in the incarnations of these controlling, uptight feminists who use feminist issues such as a critique of sexualized looking to proscribe gender appearance and behavior. This othering of feminism is apparent in the *Ally McBeal* narrative structures and visual conventions that diminish feminist storylines, vilify feminist characters, and, in turn, maintain the constituent terms of the good-bad lesbian dichotomy.

The good-bad lesbian dichotomy is a collapse of two cultural binaries that mean very different things—chic versus un-chic and good versus bad. The use of chic delineates a style that is cutting edge and hip; whereas the un-chic connotes a dated and unfashionable lack of style; both chic and un-chic are associated with visual or presentational[12] codes such as appearance and dress. Examining the oppositional elements of chic vs. un-chic is pivotal for distinguishing how the characteristics of chicness are just a piece of the broader opposition of good-bad. Through this distinction we can explore how good comes to mean sweet, accommodating, and deferring, while bad signifies rough, angry, and aggressive; good and bad become associated with interactional codes such as sexual behaviors or political positionings. Differentiating between the presentational codes of chic versus un-chic and the interactional codes of good versus bad has utility for deconstructing the oppositional nuances of the good-bad lesbian dichotomy. I will explore respondent engagements with these binaries—chic–un-chic and good-bad—through two themes that highlight the criticisms of lesbian chic and postfeminism: 1. beauty standards and consumer culture, and, relatedly, sexual objectification and the male gaze; 2. representations and erasures of difference.

Chic Versus Un-Chic

The queer insistence of *Ally McBeal* was most heightened in a highly publicized episode in which Ally and Chinese American attorney Ling Woo trade lingering looks in the boardroom, stage a suggestive dance for a male line-up, and finally exchange a spec-ocularly provocative 40-second kiss. Yet, through excessive textual recuperation,[13] Ally and Ling, who both exemplify the presentational codes of temporary lesbian chicness, proclaim ad nauseam that they are normal heterosexuals who customarily find lesbianism viscerally repulsive. In Ally's words, "The idea of kissing another woman grosses me out. Ick!!"

Although all 11 *Ally McBeal* interviewees expressed an enjoyment in seeing two female characters kiss, these pleasurable constructions were mediated by critiques that recognized the televisual history of lesbian kisses,[14] which, in turn, validated the reputation of lesbian spectators for savvy deconstruction. As Laura[15] said, "Because of the patriarchy, they're trying to reach women as consumers ... but I'm still happy to see lesbians kiss on the little screen in spite of the ick." And, Danielle stated, "It's definitely, absolutely hot to see women kissing. But, it [the kiss] wasn't for me, it was for men, to imagine. It's close, but no cigar."

These two examples demonstrated a complex awareness of the consumer appeals and narrative constraints of the Ally-Ling kiss—the encoding negotiations which coordinate the constituent terms of the good-bad lesbian dichotomy. Laura, like most participants, was aware that she was probably not being imagined by the advertisers on *Ally McBeal*.[16] She further perceived, through an acknowledgment of the recuperation of "ick," that the patriarchal inclusion of chic lesbianism exploits lesbian experiences of representational exclusion. Danielle reported an eroticized pleasure in her identificatory desire for the characters. This was mitigated by Danielle's observation that the kiss was probably not constructed with her in mind via her consciousness of an extended social audience that included heterosexual men.[17] The Ally-Ling kiss was partially created as a cultural product for the imagined co-audiences who might be invested in similar expressions of sexual liminality. Yet, of particular note in the communal *McBeal* lexicon was Ally's declaration that "gay women, for whatever reason, love me. They're attracted to me!" Such overt representational salutes coupled with the program's campy excess point to the tension between respondents' heightened media savviness and their intense desire for increased visibility. This tension speaks to changes in lesbian cultural positioning, and to the potential for subverting the chic–un-chic lesbian binary.

The presentational codes of chic are depicted in the amalgam of traditional and sexualized femininity that constitutes the appearances of Ally and Ling. Their long, disheveled hair and their low cut, short skirted, and tightly fitted designer clothing emphasize their thin, well-toned bodies. The visual accoutrements of physical appearance and glamorous style are geared toward displaying the upscale affluence associated with postfeminist gender equality and sexualized lesbian chicness. Respondents surveyed Chic Ally and Chic Ling and found them appetizing or annoying for disparate reasons that were frequently attached to definitions of what a "real lesbian" looks like. Although the temporary lesbians were measured as "hot," "sexy," and beautiful," their lesbian authenticity was found variously wanting — too femme, too straight, too thin, too rich, too male-oriented, too dressed-up, too young, too apolitical, too privileged, too white, too upper class. These responses reflected the criticisms of consumer stylized lesbian chicness, but also exemplified the deep investment of many viewers in "having real lesbians play real lesbian characters." This investment is manifested in the search for the fictive essentialized "real me" that hinges on a model of fixed identity (McRobbie, 1994).

Lesbians have a historical relation to *real* that complicates the understanding of a fixed lesbian identity (Esterberg, 1996; Faderman, 1991; Walker, 1993). For lesbians, the signification of dress and style has been central in presenting self and in recognizing others in ways that, as Reina Lewis notes, are "rarely experienced by heterosexuals" (1992, p. 94). Lesbian identity in the 1970s and 1980s explicitly linked appearance to political ideologies that coupled the omnipresent lesbian uniform —flannel shirts, men's pants, work boots, cropped hair and no make-up — with a feminist rejection of patriarchy, capitalism, and consumerism. This politicized aesthetic, Arlene Stein (1992) writes, configured an "anti-style" that symbolized "a rejection of American capitalism and a refusal to use the female body in subservient ways" (qtd. in Esterberg, 1996, p. 275). The presentational codes of lesbian-feminism constituted everyday communal practices of performing what was perceived as a homogeneous identity that still looms large in contemporary rendering, both subcultural and mainstream, of *lesbian*. The model of fixed lesbian identity is problematized by two significant notions of queer theory — that identity is malleable and performative (Butler, 1990), and that subcultural identity is constructed in interaction with the dominant culture (Sedgwick, 1990).

Respondents measured themselves against chic and real in ways that illustrate the tenets of queer theory. Although one identified herself as the lipstick lesbian of consumer chic, and another as "against chic," most described themselves as falling somewhere along the chic–un-chic continuum. Several characterized their style through the ethnographic subcultural codes that one woman dubbed "The J Crew Uniform." In contrast, Alice determined, "I wish lesbians would dress better. Everybody looks like they're on a rugby team." Many were conversant in the vocabulary of gender bending and unisex clothing, which they described as the signposts of fluid identity. Chris, a self-identified "high femme," said, "I love seeing lesbians who look like me! I'm so tired of being told I pass for straight." Chris' pleasure in gendered performance was validated by the feminine chicness of the *Ally* characters, and was expressed through the observation that she typically had not recognized herself in previous versions of *lesbian* that rejected femininity on political grounds.

The marking of lesbian identity was extended through the ways in which recognition or non-recognition of self as "real lesbian" hinges on a signification of the body as illustrated by Chelsea's gay-dar: "You can see it in her [Chic Ling]. It's in the body. That one's gay from the get go." Some respondents criticized the body norms of chic, commenting upon Calista Flockhart's "disappearing body" through discussions of "lookism" that were experientially plugged into feminist ideologies about not being subservient to men. On the other hand, the negative chicness of Ally's increasing thinness gave voice to some audience members who might not have recognized themselves or found objects of desire in previous portrayals of lesbianism. For instance, Karla put forward that she was happy to see "an athletic and powerful" lesbian body in counterpoint to what Susan Bordo (1993) has called the stereotypical lesbian's "unmuscled girth." In Chic Ally's body, Karla recognized a potential for the transgressive denial of traditional femininity that she experienced in her own lanky dancer's body. This example disrupted the naturalness of the conflation of chic with femininity, and thus problematized the rejection of feminine chicness that is a cornerstone of both a fixed lesbian identity and the chic–un-chic binary.

Some expressed mixed feelings about changes in lesbian codes. Mary linked the unfixing of subcultural identity — "what a real lesbian looks like" — to the unfixing of communal identity: "Ten years ago it was very homogeneous. It was like the dykes downtown dressed the same and had the same haircut. Then a year or two later you had lipstick lesbians, so femininity was okay. You had to make all these adjustments."

Although other respondents expressed a dissatisfaction with the fragmentation of community — with "adjustments" — I was surprised to find that there was not a clear correlation between age and belief systems about constructed gender or sexual identities in opposition to the widely held perception that age is a major divisive factor in lesbian communities (Duggan and Hunter, 1995; Franzen, 1993; Green, 1997). Instead, responses suggested a tension between personal and communal practices that was paralleled in a tension between the desire for changes in the expression of lesbian mainstream portrayals and the desire for changes in the expression of lesbian everyday identities. Everyone I interviewed agreed on one thing: They would like to see more portrayals of lesbianism with elaborate storylines, better acting, and sophisticated aesthetics; the narrative and visual excesses of *Ally McBeal*— noted by respondents as "quirky," "kinky," "eccentric," and "contradictory"—fit the bill of representational complexity.

The contradictory tensions of viewer practices and desires disrupted the naturalness of the rejection of lesbian chic in relation to a fixed communal subcultural identity, and illustrated the queer tenets of a performative identity that is constructed in interaction with the dominant culture. There are, however, significant limitations in portrayals of lesbianism fabricated through only the aesthetics of feminized beauty and consumerized style, and in the celebration of performative identity and textual camp as reception strategies. As Marian, who strongly rejected lesbian chic as "not for me," simply said: "They [Chic Ally and Ling] don't look like real lesbians. I think they are stylized," a comment that she later articulated to limiting clothing purchases through a rejection of "capitalism and the patriarchy." There is some truth in the belief that the lesbian-feminist anti-style has cost the consumer industry money (Douglas 1995, p. 268). Yet, as one respondent, Alice, noted, "these types of clothes [J Crew] do not come cheap." The fixed model of the lesbian as beauty culture refugee romanticizes lesbians as a homogenous subculture, and does not account for the pleasures that many lesbians take in the images and fashions of consumer culture (see Lewis and Rolley, 1996), nor for the ways these speak to some who might not have recognized themselves or their objects of desire in previous versions of *lesbian*. For many respondents, however, the qualifiers of lesbian chic were highly problematic when considered in relation to the presentational codes associated with the passé and unfashionable un-chic.

This is exemplified on *Ally McBeal* by a recurring character, Margaret Camero (Wendy Worthington), who is narratively identified and visually positioned as the un-chic lesbian incarnate. A feminist sociologist whose aggressive reputation proceeds her, Camero expertly testifies for a progressive politics of motherhood. In one episode, she argues for opposing counsel that working mothers are discriminated against by the rigorous requirements of the corporate world. Un-Chic Camero's penetrating testimony is interrupted when senior partner and resident chauvinist Richard Fish asks her point blank if she is a *man-hating lesbian*. On another occasion, Ally runs out of her office shouting, "I am not a lesbian!" Upon smashing into Un-Chic Camero, Chic Ally screams and turns white (literally, through digital effects). Camero's progressive testimony is delegitimized through the collapse of her feminist politics with her lesbianism and with her appearance. On *Ally McBeal*, Camero is mocked and vilified through what might be described as an ethnographic portrait of lesbian-feminism — her man-tailored clothing, her bowl shaped hairstyle, her ample girth, and the ways in which, as we shall see, the presentational codes of her un-chicness become associated with the interactional codes of her feminist politics. Camero looms large in the lesbian imaginary; not only is she the un-chic incarnate, but she is the permanent lesbian.

Many respondents were "horrified" or "mortified" at the ways in which Camero reproduced and regulated long standing un-chic lesbian stereotypes. Chelsea stated, "What's looked at as the real lesbian is fat, bad hair, and bad clothes. The real lesbian is repulsive and the substitute is edible." However, Laura had a mitigated response:

> The look itself is not at all unattractive to me. I mean, she had some attractiveness as a character, but mostly she was put on as a big old dyke. You know, as a stereotype. It was the way they contextualize the look. The way they interpreted the look. But in that environment, where she's put in stark contrast to the beautiful, thin young women, it's meant to be an ugly image.

Many acknowledged that they saw versions of Camero on the streets and agreed that she did represent one version of "what a real lesbian looks like." Others unabashedly admitted that they themselves looked more like Un-Chic Camero than Chic Ally or Chic Ling. Participants expressed a contradictory pleasure in the recognition and misrecognition of other as self that elucidated how the desire to see more complex depictions interfaces with the desire to see bona fide lesbians. Gina further problematized the un-chic lesbian trope through this corporeal identification: "I hate it. This shows the negative fantasy of the lesbian body. It's the lesbian body out of control. Because it's my body, but it's not. It's the exaggeration of the lesbian body since he [Kelley] has nothing that plays against it."

Gina's ambivalence exemplified the performative quality of televisual representations of the real as well as of daily life identifications. The exaggeration of un-chic, which is heightened through Camero's deviation from the femininity of the regular *Ally* characters, constitutes another version of lesbian camp. As Ian Ang argues, such depictions reflect "a form of excess in some women's mode of experiencing everyday life in our culture ... [that] may signify a recognition of the complexity and conflict fundamental to living in the modern world" (1985, p. 158).

What can the masculine appearing, dressing, and behaving Camero tell us about lesbian engagements with consumer culture? In contrast to the ever changing fashion parade of the *Ally* women, Un-Chic Camero wears, in three out of four episodes, the same dark, dour and dated suit—with unflattering calf length skirt—with the same blue and white pinstriped shirt. Can we imagine her in different attire? While Margaret Camero is certainly not a "Mode Woman,"[18] there might be some options. Laura had an interesting take: "If they had intended to paint her in a positive way, she could have been a very positive, strong woman. Strong lesbian look. You know, get rid of the little suit, put her in a pants suit. Let her be an assertive looking butch who could be very cute. She probably is very cute. She'd look damn cute [laughs]."

The idea of giving Camero a textual makeover suggests that there might be a type of character movement where the chic–un-chic divide fluctuates through the interactions of text and audience. Another respondent, Mary, mentioned that she sees ads for Gap clothing on *Ally McBeal,* and that as a large sized professional woman she is highly irritated because Gap carries a plus size line that is only available on-line: "What are they afraid of, that customers will run screaming out of their stores if they see a size 18?" Mary further suggested that it would make all the difference to put Camero in nice silk pants such as the ones she herself buys on sale at Lord and Taylor's.

TV characters are constructed to mirror the products promoted in the advertising. Although television may construct dubious lesbian consumer pleasures, the admittedly ambivalent, yet pleasurable, recognitions of the authenticity of Camero's permanent lesbianism collapsed the idea that respondents were accepting the textual and cultural chic–un-chic binary — many enjoyed precisely the campy engagement with the real and the un-chic. There are limits, however, in how far we can go in deconstructing this character through the chic–un-chic binary, because the lines are drawn so clearly between the temporary lesbianism of Chic Ally and Chic Ling and the permanent lesbianism of Un-Chic Margaret Camero. This boundary is set more strongly when we consider the presentational codes of the chic––un-chic in relation to the interactional codes of the good-bad binary.

Good Versus Bad

Sweet, accommodating, and deferring, Good Ally's behavior frequently veers into a childlike demeanor that is augmented by Flockhart's pubescent body. At times McBeal exhibits an assertiveness that seems commensurate with a feminist agency. This transient boldness, which might be seen as straying from traditional femininity, is mitigated through the character's focus on love, romance, and fantasy. Good Ally is apolitical, and she subtly mocks feminism: in one episode, McBeal self-reflexively confesses, "I dreamed I was on the cover of *Time* as the symbol of postfeminism"; in another, the character scornfully ridicules extratextual feminist concerns, which have been expressed about Flockhart's dangerously thin body. Good Ally's erstwhile agency is emptied out from any association with feminism through the conjoined contingencies of an apolitical naughtiness and a feminine niceness.[19]

Chic Ally is a sexual adventurer, whose temporary lesbianism is associated with her presentation for the male gaze, but also, as we have seen, for the pleasure of lesbian viewers. However, Good Ally's sexualized chicness is contingent on her apolitical niceness. Ally wants to be assertive, but concurrently wants to be seen as a nice woman. When Ally kisses a woman to deter a distasteful male pursuer, she continues to be friendly and flirtatious, unable to let go of the possibility that she might be closing some doors by rejecting this man. The presentational codes of Chic Ally's sexualized appearance and upscale style are paralleled by the interactional codes of Good Ally's new traditionalist yearning for marriage and children, and by extension for heterosexuality (although marriage and family are problematized on the program). The recurring naughty, but nice interactions when coupled with Ally's good, and thus apolitical, feminine behavior mitigate the potential for the depiction of a progressive female sexual agency and of a non-recuperative lesbianism. This depoliticization happens through and reinforces Ally's heterosexuality, and Ally's naughty, but always/already niceness becomes a safe badness with clear limitations set by the character movements through the chic–un-chic and the good-bad binaries.

Respondents' search for what they termed the "real feminist" was as contradictory as the search for the "real lesbian," and was negotiated through the interactions of feminism and postfeminism. Several participants connected liberal feminism with these postfeminist classifications: "Ally is a real feminist"; "She is very independent and powerful"; and, "She has a good career and is a good role model." Others acknowledged the postfeminist disarticulation of feminism through describing Ally's feminism as "extremely limited" or "identified only with white middle class careerism." Alice noted that Ally was "absolutely apolitical!" and Chris stated, in an ironic commentary on postfeminist gender equality, that "she [Ally] is feminist in that she has it all." Is it a limitation of television that postfeminist chic can be seen only as recapitulating an apoliticized goodness, and subsequently, as emptied out from progressive feminist meaning? Can a chic lesbian be bad? Can a chic lesbian be political? Chelsea described a potential for inverting the codes of feminine chicness and goodness:

> I love being able to feel like a marauder. Using all the feminine wiles I can to get what I want. Men look at me all the time, but I know I am using those female products to get what I want — other women. I know I'm not supposed to. I know the capitalist, patriarchal drill, but that seems like such a lose-lose proposition. They [feminine codes] just make me feel good.

Chelsea's reflexive misbehavior was an alternative version of naughty, but nice. Female sexual agency was not heterosexualized — Chelsea stated that her displays were not available to men: "Men look at me all the time, but they can't have me." Through this displacement, bad lesbian was affiliated with chic lesbian. Chelsea's sophisticated response could be interpreted as a prototypical postfeminist individualistic empowerment that is devoid of any political meaning. Nevertheless, there was a distancing (although dissimilar to the distancing of Camero) from traditional femininity that disrupted the naturalness of equating chic with good. Chelsea's commentary complicated the belief that authentic lesbians and genuine feminists are beauty culture outsiders whose choice of attire and demeanor make it clear that they are not subservient to men. This belief has been a structuring principle of the personal versus collective tensions of lesbian politics that are provoked by the model of unfixed lesbian identity. Moreover, the disarticulation of chic from good illustrated how lesbians read against the suggested positions of consumer appeals in complex ways such as re-constructing their own versions of femininity or masculinity. This disarticulation further explicated the queer tenets of a performative identity that is constructed in interaction with the dominant culture.

Such responses raise questions about sexual objectification and the male gaze that relate to the criticism of sexualized images of the female body under lesbian chic and postfeminism: Is it different if another woman is objectifying a woman? How is the female or lesbian gaze different from the male gaze (see Evans and Gamman, 1995, for an overview)? Although beyond the scope of this discussion, it is important to note that respondents described experiences with ongoing community tensions that related to these questions (Duggan and Hunter, 1995). It is, perhaps, another binary, that sexual objectification is always bad, and that women and, especially, "real feminists," do not sexually objectify; this binary has been complicated through almost 30 years of visual theory. Chelsea's misbehaviors might appeal to the imaginary male spectator, but they were unavailable in ways that disrupted the heterosexual-homosexual boundary.

What can the character movements of the desexualized Margaret Camero tell us about sexual objectification and the male gaze? It is through these that the chic–un-chic and good-bad binaries are collapsed in the presentational codes of Camero's appearance. Through this collapse, un-chic becomes part and parcel of the interactional association of bad with feminist politics. Because Un-Chic Camero is manifested through the disparagement of feminists and the delegitimization of feminism, Bad Camero's smart, logical, and assertive behaviors become always and already equated with the vilification of the excessively militant, overly strident, and sexually undesirable feminist. When Richard Fish interrupts Camero's astute testimony, he does more than ask her if she is a man-hating lesbian: "Isn't it true that you want to be a man?" Fish chortles in an excess of male chauvinism, "You look like a man!" In counterpoint, when Ally is assertive or argumentative, her behavior is seen as quirky or naughty, but never unfeminine. These contradictions reveal the constituent terms of the good-bad binary through evoking the lesbian-feminist conflation. The presentational codes of Bad Camero, along with her permanent lesbian status, divorce her from femininity. This desexualizes the character, and concurrently associates her with maleness.

Bad Camero's negativity is heightened through the desexualization of feminists under the postfeminist adage that equates female success with sexualized femininity. The movement between presentational and interactional codes simultaneously delegitimizes her politics. On *Ally McBeal*, it is unfathomable that anyone would desire a woman like Margaret Camero, let alone sexually objectify her. When she sues her insurance company for coverage of in vitro fertility treatments a series of Richard Fish jokes are hooked onto the premise that sperm would not "take" in Camero's body. Fish snorts, "Just imagine the lines!" if Camero were to try conventional intercourse. Still, the portrayal of the masculinized Camero as lesbian mother — she eventually adopts a baby — is a radical image that is typically culturally unavailable. When good becomes attached to Camero through the association with motherhood, it begs the question: Can an un-chic lesbian be good? This question ruptures the chic–un-chic and good-bad divide, and temporarily changes the recapitulation that conflates feminist politics with bad.

The contradictory search for the legitimate lesbian and the genuine feminist continued. Some respondents accepted Camero's negative positioning, and variously defined her as an "overt feminist," and as an "old time 1970s lesbian." Others read against Camero's vilification through strong feminist identifications: as Marian said, "the character was horribly misogynist." Others subverted the good-bad binaries and rejected the delegitimization of Camero: Alice stated that "she is a smart opponent who fights and wins [the exchanges with Fish]." Several participants noted the Camero as lesbian mother motif with recognition of a progressive image that "takes up space in a positive way." One woman, Chris, expressed, albeit with some ambiguity: "I thought they sort of presented her as empathetic, because of the character complexity. Not just a bulldyke."

It is important to remember that some viewers thought Camero had the potential to look "damn cute." A few found Camero desirable, partially because of the deviation from femininity; and several reconfigured Camero's anti-style as a highly valued butch aesthetic that is seldom seen. As noted, some participants reconstructed their own self-presentations so as to not fall into easily recognizable categories of heterosexual female or male. Not surprisingly, the characteristics of good lesbian are those allied with femininity, and with the more feminine appearing and acting femme,[20] while bad hooks up with the butch lesbian, and is negatively associated with masculinity through a rough appearance and aggressive behavior.[21] Although not an interpretation available to all respondents, Camero does suggest the potential for an eroticized butch lesbian.[22]

Camero's deviance from femininity made her the lesbian norm, at least as far as characterizations of her legitimate status; this relation to "realness" transformed the terms of the chic–un-chic and good-bad binaries. It is the temporary lesbians, Chic Ally and Chic Ling, that are transgressive in relation to Un-Chic Camero's permanent lesbianism. This elaborates on the signification of body performativity because it has been aberrant in some versions of lesbian identity to be svelte and beautiful — to be chic. In contrast, in the heterosexual world, it is Camero's "unmuscled girth" that is deviant, even grotesque. Thus the terms of the chic–un-chic and the good-bad become contextual: Camero is positioned as grotesque, but to many lesbians she is the real thing. The chic–un-chic and the good-bad binaries are denaturalized in the acceptance of Camero as real or as the norm in the fixed lesbian lexicon; in turn, Ally and Ling become transgressive. The binaries are further inverted when the "anti-erotic"[23] of Camero becomes desirable, which in turn, suggests complications for understandings of sexual objectification.

Racializing the Binaries

Character movements are intertwined with racialized othering on *Ally McBeal* and with respondent discussions of diversity and stereotypes. *Ally McBeal* constructs a multicultural world in which differences no longer matter, and are in fact purposefully ignored. "In my naive dream," David E. Kelley states, "I wish that the world could be like this" (qtd. in Braxton, 1999, p. 28). Despite the inclusion of two women of color, Ling Woo and Renée Radick, difference and discrimination are never acknowledged. Like gender equality under postfeminism, race relations are presented as done deals. This non-issue approach subtly maintains a white heterosexuality that is sustained through the interactions of the chic–un-chic and good-bad binaries. What counts as bad on *Ally McBeal* is often articulated by way of the exoticized codes of the non-white characters.[24]

The movements of Chinese American attorney Ling Woo are manifested in what Cynthia Liu has termed the "twin legacies" of the Dragon Lady and the Lotus Blossom: the villainess and the victim (2000, p. 24).

Chic Ling embodies a sexualized consumer femininity and an exoticized racial othering. A fierce temptress with a vast repertoire, Ling performs a "hair trick" on her boyfriend, Richard Fish, which connotes the sexual secrets of the Orient that are so attractive to white men. Angry, harsh, and anti-male, Bad Ling personifies the not-to-be-trusted outsider who carries the legacy of the archetypal Asian Dragon Lady as shifty spy, and she is emphatically disliked by the other *Ally* women who scream when she enters a room accompanied by the Wicked Witch theme from *The Wizard of Oz*. The Dragon Lady legacy is reinsured when Bad Ling, through the special effects that constitute part of the program's excess, emits dragon-like sounds and breathes real fire. In contrast to Good Ally who argues recurrently for love and fantasy, Bad Ling is a dangerous and brilliant legal adversary. When she is sued (by a feminist group) for owning a mud wrestling club, Ling employs the postfeminist defense — "sex is a weapon" — that it is a woman's right to use whatever ploys she has, especially her sexuality, for monetary advancement. Like the Dragon Lady, Bad Ling traffics in the sexually taboo— in another episode, she is brought up on charges for running a male escort agency.

Yet, Ling does not like conventional sex, which could be interpreted as a cultural reminder of the delicate, blushing, and innocent good Asian woman. At the same time, Ling's desexualization has a negative attribution that crosses the chic–un-chic and good-bad divide. Chic becomes analogous to bad, and takes on both positive and pejorative connotations depending on the association with boundaries of femininity and heterosexuality. When Ling is flirting with temporary lesbianism, she is still sexually available to the male characters, and thus there is a sexualized bad chic. This contradictory hypersexualized and hyperracialized bad chic is enhanced through the taboo of interracial desire. At other times, Ling is negatively desexed: first, by her scornful demeanor, which distances the character from traditional femininity; and second, by her dislike of conventional sex, and of men in general, which breaks down the heterosexual boundary. However, this is a temporary negativity because sexualized chicness is still attached to the character, partially because ultimately Ling is heterosexual (unlike Camero); and partially, although in contradiction, because of the exoticized bad chicness associated with racialized othering.

Because of the scarcity of popular depictions of non-white recurring female characters, respondents were highly verbose about Ling, and about the interracial Ally-Ling kiss. Pam stated, "So, there was that kind of aspect of watching the *Ally McBeal* thing, that was like wow, this is happening on a prime time major network! And that this was happening between a white character and an Asian character." One respondent, Karla, related that she and her other Asian American friends enjoyed watching and criticizing the campy, stereotypical aspects of Ling:

> Many people see Ling as this really progressive character. Because she's not a victim. And we think it's very interesting and fun to see how the character works against that because it's the Dragon Lady in this modern form. And so much a part of that is that exoticizing thing she does with her hair.

Jane Feuer (1999) suggests that culturally scarce characters such as Ling might transcend critiques of the unfashionable notion of positive images. The personal and communal pleasures invested in Ling validated Feuer's hypothetical argument: That complex and infrequent depictions were highly desired by differentiated viewers. These positive experiential identifications were enlarged upon by respondent awareness of the history of raced stereotyping and by their search for the authentic Asian lesbian through the contradictory dimensions of difference. Marian astutely comprehended that [Kelley] "does not show Chinese lesbians because he wants to be multicultural or wave a Rainbow flag." In a evocation of cultural competency, Karla commented, "I liked it that Ling is strong and not a victim who mixes up her L's and R's, but nobody ever thinks I look like that."

Karla's appreciation of Ling's strength inverted the good-bad binary through the intersecting subversions of traditional femininity and of the one-dimensional submissive Asian victim. In an interesting commentary on the ways that underrepresented viewers might follow the extratextual movements of an actress, Karla recalled seeing Lucy Liu on *ER* playing "the victim of some war, from a refugee camp," and noted how inconsistent this was with the actress's martial arts expertise in contemporary action films that included *Charlie's Angels*. And Pam described an amalgam of experiential and extratextual knowledge that articulated lesbian chic with Asian chic:[25]

> There are becoming a lot more Asian women characters passing through film and television now. Like the lesbian passing through. Asian chic? It's an "in" type of stereotype. And it's still that piece of it that's nice, but it's still not real. And like anything else, it will pass.

These identificatory matches and mismatches highlighted how marginalized viewers reread stereotypes through the desire to see some version of self as real. Participants refused some dimensions of interpellation, while simultaneously transforming others, and made use of Ling to turn negative stereotypes on their heads. Feuer stresses the interactive dimensions of identifying and writes that because of "visual oppression, representation is the first step towards liberation" (p. 198). Even if somewhat recuperable by raced stereotypes, the character of Ling interferes with recuperation, especially when read by a woman of color, or a viewer who does not fit into conventional versions of femininity.

Although the Ally-Ling kiss portrays a highly desired, yet culturally taboo same sex interracial romance, Ling was problematized for embodying otherness. However, Ling's contradictory outsider status is the site of a destabilization of heterosexuality, which suggests openings for differentiated viewers. Chris was thrilled by the narrative and visual hinting at a suggestion of a bisexuality — Ling's — which is rarely allotted airtime due to the cultural necessity of maintaining the heterosexual boundary. Danielle commented on how she appreciated the extension of a butch aesthetic through Ling's assertive body language and aggressive sexuality, that she linked intertextually to favorable comments about the episode where Ling cross-dressed and danced with another woman. A cross-dressing Ling becomes a chic butch in counterpoint to previous depictions where chic has been associated only with femininity and passivity, and un-chic with masculinity and aggressiveness.

Subverting the Binaries

African American attorney Renée Radick's movements across the chic–un-chic and good-bad divide are overtly manifested by way of the tension between two racially marked stereotypes: the hypersexed, exotic, scheming, and bad Temptress and the nurturing, amiable, gentle, loving, good Mammy (see Bobo, 1995; hooks, 1992; 1996). Renée's affluent success, class mobility, and sexualized otherness link up with chic, yet aspects of her appearance — her well-endowed figure, overt display, funky hairstyle and campy dress — lean towards the un-chic. Renée does not have the presentational codes of light skin, straight hair, European features, and thin body of many black (or bi-racial) actresses — such as Lisa Bonet (*The Cosby Show*), Michelle Michael (*ER*), and Academy Award-winning Halle Berry who have gained Hollywood fame. Moreover, the class and race lines on *Ally McBeal* are marked by the performance of the female bodies through shape, size, dress, and behavior. The only women who display a full cleavage are Renée, the one black female, and Elaine, the one regular working class character.[26] Through the fluctuations of chic and un-chic, the hyper-racialized Renée, like the butch Camero, is positioned as the embodied, even abject other. This not only distances Renée from traditional femininity, and normative heterosexuality, but when coupled with the codes of good and bad, equates her with maleness.

This association is heightened when Bad Renée argues with savvy acumen for postfeminist negotiations of gender and sexual politics, always one-upping her male antagonists. Even in the courtroom Renée proudly displays her ample cleavage — in push-up bras, plunging necklines, and tight jackets— with a camp hyperfemininity that simultaneously reifies the primitive sexuality and aggressive behavior equated with the size and shape of black women's bodies. Bad Renée crosses other lines of proper femininity. Depicted as an exotic, promiscuous seductress, she is charged with sexual violence for seriously injuring a date who would not take no for an answer, and Renée's one fleeting alliance is with a married man. Renée has the maternal body associated with the mothering black woman, but Bad Renée is decidedly not a nurturing character. Like Bad Ling, Renée is depicted as isolated, except for her temporary lesbian flirtations with roommate Ally McBeal. Renée's character movements across the good-bad divide are heightened by the history of stereotyping women of color as hypersexualized, and as we have seen with Ling, this positions Renée as sexually aberrant. Unlike Ling, because of the raced markers of un-chicness, and the gendered markers of unfeminine behavior, Renée resides in a more permanent state of sexualized badness, that is not recoupable through her heterosexuality. In fact, at times, Renée is almost deheterosexualized.

Respondents reported a communal and campy appreciation of the unconventional Renée's negotiated authenticity. Esther stated, "Renée? She sings, she dances, she's beautiful. She's kind of like violent sometimes and very oversexed. Some of my friends think she's this really great character, but she wears revealing clothes and she's supposed to be this great lawyer?" Another participant, Arline, compared Renée's to other black television characters: "No, I didn't like Julia, didn't like her at all. She was too white, too white. It was like, yeah right. Either that, or I just never met a middle class black people so when I saw her, she just reminded me of a white person." Others related Renée to experiential identifications. Danielle stated, "She [Renée] just stands out. When I was a child, I mostly knew women of African descent. You really look different if you're the only black woman of size in a room with white women."

The casting of a full breasted and dark skinned African American visually embodies the subtle reinforcement of a white, middle class norm and illustrates how the dimensions of identifying — the search for the genuine African American lesbian — are complicated by an intersection with a history of stereotyped sexualized raced markers. Danielle further stated, "As black people, we're either visible or invisible. And we're visible when there's negativity and cliché, and we're invisible on any other level." And Esther noted, "When they show it, it's not a black producer, [there's] this stereotyping. It's like you either got your Mammy, or you got your Jezebel. And, you know, we don't come in just those two roles. It's so maintaining that kind of image."

However, such depictions do have progressive dimensions even if they partially reinsure negative stereotyping. Renée might be seen as transgressive especially when read by a lesbian of color or a woman who does not fit into traditional versions of feminine beauty ideals and body norms. And, because of the overt character movements across the chic–un-chic and the good-bad divide, Renée's unconventional behavior suggested other types of openings for lesbian viewers. For instance, issues of taking space were important to the construction of identifications. Chelsea said:

> She's not a stereotypically blond thin actress type. And I think she herself probably has to work harder [to] make it in Hollywood. I like bitchy women who don't apologize ... a fat woman with dark hair, who's blowing someone over, or taking space for herself.

And Mary,

> If you're loud or big, you are seen as too aggressive or too large, and taking up too much space.

Issues of occupying space, and particularly of Renée's spatial appropriation, were significant. Renée displays her proud cleavage recurringly in *Ally McBeal* storylines that self-consciously make commentary on feminist critiques of sexual objectification and the male gaze. In one of many sexual harassment cases, Renée, co-counsel for the defense, is attired for her day in court in a tight white suit. Renée, proudly displaying her own cleavage, argues through a discourse on individualistic freedom for the right of women to display their bodies. In this scene, power is attributed to provocative female clothing, and by extension to female breasts in same way that power is attributed to the phallus; in counterpoint to the missing penis, it is the female breasts that are the symbol of power in this episode.

Lewis maintains that a bodily performance such as Renée's has the potential to be "'de-objectified' through the model's ownership of her self-display" (1992, p. 101). Although there is a subversion of the sexualized gaze inherent in Renée's contestation, it also rings a postfeminist bell that equates female empowerment with sexualized chicness. Yet, for certain spectators, at certain times, there might be a need to embrace the variabilities of sexual objectification. Feuer reasons that such portrayals are so in demand by differentiated audience members that not only are negative stereotypes turned on their heads, but that negative aspects of sexual objectification are refused and transformed.

In one temporary lesbian scene, Ally confesses to Renée that Ling has asked her out on a date and that she is worried about her heterosexuality. Renée flirtatiously suggests that Ally is nervous precisely because "opportunity and curiosity might collide." Her teasing commentary is conflated with the eroticization of the Ally-Renée relationship, and this is underscored through the aggressive performance of Renée's full-bodied circuitous movement through the one-dimensional diegesis of the televisual screen. Gina reported, "I drooled over that scene. Partly because she was the Mama figure with the big bosoms. She was a strong, survivor, sort of like butch and femme in the same package."

Renée's breast display pointedly endorses the lesbian camp of female friendship and complicates postfeminist versions of female desire and desirability through the denial of both traditional femininity and normative heterosexuality—"butch and femme in the same package." Gina's complex identification illustrated the importance of body performativity in constructing the multiple dimensions of identification and desire, and of aspects of sexual objectification in visually subverting narrative constructions of gender and sexuality. Of further transgressive note are the interactions of Renée and a black plaintiff in the above noted sexual harassment suit. In an over-the-top cross-examination about the display of cleavage, Renée in her revealing white suit coyly asks: "Am I putting out a sexual signal right now?" Pam, similar to other participants who read this exchange through a lens of lesbian sexuality, remarked on the cultural scarcity of this visual and dialogic union:

> If there is a woman of color in a movie, then that's the quota. Then the girlfriend is always white.

One might suggest, and one participant did, that Renée was "the only real lesbian on the program." Arline commented further on the scarcity of such representations:

> First of all I thought that, again, that there was no real people of color on that program. And that really pisses me off, 'cause I'm not lookin' for tokenism either. I mean it's a real fine line. I just find it really frustrating that, you know, people should have more range. So it gives that stereotype again that it's just white lesbians. And sometimes I get angry that more of a range of people are not being identified.

Accordingly, the movements of Renée through textual and cultural space subverted raced, sexualized, and gendered oppositions: A portrayal of hyperracialization does not always constitute a negative stereotype; a distancing from traditional femininity and heterosexuality does not always recapitulate desexualization. Furthermore, Renée's spatial appropriations were significant markers of the interactions of feminism and postfeminism. Issues of body size, physical space, and cultural power have been important to lesbian-feminist politics. This demonstrates how postfeminist tenets—empowerment through body display—can work hand-in-hand with feminist tenets—empowerment through body ownership. Although Renée's arguments and displays might be seen as buttressing a negative aspect of postfeminism, it is not so easy to dismiss the contradictory and unconventional Renée under the umbrella of a delegitimized feminism. Notably, several respondents allied Renée with Margaret Camero and categorized both as "positive feminists." The feminist classifications of Renée and Camero were interestingly similar given the dissimilarities of the positionings of the two characters, and suggested a reconfiguration of feminism and postfeminism.

Conclusion

I do want to acknowledge that the hegemony of the recuperative aspects of *Ally McBeal* is powerful, and that the depoliticizing of feminism and vilification of feminists are problematic. However, the queer insistence of *Ally McBeal* opens up possibilities for other expressions through shifts in longstanding lesbian stereotypes. A dismissal of the program does not account for the ways in which lesbian viewers take up and transform these changes in suggested subject positions. Yet, I have been haunted by a question throughout this essay: Do viewer responses have any political efficacy? This raises larger issues that are beyond the scope of this analysis—about resistance and agency and about the personal and the political—that speak to significant research in feminist cultural studies (see Dow, 1996; Scodari, 1998; and Haralovich and Rabinovitz, 1999, for overviews). While my focus has been on complicating different dimensions of lesbian identifications, this essay is part of a larger project that examines how anti-hegemonic readings translate into concrete collective practices. Also beyond this essay's parameters are the ways in which respondents defined the terms political or action or themselves as political or activists. Nevertheless, the ways that participants complicated the portrayal of feminists on *Ally McBeal* does speak to how oppositions such as apolitical and political are framed.

As noted, the search for the "real feminist" (and, perhaps, for the legitimate feminism) was as fraught with contradictions as the search for the "real lesbian"; both were negotiated through the discursive interactions of feminism and postfeminism. I found no fixed correlation between feminist identifications and age in contrast to my pre-interview assumptions, and a media critique did not necessarily connect with a feminist identification. Furthermore, the use or disuse of the languages of feminism and postfeminism did not hook up with respondents' own feminist identifications, or lack thereof. Instead, there was an interplay, not so surprising given that postfeminism stands on the shoulders of feminism, that complicates the typical critical and popular positioning of postfeminism as in a somewhat adversarial relationship to feminism. Respondents noted that differences in feminist identifications have been and were an ongoing source of communal tensions, and this was reinforced by fragmented understandings of feminism — expressed variously as "ambiguous," "indefinable," and "reframed."

The fragmentation of both lesbian and feminist identities speaks to a breaking down of oppositions. It was this fragmenting —*queering*— of categories that first drew me to *Ally McBeal,* and this queering was a presence throughout respondent engagements with the constituent terms of the good-bad lesbian dichotomy. The division of chic–un-chic from good-bad has implications for unpacking the question of the apoliticizing aspects of lesbian visibility. In the broader good-bad lesbian dichotomy, politics become part and parcel of the dichotomy and that is very different than the depoliticized labeling of chic, which is framed only through the aesthetics of style. In other words, the binary of apolitical-political is perceived as recapitulating the undivided good-bad dichotomy. As we have seen, respondents disarticulated the terms of the good-bad lesbian dichotomy through differentiated lenses. The disruption of the presumed collapsing of the bad with feminist and the un-chic with political complicates the politics of lesbian identifications.

Some have suggested that recent changes in lesbian visibility might mean considering an expanded notion of the political that takes into account the political dimensions of self presentations and cultural images (Lewis, 1992; Walker, 1993; Esterberg, 1996). Arlene Stein writes that "we need a political language that acknowledges our diversity as well as our commonality, that embodies playfulness along with rage, and that faces outward as well as inward" (1992, p. 438). Many lesbian and gay activists believe that increased visibility will result in changes in public acceptability.[27] It is further posited that this acceptance will be developed socially and politically in contexts such as the workplace and hate crime legislation. Furthermore, the presentation of lesbian selves in everyday life and in the media is a challenge to normative categories of sexuality and gender.

Although the discussions of lesbian authenticity could be interpreted as typical subcultural or oppositional readings, breaking down such oppositions as apolitical-political, chic–un-chic, and good-bad might also mean rethinking the ways we think about such readings. As Reina Lewis argues, "The problem becomes one of relationships *between* meanings in which the viewer's decoding activities may operate from a variety of positions each of which utilizes a different set of competencies that may be addressed by the text" (1992, p. 105). Respondents not only read *against* the grain of binary divides, but they read *across* the divides to transform the binaries of lesbian representation. They constructed their own amalgams of identities that subverted the oppositional terms of chic–un-chic and good-bad through developing "relationships *between* meanings" by bringing in "a variety of positions" and "different competencies" such as body size, personal style, and gender and race identifications. This does not mean that there is no determination, but rather that respondents made sense of *Ally McBeal* in different ways. It is through these differences that they constructed shared, albeit fragmented, social identities within a historical and cultural framework. Disrupting the naturalness of the good-bad lesbian dichotomy means also disrupting the notion of a fixed, subcultural lesbian identity. The queer insistence of *Ally McBeal* is a productive context for examining other dimensions of identifying because it exemplifies the expansion of the lesbian cultural lexicon.

Through components of self-imaging that use ontological identifications such as gender and sexual orientations, body size, and race identifications, respondents moved between and across historical and cultural stereotypes to construct a space of their own: a cultural occupancy. Creekmur and Doty (1995) suggest that a central theme of queer popular culture research is about how to negotiate a place as both producers and consumers of meaning: "How to occupy a place in mass culture, yet maintain a perspective on it that does not accept its homophobic and heterocentrist definitions, images, and terms of analysis" (p. 2). Rather than castigate popular culture, this study examines how differentiated viewers engaged with suggested and differentiated subject positions. McRobbie (1994) writes that feminist politics "must therefore imply subjectivities in process, interacting and debating" (p. 70). An entrance into the cultural imaginary even if through the entry point of a consumer aesthetics or a sexualized gaze speaks to transformations in how audience members might use representational modifications to re-imagine themselves and take up a position of cultural occupancy. Although *Ally McBeal* ultimately reifies a hegemonic position on sexual and gender politics, it also opens up possibilities for other forms of expressions through shifts in long standing stereotypes and narrative limitations. Changes in suggested subject positions speak to lesbian desires for sexual visibility, identity variation, representational acknowledgment, and consumer validation. These respondents together constructed a space for cultural occupancy through their self-reflexive awareness of fragmented, incoherent, and mediated identities.

Notes

1. I conducted 11 in-depth individual interviews between February 2000 and February 2001, asking questions about *Ally McBeal* and lesbian identifications. Each interview lasted at least two hours and following such feminist researchers as Press (1991) and Radway (1984), I utilized a

conversational format with a reflexive awareness of interview politics. The participants were part of a sampling of 30 derived from a larger work in progress, and applying the method of snowball sampling, each was chosen serially, using consecutive interviews as a source for networking suggestions and potential respondents. The 11 *Ally McBeal* viewers were aged between 20 and 59, and four identified as working class, six as middle class, and one as upper-middle class. One was a high school graduate, three had completed some college, three were college graduates, and four had obtained graduate degrees. Eight self-identified as lesbian, two as queer or queer-identified, and one as bisexual. Nine reported that they were feminists. Two had been previously married, eight were currently in relationships, one had grown children, two had young children, and one was trying to get pregnant. Two women identified as African American, one as Korean American, one as Japanese American, one as Puerto Rican, and two as Jewish; all others self-identified as Caucasian. All respondents lived in the Northampton, Massachusetts, area.

2. Most previous discussions of lesbian viewers are text based with a hypothetical, homogeneous audience and theoretical debates about how to fit spectatorship or reception into psychoanalytic, queer, or ideological frameworks. See deLauretis, 1994; Doty, 1993; Henderson, 1999; Mayne, 1991; Nataf, 1995; Stacey, 1988; Traub, 1995; Whatling, 1997; White, 1991; and White, 1999. The limited inquiries into how actual lesbian viewers interpret popular cultural texts do not problematize the construction of lesbian identities: see, Straayer, 1984; and Ellsworth, 1986. Lewis' 1992 study of changes in lesbian readings begins to explore the nuances of subcultural readings. What these studies do agree on is that lesbian viewers are savvy deconstructors who read against the grain of textual hegemony to construct what are variously termed subcultural, resistive, or oppositional readings. Although it is beyond the scope of this project to address the mechanistics of the encoding-decoding model (Hall, 1980), I do want to cite the importance of cultural studies, and feminist cultural studies in particular, for my methodological framework.

3. I acknowledge the complexities and instabilities involved in the term lesbian and in community, and I use both with an awareness of indeterminacy. The ways that *lesbian* is experienced, defined, and recorded are bound up with historical and cultural specificity. For examples, see Beemyn, 1997; Faderman, 1991; and Traub, 1995.

4. Queer theory seeks to interrogate identity categories as a way to displace the traditional notion of what it means to belong to a particular group. In queer theory, identity is seen as constructed and fluid, and normative categories of gender, sexuality, and sexual orientation are problematized. Instead of two gender roles, or two sexual orientations, queer theory argues that a range of possibilities exists within and outside these categories. Of use is Rosemary Hennessy's elaboration: "queer theory calls into question obvious categories (man, woman, Latina, Jew, butch, femme), oppositions (man vs. woman, heterosexual vs. homosexual), or equations (gender = sex) upon which conventional notions of sexuality and identity rely" (1993, p. 964). Queer theory also suggests that traditional models of gender and sexuality create a hierarchy in which some categories are privileged over others (Gayle Rubin, 1993).

5. Academic feminists have long suggested the need for a feminism that included race and class politics and a model of diffuse power rather than the broad umbrella of patriarchy (Press, 1991). Others note the need for a movement that speaks to young women who have grown up with changes in gendered economic parity and professional access (McRobbie, 1994).

6. Class currency refers to Pierre Bourdieu's (1984) significant discussion of how a politics of taste and aesthetics correlates with a politics of class position and privilege.

7. This is well illustrated in Julie D'Acci's (1994) discussion of the 1980s program *Cagney and Lacey,* in which the encoding negotiations of femininity and feminism converged in the need to have the female characters read as heterosexual.

8. Beginning in the mid-eighties, representations of lesbian took on different forms of popular visibility, as explicit images of and overt references to lesbians appeared in a range of cultural sites. Headlines such as "Lesbian Chic" (Kasindorf, 1993) and "The Power and the Pride" (Salholz, 1993) were touted in the national magazines *New York* and *Newsweek;* same sex kisses were exchanged on the television programs *Roseanne* and *Ally McBeal;* and out lesbian stars Melissa Etheridge and k.d. lang were given prominence in gossip columns. Reaching a pinnacle with the coming out of Ellen DeGeneres in the spring of 1997, a heightened cultural conversation about lesbians produced the appearance that lesbians, to put it simply, were in style.

9. The notion of a "temporary" sexuality is from Chris Straayer's (1995b) discussion of transgendered film.

10. The program ran for five seasons: Fall 1997-Spring 2002. This analysis utilizes examples from and publicity about the first three seasons.

11. An excess of behavior, style, and music has been associated traditionally with the textual

slippages of the melodrama of soap operas and romantic comedies (Elsaesser, 1986; Fiske, 1987). Excess relates to camp, which has been a strategy used by gay men (and sometimes lesbians) to experience and negotiate mass culture through the use of an ironic humor (Creekmur and Doty, 1995). Camp disrupts, enlarges upon, and makes visible the mechanisms of gender and sexual identities (Robertson, 1996).

12. Kristen Esterberg (1996) writes that there are two different types of cues—"visual/presentational" cues and "interactional" cues—that lesbians use for everyday identifications of other lesbians (p. 270). I have extended Esterberg's distinction to televisual codes.

13. On television, lesbian sexuality has been traditionally understood to be hinted at through narrative ambiguity while subverted or limited through narrative recuperation (Meg Moritz, 1999, p. 318).

14. The Ally-Ling kiss is somewhat overdetermined by the recuperative history of lesbian televisual kisses: the *L.A. Law* bisexual kiss (1991) between Amanda Donahoe and Michelle Greene, which was immediately followed by the reaffirmation that they both liked men; the *Picket Fences* kiss (1993) between two teen girls, which was shot in full lighting, yet aired in darkness so that viewers could only hear the exchange; the *Roseanne* kiss (1994), which only showed the back of Mariel Hemmingway's head and a subsequent recuperative shot depicting Roseanne wiping her mouth on her sleeve; and the *Ellen* kiss (1997), which was decried by conservatives and related by many to the program's subsequent cancellation. It is significant that *Ally McBeal* creator and auteur David E. Kelley was the producer and writer on *L.A. Law* and *Picket Fences*.

15. I cite respondents only through confidential pseudonyms, and because Northampton is a small city, I am careful not to *out* individual participants. Yet, I do not mean to suggest that there was no relationship between the interactive trajectories of identities such as race, class, or age. The sampling diversity does not represent a comprehensive sampling of western Massachusetts or of the Northampton lesbian population, and no claims were made about the correlation of respondent identifications with audience readings.

16. This raises questions about whether or not lesbians are being constituted as a commodity audience and if they are being pitched as such to advertisers. That discussion is beyond the scope of this analysis, but what is important is how the *Ally McBeal* flirtations with lesbian chic are positioned so as to appeal to audience members. See, Chasin, 2000 and Sender, 2001 for comprehensive discussions of gay consumer address.

17. The kiss episode aired on the Fox Network during the November 1999 sweeps week and received the highest ratings ever, 17 million viewers, which were largely attributed to the increase in male viewers.

18. *Mode* is a contemporary periodical geared toward the plus sized female demographic featuring large models in feminine, fashionable clothing.

19. I am indebted to Reina Lewis (1992) for her engaging discussion of a fashion spread that negotiated the terms of *naughty, but nice* in a British magazine geared toward the lesbian subcultural demographic.

20. Good Ally reifies the passivity which has been used historically to negatively associate more feminine appearing lesbians, *femmes*, with acquiescence. The apoliticized Ally's naughty, but niceness is in contraction to the bad (and highly eroticized) femme-fatale of film noir that has been historically read against the grain as lesbian, and which has a parallel in Ling, partially because of the racialized othering of the character.

21. Butch and femme identifications impacted strongly on participant discussions of lesbian authenticity. It is beyond the reach of this essay to discuss the historical and contemporary significance of butch and femme role-play, and how this is embedded in the politics of lesbian style (and class relations). This role-playing was rejected by lesbian-feminists in the 1970s and 1980s because it was seen as replicating traditional heterosexual gender relations. In the late 1980s, and through the 1990s, there has been a reclaiming of butch and femme, which some respondents saw as a transgressive strategy that worked against normative gender roles. See Faderman, 1991; Nestle, 1992; and Walker, 1993.

22. Gender identifications were especially complex for respondents who identified through the modalities of female masculinities. For a sophisticated analysis, see Halberstam, 1998.

23. The *anti-erotic* of a character such as Margaret Camero is a phrase suggested by Lewis, 1992.

24. I would like to briefly note the unmarked "whiteness" of the character, Ally McBeal. It is interesting to consider how this unmarking becomes part and parcel of Ally's naughty, but nice, distancing from lesbianism in the previously mentioned scene when Ally screams and turns white (literally, through special effects) when she crashes into Margaret Camero.

25. See, Chihara, 2000, for a fascinating discussion of Asian chic.
26. Unfortunately, it is beyond this essay's scope to discuss the complex class and age identifications of respondents.
27. Of particular note is the political activism of GLAAD — the Gay and Lesbian Alliance Against Defamation.

References

Ang, I. *Watching Dallas: Soap Opera and the Melodramatic Imagination.* New York: Methuen, 1985.

Beemyn, B., ed. *Creating a Place for Ourselves: Lesbian, Gay, and Bisexual Community Histories.* New York: Routledge, 1997.

Bellafante, G. "Feminism: It's All About Me!" *Time* (June 1998):54–62.

Bobo, J. *Black Women as Cultural Readers.* New York: Columbia University Press, 1995.

Bordo, S. *Unbearable Weight: Feminism, Western Culture, and the Body.* Berkeley: University of California Press, 1993.

Bourdieu, P. *Distinction: A Social Critique of the Judgment of Taste.* Trans. Richard Nice. Cambridge, MA: Harvard University Press, 1984.

Braxton, G., "In Ally's Romance, Race a Nonissue." *The Daily Hampshire Gazette,* 15 February 1999.

Butler, J. *Gender Trouble: Feminism and the Subversion of Gender.* New York: Routledge, 1990.

Castle, T. *The Apparitional Lesbian: Female Homosexuality and Modern Culture.* New York: Columbia University Press, 1993.

Chasin, A. *Selling Out: The Gay and Lesbian Movement Goes to Market.* New York: St. Martin's Press, 2000.

Chihara, M. "There's Something About Lucy." *Boston Phoenix,* 24 February–2 March 2000.

Clark D. "Commodity Lesbianism." In *The Lesbian and Gay Studies Reader,* edited by H. Abelove, M.A. Barale, and D. Halperin, 186–201. New York: Routledge, 1993.

Cottingham, L. *Lesbians Are So Chic: That We Are Not Really Lesbians at All.* New York: Cassell, 1996.

Creekmur, C., and Doty, A., eds. *Out in Culture: Gay, Lesbian, and Queer Essays on Popular Culture.* Durham: Duke University Press, 1995.

D'Acci, J. *Defining Women: Television and the Case of Cagney & Lacey.* Chapel Hill: University of North Carolina Press, 1994.

de Lauretis, T. *The Practice of Love: Lesbian Sexuality and Perverse Desire.* Bloomington: Indiana University Press, 1994.

Doty, A. *Making Things Perfectly Queer: Interpreting Mass Culture.* Minneapolis: University of Minnesota Press, 1993.

Douglas, S. *Where the Girls Are: Growing up Female with the Mass Media.* New York: New York Times Books, 1995.

Dow, B. *Prime-Time Feminism: Television, Media Culture, and the Women's Movement since 1970.* Philadelphia: University of Pennsylvania Press, 1996.

Duggan, L., and N.D. Hunter, eds. *Sex Wars: Sexual Dissent and Political Culture.* New York: Routledge, 1995.

Ellsworth, E. "Illicit Pleasures: Feminist Spectators and Personal Best." *Wide Angle* (1986):8(2), 45–56.

Elsaesser, T. "Tales of Sound and Fury: Observations on the Family Melodrama." In *Film Genre Reader,* edited by B. Grant, 278–308. Austin: University of Texas Press, 1986.

Esterberg, K.G. "'A Certain Swagger When I Walk': Performing Lesbian Identity." In *Queer Theory in Sociology,* edited by S. Seidman, 259–279. Cambridge, MA: Blackwell, 1996.

Evans, C., and L. Gamman. "The Gaze Revisited, or Reviewing Queer Viewing." In *A Queer Romance: Lesbians, Gay Men and Popular Culture,* edited by P. Burston and C. Richardson, 13–56. London: Routledge, 1995.

Faderman, L. *Odd Girls and Twilight Lovers: A History of Lesbian Life in Twentieth-Century America.* New York: Columbia University Press, 1991.

Faludi, S. *Backlash: The Undeclared War Against American Women.* New York: Crown, 1991.

Feuer, J. "Averting the Male Gaze: Visual Pleasure and Images of Fat Women." In *Television History, and American Culture: Feminist Critical Essays,* edited by M.B. Haralovich and L. Rabinovitz, 181–200. Durham: Duke University Press, 1999.

Fiske, J. *Television Culture.* London: Metheun, 1987.

Franzen, T. "Differences an Identities: Feminism and the Albuquerque Lesbian Community." *Signs* (1993):18(4), 891–906.

Green, S.F. *Urban Amazons.* New York: St. Martin's Press, 1997.

Halberstam, J. *Female Masculinity.* Durham: Duke University Press, 1998.

Hall, S. "Encoding/Decoding." In *Culture, Media, Language: Working Papers in Cultural Studies,* edited by S. Hall, D. Hobson, A. Lowe, and P. Willis, 128–138. London: Hutchinson, 1980.

Hamer, D., and B. Budge, eds. *The Good, the Bad and the Gorgeous: Popular Culture's Romance with Lesbianism.* London: Pandora, 1994.

Haralovich, M.B., and L. Rabinovitz. Introduction to *Television, History, and American Culture: Feminist Critical Essays,* edited by M.B. Haralovich and L. Rabinovitz, 1–16. Durham: Duke University Press, 1999.

Harris, D. *The Rise and Fall of Gay Culture.* New York: Hyperion, 1997.

Henderson, L. "Simple Pleasures: Lesbian Community and *Go Fish.*" *Signs* (1999):25(1), 37–57.

Hennessy, R. *Materialist Feminism and the Politics of Discourse.* New York: Routledge, 1993.

hooks, b. *Black Looks: Race and Representation.* London: Turnaround, 1992.

_____. *Reel to Reel: Race, Sex, and Class at the Movies.* New York: Routledge, 1996.

Inness, S.A. *The Lesbian Menace: Ideology, Identity, and the Representation of Lesbian Life.* Amherst, MA: University of Massachusetts Press, 1997.

Kasindorf, J. "Lesbian Chic: The Bold, Brave, New World of Gay Women." *New York Magazine* (May 1993):31–37.

Kilbourne, J. *Slim Hopes.* Media Education Foundation, Videocassette.

Lewis R. "Looking Good: The Lesbian Gaze and Fashion Imagery." *Feminist Review* (1992):(55), 91–109.

_____, and K. Rolley. "Ad(dressing) the Dyke: Lesbian Looks and Lesbians Looking." In *Outlooks: Lesbian and Gay Sexualities and Visual Culture,* edited by P. Horne and R. Lewis, 178–190. London: Routledge, 1996.

Liu, Cynthia W. "When Dragon Ladies Die, Do They Come Back as Butterflies? Reimagining Anna Mae Wong." In *Countervisions: Asian American Film Criticism,* edited by D. Y. Hamamoto and S. Liu, 23–29. Philadelphia: Temple University Press, 2000.

McRobbie, A. *Postmodernism and Popular Culture.* London: Routledge, 1994.

Mayne, J. "Lesbian Looks: Dorothy Arzner and Female Authorship." In *How Do I Look?: Queer Film and Video,* edited by Bad Object-Choices, 105–143. Seattle: Bay Press, 1991.

Moritz, M. "Lesbian Chic: Our Fifteen Minutes of Celebrity?" In *Feminism, Multiculturalism, and the Media: Global Diversities,* edited by A.N. Valdivia, 127–145. Thousand Oaks, CA: Sage, 1995.

_____. "Old Strategies for New Texts: How American Television is Creating and Treating Lesbian Characters." In *The Columbia Reader on Lesbians and Gay Men in Media, Society, and Politics,* edited by L. Gross and J.D. Woods, 316–326. New York: Columbia University Press, 1999.

Nataf, Z.I. "Black Lesbian Spectatorship and Pleasure in Popular Cinema." In *A Queer Romance: Lesbians, Gay Men and Popular Culture,* edited by P. Burston and C. Richardson, 57–80. London: Routledge, 1995.

Nestle, J., ed. *The Persistent Desire: A Femme-Butch Reader.* Boston: Alyson, 1992.

Press, A. *Women Watching Television: Gender, Class, and Generation in the American Television Experience.* Philadelphia: University of Pennsylvania Press, 1991.

_____, and T. Strathman. "Work, Family, and Social Class in Television of Women: Prime-Time Television and the Construction of Postfeminism." *Women and Language* (1992):16(2), 7–16.

Probyn, E. "New Traditionalism and Post-feminism: TV Does the Home." *Screen* (1990):31(2), 147–169.

Radway, J. *Reading the Romance: Women, Patriarchy, and Popular Literature.* Chapel Hill: University of North Carolina Press, 1984.

Rich, R. "Lethal Lesbians: Lesbian Representation in Popular Contemporary Film." Lecture, Mount Holyoke College, Holyoke, MA. April 18, 1996.

Robertson, P. *Guilty Pleasures.* Durham: Duke University Press, 1996.

Rubin, G. "Thinking Sex: Notes for a Radical Theory of the Politics of Sexuality." In *The Lesbian and Gay Studies Reader,* edited by H. Abelove, M.A. Barale, and D. Halperin, 3–44. New York: Routledge, 1993.

Salholz, E. "Lesbians Coming Out Strong: The Power and the Pride." *Newsweek* (June 1993):54–60.

Scodari, C. "'No Politics Here': Age and Gender in Soap Opera 'Cyberfandom.'" *Women's Studies in Communication* (1998):21(2), 168–187.

Sedgwick, E.K. *Epistemology of the Closet.* Berkeley: University of California Press, 1990.

Sender, K. "Producing the Gay Market: Sex, Sexuality, and the Gay Professional-Managerial Class." Dissertation, University of Massachusetts at Amherst, 2001.

Shalit, R. "Canny and Lacy (Betrayal of Postfeminism in TV Portrayals of Women)." *The New Republic* (April 1998)27–33.

Sheldon, C. "Lesbians and Film: Some Thoughts." In *The Columbia Reader on Lesbians and Gay Men in Media, Society, and Politics,* edited by L. Gross and J.D. Woods, 301–305. New York: Columbia University Press, 1999.

Spigel, L., and Mann D., eds. *Private Screenings: Television and the Female Consumer.* Minneapolis: University Press of Minnesota, 1992

Stacey, Jackie. "Desperately Seeking Differences." In *The Female Gaze: Women as Viewers of Popular Culture,* edited by L. Gamman and M. Marshman, 112–129. London: The Women's Press, 1988.

Stein, A. "All Dressed Up, but No Place to Go? Style Wars and the New Lesbianism." In *The Persistent Desire: A Femme-Butch Reader,* edited by J. Nestle, 431–439. Boston: Alyson, 1992.

Straayer, C. "Personal Best: Lesbian/Feminist Audience." *Jump Cut* (1984):29, 40–44.

_____. "The Hypothetical Lesbian Heroine in Narrative Feature Film." In *Out in Culture:*

Gay, Lesbian and Queer Essays on Popular Culture, edited by C. Creekmur and A. Doty, 44–59. Durham: Duke University Press, 1995.

_____. "Redressing the Natural: The Temporary Transvestite Film." In *Film Genre Reader II,* edited by B.K. Grant, 402–427. Austin: University of Texas Press, 1985.

Traub, V. "The Ambiguities of 'Lesbian' Viewing Pleasure: The (Dis)articulations of Black Widow." In *Out in Culture: Gay, Lesbian, and Queer Essays on Popular Culture,* edited by C. Creekmur and A. Doty, 115–136. Durham: Duke University Press, 1995.

Walker, L.M. "How to Recognize a Lesbian: The Cultural Politics of Looking Like What You Are." *Signs* (1993):18(4), 866–890.

Walters, S.D. *Material Girls: Making Sense of Feminist Cultural Theory.* Berkeley: University of California Press, 1995.

_____. *All the Rage: The Story of Gay Visibility in America.* Chicago: The University of Chicago Press, 2001.

Whatling, C. *Screen Dreams: Fantasising Lesbians in Film.* Manchester, UK, and New York: Manchester University Press.

White, P. "Female Spectator, Lesbian Spector: *The Haunting.*" In *Inside/out: Lesbian Theories, Gay Theories,* edited by D. Fuss, 142–172. New York: Routledge, 1991.

_____. *UnInvited: Classical Hollywood Cinema and Lesbian Representability.* Bloomington and Indianapolis: Indiana University Press, 1999.

4

The Comic and Burlesque: A Frame Analysis of Post-Feminist Values and Female Professionalism in *Ally McBeal*

Michele Hammers

David E. Kelley's hit television series *Ally McBeal* (*McBeal*) raises issues by highlighting the raised hemlines and waifish beauty of its title character, Ally. While *McBeal* cannot really claim to be a show about the practice of law, it also cannot deny the fact that its setting — a small Boston law firm and the Boston court system — invites viewers to think about Ally, and her female counterparts, in terms of their professional identities. When young female lawyers complain that their male clients actually refer to them as a "little Ally McBeal," we have to concede that Kelley's fictional creation has made its way into a variety of different discourses. As Bonnie Dow argues, the media have a powerful impact on cultural and political discourses surrounding feminism and femininity (Dow, *Feminism*, xv). Specifically, Dow argues that media texts, particularly the sitcoms of the last 30 years, "have done important cultural work in representing feminism for the American public" (Dow, *Feminism*, xv). Other scholars have commented on the role that the media plays in the construction of social identities — particularly those identities based, even in part, on notions of gender (Trethewey, 424; Harrington, 152–153).

Since the 1996 publication of Dow's book, which covered television series ranging from *The Mary Tyler Moore Show* to *Murphy Brown*, the working-woman sitcom has received an overhaul in the form of *McBeal's* glossy production values, song and dance numbers, and animated fantasy scenes. In addition to these formal revisions, *McBeal* also (re)presents a different version of feminism, femininity, and feminine identity than its predecessors. Recent criticism and commentary has focused on *McBeal* as a representative icon of contemporary feminist discourse(s) (see Shugart, Vavrus). For example, in June of 1998, *Time* magazine's cover asked the question "Is Feminism Dead?" The related article, written by Gina Bellafante, takes Ally McBeal to task for being "ditsy." Bellafante places Ally in the middle of a "popular culture insistent on offering images of grown single women as frazzled, self-absorbed girls" (Bellafante, 58). Comparing Ally with the title character of Helen Fielding's *Bridget Jones's Diary* (which is now a major Hollywood movie), Bellafante complains that "the problem with Bridget and Ally is that they are presented as archetypes of single womanhood even though they are little more than composites" of broadly drawn and stereotypically "female" neuroses (Bellafante, 58).

Despite this type of critical response, the *McBeal* series, particularly in its first two years, was a popular hit. This popular success is not likely to be unwound in the few pages available in this chapter. However, it is possible to begin exploring what this appeal indicates about the larger discourse surrounding post-feminist politics, female professionalism, and the ongoing importance of the female body as a site for identity formation. One way to begin making sense of Ally as a point of identification and viewing pleasure for women (and men) is to consider the frames of reference operating within and around the show. This analysis emphasizes *McBeal's* significance in terms of its intersection of the feminine and the professional.

Comic and Burlesque Possibilities

A person's frame of reference is his or her attitude toward, or approach to, reality. Reality, for Burke, is largely a product of social interaction and symbolic construction (see Burke, *Permanence*, 5–36). Thus, one's attitude toward reality takes on a great deal of significance. Ultimately, how we name something affects not just how we think about it, but how we will act toward it (Burke, *Attitudes*, 92). Acceptance frames have a primarily optimistic view of the social order (Burke, *Attitudes*, 28, 42–43; Carlson, "Gandhi," 448). These frames are designed to "make men at home in their world" through either resignation or enlightenment (Burke, *Attitudes*, 35). Of the acceptance frames, Burke placed particular emphasis on the comic frame, which accepts the fact that no social order is ever broad enough to encompass all "necessary attitudes" and be without flaws (Burke, *Attitudes*, 40). The comic frame promotes awareness of these imperfections and deals with them in a manner that operates as "sanctioned doubt" (Moore, 108, 110–111).

The comic frame deals with problems or tensions within the social order through dialogue that emerges from the education or reeducation of a "clown" (Burke, *Attitudes,* 41–42; Carlson, "Limitations," 312; Carlson, "Gandhi," 448).

The comic clown has counterparts in the rejection frames, which do not see the existing social order as primarily redeemable (Moore, 108–110; Carlson, "Limitations," 314). Rejection frames do not take a charitable view toward the social order or toward the clowns who serve as repositories for the social order's ills (see Hubbard, 355). For example, in the burlesque frame the clown uncharitably represents social ills in their most extreme and ludicrous forms (Burke, *Attitudes,* 53–55; Moore, 109, 111–112). The burlesque clown is not temporarily ostracized as a means toward redemption; instead, the burlesque clown is thrust from the group with no hope of ever being returned (Moore, 112; Carlson, "Limitations," 317). The burlesque clown still serves the purpose of purging the social order of its flaws; however, this purging takes place through the clown's utter humiliation and an outright rejection of the things that the clown comes to represent (Moore, 111–112).

As this theoretical overview indicates, a critical difference between the two frames is how the dominant social order behaves toward its clowns. A comic clown is laughed at, to be sure, but the laughter and the distancing that comes with it set the stage for the clown to learn her lesson and be readmitted into the social order. On the other hand, the burlesque clown is looked upon as being beyond redemption; the laughter directed at such a clown holds out no hope, nor desire, for the clown to be returned to the fold. Thus, largely comedic series such as *McBeal* raise the question: "Just what is the deeper attitude at work beneath the laughter?" Here, structural questions of genre — such as comedy and melodrama — intertwine with the attitudinal aspects of Burke's frames of reference to provide for rich, and complex, readings of the *McBeal* series.

Murphy Brown: *Rejecting Liberal-Feminist Politics and Values*

In her 1992 article "Femininity and Feminism in *Murphy Brown,*" Dow argues that Murphy is an example of a scapegoat and is used to control the threat of liberal feminist values and politics. Dow begins her analysis by stressing that Brown is a comedy series that taps into the conservative potential of comedy as a genre (Dow, "Feminism," 146–147). Reading the series in light of this conservative potential and with reference to Burke's concept of the scapegoat, Dow argues that the series puts Murphy forward as an apparently "progressive" representation of a successful career woman, but actually limits the "approval" that she receives (Dow, "Feminism," 147). Thus, Dow reads Murphy as a symbol of society's unappealing construction of liberal-feminist values and its efforts to reject those values through repeated punishments and humiliations.

In order to contextualize *Murphy Brown* politically, Dow notes that when the series aired on prime time, liberal-feminism dominated the mainstream feminist agenda. Dow explains liberal-feminist values and assumptions as follows:

> Generally, liberal feminism emphasizes evaluation of the position of women on the basis of their equality with men within dominant cultural systems.... Key characteristics of this view are that it accepts as desirable the cultural standards established through male dominance and it focuses almost exclusively on women's equality in public life [Dow, "Feminism," 145].

Dow's article then provides a rich textual analysis of the ways in which the series represents Murphy's liberal feminist values and characteristics in a negative fashion and then punishes her for those values and characteristics. For example, Dow illustrates the ways in which the series associates Murphy with extreme caricatures of aggressive and competitive behavior and then contrasts those caricatures with representations of more traditionally feminine behaviors and attitudes (Dow, "Feminism," 148–152). Whenever Murphy is set directly alongside her more feminine foil (the character of Corky Sherwood-Forrest), Murphy is typically depicted in a negative light. The series' ultimate message, according to Dow, is that Murphy's excessively masculinized behaviors are the key to her professional success but are also the cause of her failure in more traditional feminine venues (Dow, "Feminism," 148 and 150).

Ally McBeal: *TV and Feminism after* Murphy Brown

Close on the heels of *Murphy Brown,* the working-woman sitcom received a sleek, fantasy-driven, updating for early 21st century prime time. *McBeal*'s glossy production values, computer animated fantasy scenes, and choreographed song and dance routines make it a different spectacle than its precursors *Mary Tyler Moore* and *Murphy Brown.* From the outset, with *McBeal,* one gets the distinct impression of having landed somewhere down Alice's proverbial rabbit hole. This fantasyland spectacle is further perpetuated by the extreme characteristics embodied by Ally and the show's other characters. More caricature than character, these individuals—both male and female — tend to emphasize human foibles and pathologies. This provides much of the comedy in the series; it also permits the series to address potentially volatile political and social issues with a tongue-in-cheek mocking that is displaced onto the characters themselves.

Ally McBeal's title character is a young, Harvard-educated litigation associate at a small, eccentric Boston law firm. Ally's primary character traits revolve not around her professional persona, but around her tumultuous personal life, romantic dreams, and myriad neuroses. A panel discussion held with eight professional women in the Boston area reveals that the women do not take Ally McBeal "seriously as a lawyer." One panelist, an associate at a large Boston law firm, commented:

> A lot of us at my firm watch it religiously. We don't watch it as a show about law. We watch it as a comedy about this neurotic woman who makes us feel better about ourselves [Chambers, 59].

However, the personal and professional do not separate so easily in real life. In fact, they do not separate that easily on the television series; Ally's private insecurities, romantic dilemmas, and otherwise chaotic personal life constantly spill over into her professional behavior.

This blurring of private and professional is particularly troubling to those who have written about the series from a critical feminist standpoint. Ruth Shalit focuses her criticism of the series on a few of its recurring representations of Ally. First, she notes that Ally has an opportunistic attitude toward her own sexuality (Shalit, 31). In addition to criticizing Ally's manipulative sexuality, Shalit also calls into question the series' depiction of Ally's emotional instability as a professional asset:

> As David E. Kelley has set things up, Ally's [emotional] imbalance is a badge of honor. The Boston legal scene is a kind of difference-feminist utopia, and Ally McBeal is a Carol Gilligan heroine.... Here is a lawyer who is valued not for her legal acumen, but for the weepy integrity of her ruined dreams [31].

Finally, after noting that *The New York Times* has praised the series for "training public attention on the myriad problems faced by working women," Shalit goes on to criticize the childish way in which Ally handles these problems (30). On this point, she argues that Ally's insistence on seeing herself as a "fuddled schoolgirl" is actually a case of "arrested development" (Shalit, 30).

The shift from *Murphy Brown*'s ambivalent portrayal of liberal-feminist to *McBeal*'s similar depiction of post-feminist values can be seen in three primary aspects of Ally's character and characterization. First, there is the series' tendency to infantalize Ally. Ally is, like Mary Richards from the *Mary Tyler Moore Show* was before her, primarily situated within a workplace family, where she plays traditionally "feminine" roles vis-à-vis her coworkers and friends (see Dow, *Prime-time*, 25, 31, 37–38, 48). However, unlike Mary Richards, who was largely supportive in her office relationships, Ally has been highly infantalized and is typically the object of a large expense of energy and attention by the other characters. This infantalization, which is both physical and emotional, works toward a direct reversal of Murphy's masculinization. While Murphy embodied the dangers inherent in liberal-feminism's excessively masculine values and behaviors, Ally shows us the problems inherent in a return to overtly feminine and usually childlike (or even childish) behaviors and characteristics. For instance, an early episode displays Ally expressing her refusal to attend a meeting with clients because it made her feel like a "little girl." This expression of insecurity had a visual counterpart in the "fantasy" image of Ally shrinking in size to be engulfed by a large leather chair. Thus, Ally's emotional (and professional) immaturity is complemented by a physical diminution.

Further adding to her infantalization are the scenes in which she dances around her apartment with a life-size, blow-up "boyfriend" while wearing cow-print pajamas— scenes that are reminiscent of adolescent slumber parties. Moreover, Ally has trouble walking in the high-heeled shoes that she insists on wearing and spends a good part of the first season falling down — typically in front of male co-workers or clients. Combined with her tiny frame, large dewy eyes, and tendency to bite her lower lip, the picture presented is of an immature girl, not a grown woman. This infantalization of Ally arguably has increased over the series' run. Third season episodes even went so far as to put Ally in situations where she dated a teenage boy via the Internet (believing him to be an adult) and was attracted to another teenage boy she met through a court case. The association of Ally with these young men —combined with her inability to maintain successful long-term romantic relationships with adult men — works to undermine her viability as an adult.

Fueling this increased infantalization is the fact that Calista Flockhart, the actress who portrays Ally, has become increasingly thin over the series' last few seasons. Ally now more closely resembles a preadolescent boy — flat-chested and slim-hipped — than a full-grown woman. Recent press coverage has noted that Ally's emotional immaturity has become increasingly coupled with images of her emaciated, preadolescent-looking body (Kinnes, Moran). Moran argues that the series capitalizes on confusion of "the show's child-like logic with Flockhart's increasingly childlike physical state" (Moran). This is not just about Flockhart's overt thinness— it goes beyond size to the overall presentation of Ally's physical presence:

> She's worn no discernible make-up throughout the latest (season), and her hair, previous a smart New York bob, is now that stringy, nothingy mid-length all girls have when they're 12. Her blouses are becoming very school-like, the

teeny miniskirts reveal legs that taper upwards from the knee, and she holds mugs with both hands while peering over the rim with eyes as big as windmills [Moran].

In this way, Ally's physical body — just like Murphy's masculine dress and demeanor — is used as a reflection of her interior status. This interior status, unfortunately, falls short of current expectations for mature, professional women.

Thus, Ally has come to represent a new version of femininity — selfish, insecure, and overwhelmed. As Shalit has put it:

> As an upscale exercise in female interiority, Ally McBeal is less Mary Richards than Angela Chase, the frazzled pubescent played by Claire Danes in the recent high school weepie, *My So-Called Life*.... But there is a difference. When Angela Chase lets fly with one of her girlish temper tantrums, it is cute.... In a 30-year-old attorney, however, it is not cute. It is manipulative and infantile and demeaning [30].

Television has returned the professional woman to the family fold, only to reconstruct her as immature and emotionally demanding. This links overt "femininity" with behaviors that are uniquely problematic in a professional setting.

The relationship between Ally's emotional nature and her professional performance introduces the second way in which the series' depiction of Ally is problematic. Ally not only represents a reversal of Mary Richards' largely positive rendition of the traditionally feminine, supportive role in the workplace, but she also represents a reversal of Murphy Brown's masculinized approach to professional competitiveness. In contrast to Murphy's aggressive, insensitive careerism, Ally is childlike, overly sensitive, and absorbed in her personal life. While Murphy was punished for being too much like a man, Ally is punished because of the female-gendered professional standards she represents. Ally, while usually "successful" in court, is not depicted as a necessarily strong or capable lawyer (when judged by prevailing standards). In fact, her professional success is usually due to her emotional vulnerability and romantic notions; the television show romanticizes her overly emotional approach to the practice of law. Ally's value as a lawyer is her emotional nature *not* her legal acumen:

> Ally's romantic idealism, her emotionalism, her girlish indifference to such manly concerns as law and logic and reason, do not just make her a superior person. They also make her a superior lawyer. Like a killer precedent of a surprise witness, her neurosis is a passport to truth [Shalit, 31].

So Ally's success comes with the clear message that she is practicing law "like a woman" and not in the traditionally accepted — "masculine" — way. Where

Murphy succeeded in a male-dominated profession by beating men at their own game, Ally plays the equally male-oriented game of law like a woman. Sometimes this works for her, but it always leaves her looking a little foolish when compared to existing standards for actual professionalism. While a generously comic reading of these incidents might argue that the message of *McBeal* is that we should value "difference," the alternative implication is that one cannot be emotionally in touch and idealistic (read "feminine") and *also* be legally astute. This mirrors the tension set up in *Murphy Brown* between Murphy and Corky, between "real" journalism and "soft" news— in short, between competent male professionalism and merely "interesting" (or, at best, occasionally useful) female emotionality (see Dow, "Feminism," 147, 151). Ally's excessive emotionality — which is always, already linked by cultural association to her excessive femininity —fares no better than Murphy's excessive masculinity. Both women fall short of accomplishing complete success: Ally because she is too much like a woman and Murphy because she is not woman enough.

The truth is that Ally never really wanted to be a lawyer in the first place. Not surprisingly for someone whose happiness appears to be wrapped up in her romantic life, Ally followed her boyfriend at the time to law school. Thus, Ally's whole association with the law is tinged with romantic expectations and a quest for personal satisfaction that is unrelated to the demands, challenges, and rewards of the profession itself.

This connection between Ally's career choice and her romantic nature raises the final problem with the series' depiction of her personal and professional character. This problem involves the complicated tensions that surround women, romance, and sex. It is important to note that both Ally and Murphy are largely unhappy in their romantic relationships. However, Murphy was depicted as romantically impaired because of her "inappropriate" dedication to her career (Dow, "Feminism," 150–151). Ally, on the other hand, is romantically unhappy due to a series of personal neuroses and a lack of good judgment. Her idealism, which sometimes makes her a powerful "force" in the TV version of a courtroom, makes her difficult to please in her personal life. At the end of the series' second season Ally had withdrawn to her bedroom in order to live in a perpetual fantasy concerning singer Al Green. Again, Ally's emotional instability ends up requiring the attention of almost everyone in her office — including several of the other lawyers who go to the apartment to try to "cheer" Ally up. The implication in Ally's case is not that her professional ambitions keep her from personal happiness— instead her personal unhappiness finds its way into her professional arena. This presents an interesting alternative to Murphy's message that women who are "too" successful are doomed to live lonely lives. Instead, Ally's message is that women — especially single, romantically inclined, women — are doomed to struggle with problems on the job. *McBeal* represents a retreat from *Brown*'s harsh treatment of professional success as incompatible with personal happiness (for women). However, it also represents a departure from depictions of women as capable of professional success on par with their male counterparts.

An interesting addition that *McBeal* makes to the representation of prime-time feminism and femininity is the series' emphasis on Ally's sexuality. Where Mary Richards' sexual activity, or lack thereof, was merely hinted at in that series, and where Murphy's on-off romantic liaisons were subtly sexual (she did have a child during the series' 1991–1992 season), but were not featured for that content, Ally's sexuality — and that of the other characters (primarily the women characters) — is played up as part of the series' popular appeal. Ally makes bold strides in bringing female sexuality into the limelight. For example, various episodes revolve around Ally's brief "affair" with a male model that Ally dates for purely physical reasons. The series makes frequent use of "fantasy" scenes in which Ally (or another woman on the show) overtly reacts to an attractive man (usually with a "tongue" that lasciviously hangs from the woman's mouth in the fantasy image). Most recently, during the series' third season, two episodes have played with the erotic taboos surrounding lesbian fantasies. The first indulged in a sensual dance scene between Ally and Ling and the other showed them engaged in a lingering kiss. This attention to virile female sexuality has the potential to be liberating. However, this version of female sexuality has a darker side when considered in light of its relationship to popular discourse surrounding female professionalism.

Ruth Shalit, in her article in the *New Republic,* notes that Ally has an opportunistic attitude toward her own sexuality. For example, in one episode Ally used her sexuality to "fluster a hapless [male] opponent" and in another she engaged in a flirtation with a potential client in order to get his business for her firm (Shalit, 31). In light of the cultural associations that link women with their bodies and deny them the authority of the "mind," Ally's attempt to manipulate her sexuality for a "business" purpose is a troubling representation of a woman professional. Notably, Ally is not the only one of the women lawyers on the series to adopt this careerist sexuality at one time or another. Nell, Ling, and Renee all have been featured in story lines that revolved around their use of their sex appeal to gain a professional advantage over a male colleague. For example, in one episode Nell used her attractiveness to manipulate a male IRS agent into giving her the legal concessions that she wanted for her client. Nell is herself repulsed by this course of action, but she, apparently, values winning over all else. This careerist approach to female sexuality serves to confirm the association of women with sex and the body, as opposed to the culturally approved, professional traits of reason and competency.

Ally and Murphy represent different versions of female identity and feminist values; however, both women serve as clowns from a Burkean perspective. Both women are burdened with problematic characteristics associated with women who intrude upon the primarily masculinist professional arena. Both women are ridiculed and punished; while Murphy was punished for being too much like a man, Ally is punished because of the female-gendered professional standards she represents.

The Question of Genre: This Is Supposed to Be a Comedy, Right?

All of this talk about ridicule, punishment, and problematic representations, begs the question "where is the humor?" More importantly, it begs the question "why is all of this funny?" Part of the answer to both of these questions can be found in the very nature of "comedy" itself. Comedy, especially the sitcom genre, has a potentially conservative impact on social attitudes. While not typical of the 30-minute sitcom genre that characterized *Brown*, *McBeal* does provide many of the same pleasures as a traditional comedy series:

> Situation comedies ... [position] the subject, not in suspense but amusement and laughter ... the viewer's pleasure does not lie in the suspense of puzzle solving nor in the suspense surrounding the hero's ability to cope through action with various tasks and threats. Rather the tension of the narrative to which the viewer responds revolves around the economy or wit with which two or more discourses are brought together in the narrative. The pleasure of situation comedy is linked to the release of that tension through laughter [Woolacott, 171].

In many ways, *McBeal* fits the sitcom model nicely. Each episode brings together a variety of subplots and their related discourses, usually revolving around some intersection between personal issue and broader "social" topics, in a fashion that lends itself to a comic resolution. Frequently, the series employs moments of more substantial tension — giving it a more serious tone, which feeds its melodramatic undercurrent — but the "pleasure" of the series remains firmly linked to its moments of laughter.

Interestingly, despite this basic compliance with the above model, the *McBeal* series does frustrate the expectation created by the sitcom format that everything will have a happy ending. While typically resolving the immediate issues raised by a particular story, the series leaves the issues of

Ally's romantic and emotional discontent and the other characters' vague dissatisfactions with their lives unresolved. In this way, the series nurtures a somewhat darker mood than the typical sitcom. As noted above, Ally's perpetual struggle with her romantic troubles lends a melodramatic flavor to her character. This melodramatic flair works within the confines of the comedy genre to promote ongoing identification with Ally as a heroine — and, ultimately, as a clown.

Despite the series' heavy reliance on the viewer's identification with Ally, the humor of the series largely derives from her neuroses and foibles. Most obviously, the series frequently employs fantasy scenes that purport to reveal Ally's inner world and serve to subvert narrative cohesion to playful imagery. These scenes frequently inflict humiliating or otherwise painful experiences on Ally. Shalit argues that the images in these scenes "positively seethe with hostility" and asserts that Kelley uses these images to make Ally look "foolish and incompetent" (30). For example, Shalit cites two of the most popular fantasy images from the show. The first is Ally "with a giant foot stuffed in her mouth" and the other showing Ally "being unloaded by a dump truck" (30).

Even when the fantasy scenes themselves are not overtly hostile toward Ally, they frequently interfere with her "normal" functioning in the "real" world. During the first season Ally was plagued by visions of a dancing baby. Eventually, the baby began to roller skate past Ally and ultimately, it began throwing spears at her. On several occasions Ally was depicted as actually ducking out of the way of the spears thrown by her imaginary persecutor. In another episode, Ally attempted to kick the baby and ended up kicking a young boy who had just stepped off the elevator into her firm's office.

The series' use of humor that is frequently physical and usually humiliating is open to more than one reading. On the one hand, it may actually work to heighten the viewer's empathetic identification with Ally. On the other hand, the harshness of the comedy tends to have a critical feeling to it. Ally's comic moments are born of her failings as a lawyer and as an adult woman; the viewer is asked to laugh at her because she has been made ridiculous beyond a point that is acceptable in everyday life.

This tension between identification and rejection has been explored in relation to other television shows. Specifically, Ien Ang looked at female viewers' attitudes toward the women portrayed on the prime-time series *Dallas*. Ang argued that women identified with the character of Sue Ellen Ewing, despite the fact that she was seen as a poor role model, because the women viewers used Sue Ellen as a surrogate for experiencing a subject position that was actually unacceptable in real life (Ang, 92, 94–95). Ang theorizes that this type of "melodramatic" identification takes place when a series combines three characteristics: an emphasis on personal experiences, usually fraught with high drama, disappointment, and frustration; convoluted plots, which treat "extraordinary" events as commonplace; and the potential for little or no progress (Ang, 88–90). Arguably, despite its status as a comedy, *McBeal* meets these melodramatic conditions. The potential for Ally to serve as a source of melodramatic identification has to be considered in conjunction with the overall comedic strategy of the series.

In addition, the role of melodramatic identification in explaining Ally's potential appeal and popularity can also be related to her potential positioning as either a comic or burlesque clown. Recall that Burke's comic frame requires a simultaneous identification with and rejection of the clown. This asks people within the social order to see in the clown a shared experience, value, or flaw. Through his or her foibles the clown is made humorous, but the laughter directed at the clown has a distancing effect. The ultimate purpose of laughing at the comic clown is to open a dialogue around the problems that the clown represents. This dialogue is possible only because the people within the social order — the non-clowns — identify with the clown and his or her failings (Carlson, "Gandhi," 447). At this point, the importance of Ally's melodramatic appeal comes into play. By *rejecting* Ally — the clown — as a role model while still identifying with her as a possible, but impractical, subject position, viewers are able to experience Ally as a comic clown. Ally remains within the scope of redemption because, and only to the extent that, she remains someone with whom viewers can identify.

On the other hand, the series' ultimately harsh treatment of Ally also has tendencies toward the burlesque. In the burlesque frame, the clown is made to look "as ridiculous as possible" and there is no effort made to understand his or her motivations:

> There is no sense of identification with the clownish figure here, for that would be to admit that we have a share in the folly. There is no need to feel sympathy for the clown, for we do not want to welcome the renegade back to the fold under any circumstances [Carlson, "Limitations," 317].

The humor of the burlesque is in the fact that "externals of behavior" are logically reduced to "absurdity" (Moore, 108). One result of the burlesque frame is that the possibility of change or growth is largely eliminated. Most importantly, the burlesque clown does not learn (Moore, 108).

This lack of change, the burlesque inability to learn from and redress mistakes, is prevalent in the *McBeal* series. This may be partially due to the serial nature of the series, which leaves little room for growth and change. The burlesque nature of the series however is not colored merely by this lack of growth, but also comes from the troubling nature of the status quo that the series preserves as normal. The *McBeal* series largely has established the troubling *failures* of Ally — and to a lesser extent its other characters — as the norm. Not only does Ally not learn, but the viewers also are reminded of this fact in almost every episode. In fact, since melodrama necessarily requires a repetition of mistakes — "process without progress" — Ally's potential role as a *burlesque* clown arguably is also augmented by the melodramatic nature of her popular appeal.

Conclusions: Possibilities and Tendencies

Ultimately, what one makes of the harsh humor at work in *McBeal* may depend on whether the series is seen as performing within a comic or burlesque frame of reference. A preference for one frame over the other has to do with where the viewer is willing to "draw the lines" and where, upon reflection, the viewer assumes that the series is drawing its own lines (see Burke, *Attitudes,* 92).

Looking specifically at the first two seasons of *McBeal,* a shift from the comic toward the burlesque can be seen in the series' treatment of Ally's romantic notions and emotional imbalances. While Ally was rejected as a model of how women ought to perform their roles as women (and as lawyers), she remained a sympathetic — if not necessarily likeable — character. Moreover, Ally's romantic notions, while out of line with the expectations of the real world, have been put to good use in the television courtroom. In fact, her ability to use her romanticism as a tool for redeeming the law from its bottom-line emphasis on rationality and efficiency, is on occasion held up to be an admirable thing. In this way, Ally's nonrational approach to the law brings into question the role of pure objectivity and rationality within our legal system. Arguably, Ally's role as a clown who goes about practicing law in a different way requires her to be rejected, but it also opens a space for a dialogue about why emotion, idealism, and passion have been pushed so far outside the sphere of "good" lawyering.

During the show's first season and into its second, Ally was repeatedly punished for her romantic notions and overly sentimental approach to her job and her life. But, on the other hand, she was often redeemed and — even when not fully redeemed — she remained able to return to the world of the regular social order. From this perspective, Ally *had the potential* to function as a comic clown. However, more often than not this potential was not exploited and the series chose, instead, to retreat from the opportunity of promoting change through its treatment of issues and to re-inscribe more traditional ideas of femininity instead.

Furthermore, this comic potential began to fade during the series' second season. Over time Ally's personal romanticism took a more dysfunctional turn — leaving her personally devastated and professionally crippled. More and more episodes began to end, not with Ally dancing with her friends at their favorite bar, but sitting alone in her office or walking alone down the dark city streets. Ally's inability to maintain a working romantic relationship became the center of increased attention. After her feelings for Billy contributed to their short-lived romantic fling (which never got beyond a kiss), Ally loses her boyfriend Gregg — proving, again, that she is doomed to "process without progress." By the end of the second season Ally has withdrawn into her room where she can live in her fantasy world without interruption. At this point, her inability to cope in the real world has become a painful parody of her own supposedly sensitive nature. In addition to rendering her personally dysfunctional, this emotional breakdown also affected her ability to perform as a professional; when Ally takes to her room to hide in her dream world, she manages to disrupt the workings of her law firm and require the attention of all of her colleagues. This blurring of personal and professional, with negative effects on the professional, calls into the question the post-feminist ideal that women can now "have it all" — romance, sex, power, and a successful career. While it may not be the case that Ally has become completely unsympathetic, the second season's finale is definitely a move toward the harsher burlesque frame. One might still laugh at Ally's romantic fantasies, but identification with her was made potentially more difficult. The melodramatic repetition of Ally's mistakes eventually began to work against — instead of for — the melodramatic appeal that potentially kept her popularity high.

Of course, not everyone likes Ally. Even in the show's more positive moments, the shadow of rejection looms large. And, for people who see very little that is funny about a grown woman ducking imaginary spears and falling down in front of clients, the relevant frame of reference for viewing the show is probably more akin to burlesque. By reading the images of Ally as hostile and unforgiving stereotypes of female behavior and post-feminist values, the burlesque viewer will find little hope for change-through-dialogue in the images of Ally McBeal. These viewers will not identify with Ally's melodramatic fragility and will, instead, reject her as an absurd caricature — a collection of mannerisms that lie, professionally speaking, beyond redemption.

Works Cited

Ang, Ien. *Living Room Wars: Rethinking Media Audiences for a Postmodern World.* London and New York: Routledge, 1996.

Bellafante, Gina. "Feminism: It's All About Me!" *Time Magazine,* (1998, June 29): 54–60.

Burke, Kenneth. *Attitudes Toward History.* 3rd ed. Berkeley, Los Angeles, and London: University of California Press, 1984.

_____. *Permanence and Change.* 3rd ed. Berkeley, Los Angeles, and London: University of California Press, 1984.

_____. *The Rhetoric of Religion: Studies in Logology.* Berkeley, Los Angeles, and London: University of California Press, 1970.

Carlson, A. Cheree. "Gandhi and the Comic Frame: 'Ad Bellum Purificandum.'" *Quarterly Journal of Speech* 72 (1986): 446–455.

_____. "Limitations on the Comic Frame: Some Witty American Women of the Nineteenth Century." *Quarterly Journal of Speech* 74 (1988): 310–322.

Chambers, Veronica. "How Would Ally Do It?" *Newsweek,* (2 March 1998): 58–60.

Dow, Bonnie J. "Femininity and Feminism in *Murphy Brown.*" *Southern Communication Journal* 57(2) (Winter 1992):143–155.

_____. *Prime-time Feminism: Television, Media Culture, and the Women's Movement Since 1970.* Philadelphia: University of Philadelphia Press, 1996.

Harrington, Mona. *Women Lawyers, Rewriting the Rules.* New York: Plume, Penguin Books, 1995.

Hubbard, Bryan. "Reassessing Truman, the Bomb, and Revisionism: The Burlesque Frame and Entelechy in the Decision to Use Atomic Weapons Against Japan." *Western Journal of Communication* 62(3) (Summer 1998): 348–385.

Kinnes, Sally. "He's the Weirdo Lawyer in *Ally McBeal* Whose Nickname Is the Biscuit." *Sunday Times (London),* (2000, July 2): Features.

Moore, Mark P. "'The Quayle Quagmire': Political Campaigns in the Poetic Form of Burlesque." *Western Journal of Communication* 56 (Spring 1992): 108–124.

Moran, Catherine. "Oh, No! It's Ally, Ally-oops Again." *The Times (London),* (1999, October 29): Features.

Rybacki, Karyn C., and Donald J. Rybacki. "Competition in the Comic Frame: A Burkean Analysis of Vintage Sports Car Racing." *Southern Journal of Communication* 61 (1995): 76–89.

Shalit, Ruth. "Canny and Lacy: Ally, Dharma, Ronnie, and the Betrayal of Postfeminism." *The New Republic,* (1998, April 6): 27–32.

Trethewey, Angela. "Disciplined Bodies: Women's Embodied Identities at Work." *Organization Studies,* 20, (1999): 423–450.

Woolacott, Janet. "Fictions and Ideologies: The Case of Situation Comedy," in *Media Studies, A Reader,* edited by Paul Marris and Sue Thornham. Edinburgh: Edinburgh University Press, 1986.

5

Ally McBeal and the Death of Feminism

Kristyn Gorton

Is feminism dead? *Time* magazine posed this question in the June 1998 issue, featuring *Ally McBeal* as the reason why feminism may no longer be a viable political movement. In this essay, I will use *Ally McBeal,* the show, the character and the actress who portrays Ally, as a case study to discuss larger issues concerning the media's role in feminist politics, the slender body, and the emotional engagement viewers experience from programs such as *Ally McBeal.*

The *Time* cover, among other readings, demonstrates the media's ability to construct icons in a political movement that has struggled against such representation. What the media does, whether intentionally or not, is reduce the complexities of a movement such as feminism into a marketable success or disaster story, one that interferes directly with the practice of feminist politics. Germaine Greer acknowledges the media's damaging role in feminist politics in *The Whole Woman,* the sequel to her feminist polemic *The Female Eunuch.* In her discussion of sisterhood, she argues that "the media identified 'newsworthy' candidates for leadership and massaged their images briefly before setting up cat-fights between them. I was dubbed the 'High Priestess of Women's Liberation,' Gloria Steinem was 'The New Woman,' and Betty Friedan was 'The Mother Superior'" (Greer, 1999: 228). The triad of virgin, whore and mother that the media establishes in its dubbing of Greer, Steinem and Friedan, is emblematic of the way the media reduces political agency into easy-to-read stereotypes. The dynamics of feminism are flattened into one-dimensional characters which focus more on an individual woman's sexuality than on her political agenda.

Media tactics have not changed; they continue to identify new figures to represent feminism in order to generate what Greer appropriately calls "cat-fights." The media sets up these figures not only to encourage debate but to put a new face to a new brand of feminism, or as in the case of the *Time* magazine issue, the faces that line the cover are there to question whether feminism is still relevant. A linear progression is suggested on the cover, as well as in other media campaigns, which implies that feminism has moved from a "we" solidarity of the '60s and '70s to a "me"-based feminism in the twenty-first century. This development is suggested by positioning the faces of Susan B. Anthony, Betty Friedan, Gloria Steinem and Ally McBeal in an attempt to categorize the history of feminism in America into distinct identities from the suffragettes to "today's" feminist. The choice of all white, middle-class and presumed heterosexual representatives not only exposes the conservative underpinnings of *Time* magazine but is also reminiscent of why feminist theory divides itself between equality and difference politics. One can hardly dispute that the black and white heads are meant to represent "then" whereas the colorful McBeal represents "now."

The staring faces also appear as a reminder of the media's role in turning feminism into a kind of fashion-show politics. In the example of the *Time* cover, it is not hard to pick out the most fashionable one. There can be no doubt that one of the intentions or underlying readings is that feminism has changed its style over the years. From the severe matron-like appearance of Susan B. Anthony to the glossy, lip-sticked face of Ally McBeal, "you've come a long way, baby" springs to mind along with arguments that women today can be feminist *and* attractive. On the one hand the attention to fashion in shows such as *Ally McBeal* and *Sex and the City* presents interesting ways to talk about feminism, women's sexuality and women's relationships. However, what does it mean in terms of feminist theory? Is there a danger in "fashion coating" important and integral issues in feminist politics?

Whether the cover's designer intends to comment on the lack of authority these women have by cutting off their bodies and leaving their heads, or if she intended the line-up to spark humor in a postmodern parody, the cover reveals the media's continuing role in reducing a complex movement like feminism into a simplistic array of names and faces. The absence of bodies on the front cover is also not to be dismissed within a movement that has struggled with issues concerning the body, whether in the politics of writing the body theorized by French feminists such as Hélène Cixous and Luce Irigaray, or in prevalent issues of Western democracies like reproductive rights, anorexia and breast cancer. In feminist theory, the body is often perceived as a foundation for agency, pleasure, desire and political voice. In *This Sex Which Is Not One*, Luce Irigaray argues that: "The use, consumption, and circulation of [women's] sexualised bodies underwrite the organisation and the reproduction of the social order, in which they have never taken part as 'subject'" (1985: 84). The *Time* cover does not use, consume or circulate these women's bodies because they have been erased. Only their heads are left. Is this where feminist agency is located today? In the mind? Or does the cover's format attempt to divorce the subject of feminism from body politics?

It is impossible to separate discussions on Ally McBeal from her body. The issue of weight has been associated with Ally McBeal almost as often as the issue of feminism. The media has made much of Calista Flockhart's body — whether to sell the latest fashion or as in the case of a recent television guide in the UK, to sell the show by featuring Flockhart semi-nude on the cover under the heading "body of evidence" (2002). As in the *Times* cover, where Flockhart's name is exchanged for "Ally McBeal," articles on Flockhart often refer to her role as "Ally McBeal" instead of referring to Flockhart as an individual. Her television character is often exchanged for her personal identity.

Articles entitled "Thin, Thinner, Thinnest," (Chaudhuri, 2001) and "Ding Dong, Skinny's Dead," (www.televisionwithoutpity.com, 2002) capture only a fraction of the attention Calista Flockhart has received with regard to her figure. In June 1999, Camille Paglia wrote in the *Los Angeles Times*, "[Calista Flockhart] looks diseased. She keeps carrying on about how 'I'm fine' and 'I have no eating disorder,' but it is a disorder if you're that thin and you choose a dress that is backless" (Chunovic 1999: 31), referring to the Richard Tyler dress Flockhart wore to the Emmy awards. What is interesting here is the relationship Paglia draws between Flockhart's size and her right to wear certain fashions. In this case the right to wear backless dresses is forbidden to thin women.

Although Ally McBeal is portrayed as a sexually potent woman, the focus on Calista Flockhart in the media highlights a "diseased" or "grotesquely thin" body. The media coverage of Flockhart concentrates primarily on her thin figure or on speculations of an eating disorder. Indeed, she is better known for her body than for her acting career. All the attention to her figure suggests that Flockhart's place in the public spotlight as a sex object is a contentious one. The ridicule she receives with regard to her body may also tell us something more about the "perfect" body women in Western culture are expected to have.

Kim Chernin's "tyranny of slenderness" (1981) and Susan Bordo's "reading the slender body" (1993) both examine Western culture's preoccupation with being thin. In *Unbearable Weight,* Bordo suggests that the emphasis on slenderness masks psychic anxieties and moral valuations concerning correct and incorrect management of impulse and desire (1993: 187). Eating disorders, according to Bordo, reflect a capacity for self-denial and the repression of desire whereas the overweight body symbolizes a capitulation to consumption.

The media's obsession with Flockhart's weight seems to go beyond concerns that she is glamorizing slenderness. Initially the focus was on her weight as an eating disorder, however, more recently the attention has been levelled in humorous parodies or requests such as the "secret wish" on the "Ask Men" Web site that: "Calista, eat a cheeseburger with lots of cheese, some French fries and onion rings" (2002) or on the *Tonight Show* when Jay Leno presented the audience with the "McBeal TV Dinner," consisting of a few peas and a lima bean.

Flockhart's body has become a category of its own, beyond the slender body and yet not directly associated with the diseased body. I would argue instead that the attention to Flockhart's figure reflects a limit or boundary to how slender a woman is allowed to become. Although there is a demand for women to be slender, as Chernin and Bordo argue, there also appears to be a limit on just how slender they can be. In the same respect there is also a suggestion that Flockhart consume — that she lose some control over her own desires for consumption. If the slender body reflects a way of controlling desires, then Flockhart's body represents a non-desiring body and the reactions to it seem to demand that she demonstrate some desire to desire.

Indeed, Flockhart's relationship with Harrison Ford suggests that the media is still unwilling to accept her as a desirable woman; instead she is parodied because of the age difference between her and Ford or because of her figure. In a magazine article entitled "Indiana Jones and the Very Thin Lady" (2002), Flockhart is described as having secured the romantic lead in an upcoming *Indiana Jones* movie because of her relationship with Ford. It reads: "Naturally Flockhart, who has had few big-screen outings, will play Ford's love interest. Although we think the stick-thin actress could double up as Indie's trusty whip" (*OK*, 2002: 302). Not only does the article imply that Flockhart has received the role as Ford's love interest because of Ford and not her acting talent but it also takes the opportunity to make a crass reference to her body and to her inability to be a "love interest," whether in the movie or in reality. The implication is that Flockhart cannot be desirable or sexy because she is "stick-thin." Also in this example, Flockhart is not identified by her name nor by her character, only by the dimensions of her figure.

The treatment Flockhart has received in the media and the press point to an expectation that a woman like Flockhart, who has achieved a certain level of success and notoriety, must conform to an acceptable weight, whether that means she is expected to be thinner or, in Flockhart's case, heavier. There is no question, as Chernin and Bordo argue, that women are expected to be slender in order to be accepted as successful. However, what if a woman is considered too slender? How does this affect her success? If there is a limit to how slender a woman can become, is there also a limit to how successful she can be without risking public shame and humiliation, whether over her figure, her sexuality or her career?

If the popularity of the show or of its star character were ever in question, then the onslaught of media coverage announcing the show's ending is proof of its success. Headlines such as "Goodbye Ally McBeal, We owe you" (Lawson, 2002: Ed.) from *The Guardian,* and "Absurd, Tiresome and far too thin (but I'll still be very sorry to see Ally go)" (Heffer, 2002: 13) in the *Daily Mail* echo the success of the show, despite its inevitable doom. The articles not only lament the passing of one of the most talked about shows in the U.S. and the U.K., but also take the chance to bring up issues concerning feminism. Simon Heffer, from the *Daily Mail,* writes: "After years of TV programmes that have sought to pretend to the contrary, Ally McBeal herself repudiates the main mantra of feminism: that a high-achieving young woman has no need of a man" (2002: 13). Whatever his intention, Heffer's comment echoes the show's general premise: that a successful career woman in her late twenties or early thirties needs a man. As Amanda Rees argues in *Feminist Theory:* "Lack of a partner for the Ally McBeals of this world doesn't just imply the absence of masculine attention, but the presence of very real emotional turmoil and self-doubt; having a husband or a boyfriend, it would seem, is the real mark of success" (2000: 365).

The show's writer-producer, David E. Kelley, well known for other series including *L.A. Law* and *Picket Fences,* has been quoted as saying that: "[Ally McBeal is] not a hard, strident feminist out of the '60s and '70s. She's all for women's rights, but she doesn't want to lead the change at her own emotional expense" (Bellafante, 1998: 58). Kelley's comment forms an interesting paradox which echoes recent pop culture feminist arguments coming from writers such as Elizabeth Wurtzel and Natasha Walter.

Wurtzel, well-known for her personal memoirs on Prozac and addiction, argues that feminism has not succeeded in allowing women to be what they want to be; she writes: "Because, frankly, I have a tough time feeling that feminism has done a damn bit of good if I can't be the way I am and have the world accommodate it on some level" (Wurtzel 1999: 33). In Britain, Natasha Walter's *The New Feminism* encourages old myths of dungaree-wearing lesbians as feminists to be buried into our collective imagination. She argues that:

The reluctance that many women feel in saying that they are feminists is understandable; they feel alienated from the label because they feel it puts them in some sort of a ghetto, that it defines them as an activist or a socialist or a lesbian or somebody who is humourless or dowdy or celibate. A woman should be able to say "I am a feminist" without feeling that she is implying any of these other positions [1998: 50].

Again in Walter's take on feminism there is an underlying insistence that feminism be about *me;* in this case a white, heterosexual, feminine woman, and not these activists, socialists, lesbians and bad dressers. Feminism is addressed at the level of appearance — Walter's concerns center on what feminism means in the eyes of other people, how it defines and therefore limits her, rather than what it means to political change or ideology. To return to Kelley's comment, I would argue that the show *Ally McBeal* reflects some of the anxieties within feminism as well as within the media's coverage of feminism.

Feminism plays a central role in *Ally McBeal.* For example, in "It's My Party" (originally aired 19 October 1998), Ally is asked to represent George Madison, the editor of *La Femme* magazine. Madison has recently been fired because of his Baptist religion, although he does not consider himself to be a strict follower. The head of *La Femme* magazine believes that although the editor may not adhere to all the Baptist dogma, the fact that he is a Baptist is enough to make his position within a feminist magazine untenable. She argues that "all it takes for misogyny to survive is for men to do nothing."

The head of *La Femme* magazine is portrayed as a "hard, strident feminist out of the '60s and '70s" (to repeat Kelley's words). She is perceived by Ally and Georgia as politically incorrect in her decision to fire her editor-in-chief on the basis of his religious affiliation. As viewers, we are also led to think that her stance is misguided, particularly when she tells the defending attorney: "We're a feminist magazine. How does it look with an editor-in-chief who tolerates such a position [a presumed belief that Baptists think women should stay in the home] much less endorses it.... If a Ku Klux Klan member tells me that he personally has nothing against blacks, forgive my cynicism." Her comparison between racism in the Ku Klux Klan and chauvinism in the Baptist faith is enough to convince the judge that Madison should have his job back, and the case is won.

The case is largely about the personal (one's religious beliefs) versus the political (the stance of the magazine as feminist). It is no coincidence that Kelley chooses this topic as a background to the other issues in the episode. "Make the personal political," was a, if not *the* second-wave feminist slogan. However, in this case, a feminist magazine has fired the editor-in-chief for his personal beliefs, believing his personal choice will adversely affect the sales of their political magazine.

Kelley often focuses on second-wave feminist concerns in order to challenge and question their viability. In her essay entitled "Ally McBeal and the End of Feminism," Katherine Post argues that, "even in Hollywood, it is no longer politically correct to accept feminist dogma without question, and that represents true progress" (1999). Whether or not "true progress" can be measured by political correctness, the point of Post's comment seems to be that in questioning feminist dogma we are accepting that certain equalities have been reached, and now we must question how these "dogmas" are practised, whether in law, politics or ethics.

It is possible to see how Post's analysis fits with regards to "It's My Party." If the editor is fired because of his association with the Baptist faith, then the suggestion is that his personal association sends out a political stance, whether or not he personally agrees with the ethics he is being allied with. So, in this case, although Madison does not personally believe that a woman's place is in the home, because he identifies himself as Baptist he is accused of sending out that political message. And because the idea that "a woman's place is in the home" is not one shared within most feminist ideology, he is fired from his political position.

Turn this logic around, as Kelley no doubt expects us to, and it can also be said that by calling herself a feminist, a woman is liable to the same political readings and misreadings. That is, even though she may not agree with all the principles of feminism, by calling herself a feminist she is taking a political position that may be judged fairly or unfairly by others.

Although Post sees *Ally McBeal* as questioning feminist dogmas, I would argue that it does so in order to question the necessity or role of feminism in politics, law and ethics rather than to pose alternative feminist understandings. In other words, *Ally McBeal* is not offering its viewers a new version of feminism; instead it is playing with the way feminism has been accepted and understood in popular culture.

In the same moment that Ally successfully defends her case against the "hard, strident feminist" she is held in contempt of court for the short mini-skirt she is wearing. After being called into chambers once before for the short length of her skirt, wearing it again is enough for the judge to rule that she must serve time in jail. There are several ways to read this moment. One could say that the case represents "true progress" as Post claims, as it challenges feminist dogma, and yet, as Ally is jailed for her fashion sense, this could signify a step backward: one step forward, one step backward for feminism. On the other hand, this scene could also be read in terms of Kelley's vision of Ally McBeal, a woman who is not like the "hard, strident" feminists of the '60s and '70s, but someone who will defend her right to wear what she wants because *she* wants to wear it. In other words, she will take up a feminist cause almost by accident, as it affects her life, not because it threatens feminist ideology. There is a suggestion here, as in the *Time* article, that feminism has moved from a "we" solidarity of the '60s and '70s to a "me"-based feminism in the twenty-first century.

However before a conclusion about solidarity can be made, the show takes another turn which suggests that a different kind of feminist solidarity still exists. As a mark of support, Fish insists that the entire firm go to Ally's hearing. When Ally calls the judge a "pig," Nelle stands up in her defense. She argues that Ally has been unjustly punished for her sexually provocative fashion. Her defense suggests that women have been unfairly expected to conform to the demands of an "old boy's" club and that Ally courageously demonstrates her ability to wear what she wants despite its sexual connotations:

NELLE: Every billboard and magazine cover tells us that we should look like models, all the while we have to fight the mind set: if she's beautiful, she must be stupid. I fight it too and I bend to the prejudice. I don't have [Ally's] courage. If I did, I might come in here and let my hair down [*lets hair down*]. If I didn't care about people automatically thinking I'm a bimbo, I might not always wear jackets [*takes off jacket to reveal a sleeveless top*]. But people, men and women, draw unfair conclusions. We've come to expect the bias. But not from judges. What's most disappointing here: You saw this woman perform in court. You heard her argue. She won her case and you're still judging her on hemlines. What do we have to do?

JUDGE: Ms. McBeal, do you have anything else?

ALLY: Only, you know, the obvious, your honor.

JUDGE: Which is?

ALLY: I wish I had her hair ["It's My Party"].

Nelle's closing statement, "What do we have to do?" suggests that there *is* something more to do— the fact that women are still judged on their "hemlines" is enough to believe that feminism is necessary. As long as women are forced to "bend to the prejudice" then inequality remains. And yet in order to prove her point, Nelle must expose her sexual potency. She must prove that she is just as sexy as Ally beneath her "old boy's club" appearance.

The scene sets up a contrast between Nelle and Ally: the "ice queen" versus "the girl next door" and interestingly, brings them together under the guise of feminism. The episode begins with Ally reluctantly inviting Nelle to her party. When Nelle accepts Ally's invitation, she rolls her eyes and tells Georgia, "Look at the bright side, she's bringing us closer together," emphasizing the differences between women like Ally and Georgia ("girl next door" and "smug married") and those like Nelle and Ling ("ice queen" and "man eater"). The scene then switches to Nelle and Ling discussing Nelle's fear that none of the women in the office like her, demonstrating her self-perceived exclusion from the other women in the firm. And yet, as discussed, it is Nelle that rises to Ally's defense, not Georgia or Elaine. Nelle's defense of Ally signifies her as "one of the gang" as demonstrated in the final party scene when Ally gives Nelle a sympathetic look as if to say, "I've accepted you now." The episode not only demonstrates a different kind of feminist solidarity but also reiterates Ally's central role in the firm's social dynamics—the one that can decide whether or not you are invited to the party. Perhaps Kelley is implying that Ally's relationship to feminism is a widely accepted one or we, as critics, could read Ally's brand of feminism as representing a popular version of feminism.

It is interesting to note that Ally seems to accept Nelle more for her hair than for her feminist defense. Ally's comment, "I wish I had her hair," suggests that she was paying more attention to Nelle's sexual potency than to the message in her defense. In other words, Ally is more impressed with Nelle's beauty than her intelligence. She objectifies Nelle at the same time that Nelle is trying to get the judge to stop judging Ally on the length of her skirt. A paradox is formed here that runs throughout the series. On the one hand Ally wants to be who she wants to be and yet she does not want to have to call herself a feminist or side with a feminist viewpoint. Instead her character remains ambiguous on this point whereas Nelle's character is more two-dimensional. She is the "ice queen," playing by old boy's rules and getting ahead for these reasons. Although this characterization could be viewed as reductive, it is also possible to see *Ally McBeal* as offering a variety of feminist viewpoints. Each female character, and at times, male character, has his or her own relationship to feminism. In this way, the show demonstrates *feminisms* rather than promoting a certain understanding of feminism.

Similar to a show such as *Sex and the City*, *Ally McBeal* offers viewers several different stereotyped female personalities to identify with or enjoy. And yet, these stereotypes, like ones in the media, focus more on a woman's sexuality than on her political or ethical beliefs. The presence of these different stereotypes also poses questions such as: why does it take so many women to express the multiplicity of woman? And why do women viewers enjoy these stereotypes?

The clash between Ally's character and feminism is addressed directly in the episode "Love Unlimited" (originally aired 18 January 1999). Ally is approached by Lara Dipson, executive vice president of *Pleasure* magazine, and asked to be the 1999 role model for young professional women. Ally's immediate dismissal of such a privilege is met by Ms. Dipson's demand that she must conform to women's expectations of her:

LARA: Well that's very sweet, but I'm afraid you really have no choice. Anyway, it'll be wonderful; you'll love it. We are going to have to make a few adjustments in the way you dress. And I'd really like to fatten you up a little bit. We don't want young girls glamorising that "thin" thing.... Now my sources tell me that you feel an emotional void without a man; you're really going to have to lose that if women are going to look up to you.

ALLY: I don't want them looking at me at all.

LARA: Don't be pissy. You're a role model and you'll do what we tell you to do. Now you can start by dropping that skinny, whiny, emotional slut thing and be exactly who we want you to be. Nothing more, nothing less. Can you do that, pin head? ["Love Unlimited"].

At this point Ally growls and bites off Lara's nose.

The scene abruptly switches to John Cage and Ally in a mock therapy session. John asks: "You bit off her nose?" to which Ally replies, "Yes, and I got blood on my outfit." John is trying to decipher Ally's dream, believing it may have some connection to the intimacy issues in her relationship with Dr. Greg Butters, one in a string of many relationships Ally has within the series. Ally answers that she thinks the dream reflects her desire to be with a man in a dependent role. She tells John: "I want somebody I can be totally weak with. Somebody who will hold me and make me feel *held*." She pauses and emphasizes the "held." She adds: "I think I crave some kind of dependency and that makes me feel like a failure as a woman. You know I had a dream that they put my face on the cover of *Time* magazine as the 'Face of Feminism?'"

Several things are worth noting, both in regard to feminism and Flockhart's body. Lara Dipson, who appears as a second-wave feminist figure (complete with shoulder pads), draws attention to Ally's "skinny" body twice and imagines it as an obstacle against Ally being a healthy, positive role model for women. Indeed the whole notion of women being good role models and in having positive representation of women is constructed here as part of a second-wave agenda. Ally's reluctance to be a role model for *Pleasure* magazine can be linked to Walter's observation that women today are afraid that being feminist puts in them in jeopardy of being ghettoized as lesbian or socialist.

What the scene does best to illustrate, however, is that there is confusion over what it means to be feminist as well as what it means to be a successful woman. It also questions whether this successful woman, Ally, owes anything to her second-wave counterpart or to her post-feminist contemporaries. What Ally shares with writers like Walter and Wurtzel is ambivalence over what it means to be a feminist and a reluctance to get involved if there isn't anything in it for them personally. Instead of the two-dimensional "Lara Dipson," who Kelley clearly positions as a kind of militant second-wave feminist, Ally is struggling with her desires to be independent and to be "held." Whereas Dipson clearly knows what she wants and who she is, Ally does not. Is she a post-feminist, a third-wave feminist? Is she a feminist at all? These questions are deliberately left unanswered.

There is also an issue here regarding pleasure — it is hardly a coincidence that Lara Dipson works for *Pleasure* magazine. There is a distinction made between Dipson's character who takes "pleasure" in her professional life and Ally who "feels an emotional void without a man." As Ally tells John: "I think I crave some kind of dependency and that makes me feel like a failure as a woman." One the one hand, this reads as a frustrating suggestion that underneath every career woman is someone who just wants to get married and stay at home; however, on the other hand, it can also be read as a frustration that professional women are not expected, or perhaps even allowed, to be emotional or vulnerable. Read in this way, this scene demonstrates the work that is still left for feminism, not its death. It suggests that there is still a societal expectation of successful women to be successful in all ways, which is not always true for their male counterparts.

However, far from being "unallowed" her emotions in the workplace, Ally's vulnerability underpins the narrative and comedic edge to the program. As Jane Arthurs argues, "The melodramatic excessiveness of Ally's vulnerability tips over into its opposite in that her reactions are sufficiently intense to require accommodation. She doesn't simply fit into a masculinized workplace predicated on rationality; in fact her emotional excess becomes the dominant office code for her male colleagues" (2004: 133). One of the progressive elements of the program is an allowance for emotion and its contagious effect. It not only extends to the confines of the workplace, but also seems to reach the viewers, who take pleasure in Ally's emotional instability. For instance, Laura Morice writes in *Self* Magazine: "Let's leave the debate over Ally's impact on the women's movement to the critics and allow ourselves a rare guilty: watching a woman we can relate to—flaws and all" (www.cflockhart.com/articles). In her essay "The Ally McBeal in Us: The Importance of Role Models in Identity Formation," Judith Schroeter argues that Ally "personifies typical conflicts that arise from an increasingly individualised society — thus, conflicts we all face in our daily lives. Consequently, Ally McBeal can provide support and help us cope with them" (www.theory.org.uk, 2002). Schroeter's claim that the program actually helps viewers cope is an interesting one and points toward the importance of emotion within texts such as *Ally McBeal*. It suggests that part of the reason for the success of *Ally McBeal* lies in its ability to speak to the inherent contradictions and ambivalences women face, whether in the workplace or at home.

The failure of the last two seasons may be read as further proof that it is these inconsistencies and ambivalences that Ally's character possesses that attracts and keeps viewers engaged. Whereas the first three seasons deal with Ally's ambivalence over her status as a single woman, the final two seasons consider and resolve these ambiguities. The fourth and fifth seasons illustrate a more centered, focused Ally; she has made partner in the firm, she buys a house, finds "Mr. Right" and establishes a relationship with her long-lost daughter. Although not a conventional family as she may have once yearned for, it is all the same a family and one that suggests permanence. And yet, as Ally's life gains clarity and security, the very opposite happens to the show itself. As this new, more self-confident Ally appears the show's ratings take a nosedive. Of course other factors, such as the length of the series and introduction of new characters could be blamed for the show's decline; however, it seems possible that this Ally is not the one the viewers prefer. And if this is true, then we are left wondering why viewers, even feminist viewers, prefer the Ally who mourns her single status, who wants nothing more than to be married, who spends more time in her fantasy life than her "real" one — instead of a woman who has found emotional, financial and personal security? Instead of reading this as an inability on the viewers' part to appreciate "positive" role models, it indicates the enjoyment viewers take in watching someone "flaws and all." It further indicates the pleasure viewers take in watching someone who cannot always cope with what life offers. Instead of heralding the death of feminism, programs such as *Ally McBeal* reveal the strength of feminism to continue to offer a way of talking through the ambivalences and contradictions women face in contemporary Western societies.

Works Cited

Arthurs, Jane. *Television and Sexuality: Regulation and the Politics of Taste*. Maidenhead: Open University Press, 2004.

AskMen Website. "Calista Flockhart." *www.askmen.com*. (accessed 18 July 2002).

Bellafante, Gina. "Feminism: It's All About Me." *Time Magazine,* 29 June 1998: 54–62.

"Body of Evidence." *TV-7: ITV Digital Magazine,* February 2002 [Cover].

Bordo, Susan. *Unbearable Weight: Feminism, Western Culture and the Body*. Berkeley: University of California Press, 1993.

Chaudhuri, Anita. "Thin, Thinner, Thinnest." *Guardian Unlimited*. 18 Oct. 1999. http://www.guardianunlimited.co.u...ve/Article/0,4273,3913436,00.html.

Chernin, Kim. *Womansize: the Tyranny of Slenderness*. 1981. London: The Women's Press, 1983.

Chunovic, Louis. *The Complete Guide to Ally McBeal (Unofficial)*. London: Boxtree, 1999.

Cixous, Hélène, and Catherine Clément. *The Newly Born Woman.* Translated by Betsy Wing. Minneapolis: University of Minnesota Press, 1986.

Greer, Germaine. *The Whole Woman.* London: Doubleday, 1999.

_____. *The Female Eunuch.* 1970. London: Flamingo, 1993.

Heffer, Simon. "Absurd, Tiresome and Far Too Thin (but I'll Still Be Very Sorry to See Ally Go)." *Daily Mail.* 19 April 2002: 13.

"Indiana Jones and The Very Thin Lady." *OK Magazine,* Issue 322. July, 2002: 302.

Irigaray, Luce. *This Sex Which Is Not One.* Translated by Catherine Porter. Ithaca, NY: Cornell University Press, 1985.

Kelley, David E. "It's My Party" (1998), "Love Unlimited" (1999), and "Blowin in the Wind" (2001). *Ally McBeal.* Los Angeles: Twentieth Century Fox Film Corporation.

Lawson, Mark. "Goodbye, Ally McBeal. We Owe You." *The Guardian,* April 2002: Ed.

Morice, Laura. *Self Magazine. www.cflockhart.com/articles.* (accessed 6 August 2002).

Post, Katherine. "Ally McBeal and the End of Feminism." *The Contrarian: News and Comments on Women's Issues.* 3. 7 (1999).

Rees, Amanda. "Higamous, Hogamous, Woman Monogamous." *Feminist Theory* 1.3 (2000): 365–37.

Schroeter, Judith. "The Ally McBeal in Us: The Importance of Role Models in Identity Formation." *www.theory.org.uk/ally.htm* Jan. 2002. (accessed 6 August 2002).

Walter, Natasha. *The New Feminism.* London: Little Brown, 1998.

Wurtzel, Elizabeth. *Bitch: In Praise of Difficult Women.* London: Virago, 1999.

6

Female Representation and the "Postfeminist" Challenge

Laurie Ouellette and Susan E. McKenna

Critical scholars have long grappled with how to teach students who are already sophisticated consumers of media culture.[1] Feminist cultural studies, in particular, has stressed the importance of addressing relations between representations of women and gender in the media, and the construction of female subjectivity.[2] And yet, much feminist cultural scholarship continues to emphasize the ideologies and subject positions constructed by the media on the one hand and female spectatorship, audience identifications and pleasurable readings on the other.[3] Our purpose in this paper is to translate the contributions made by feminist cultural studies to the relations between media culture and social experience in the classroom. We begin by discussing the challenges of teaching students about feminism and media representations in a "postfeminist" political environment, and conclude by sharing pedagogical strategies for engaging undergraduate students in the critical analysis of one contemporary fictional television persona, Ally McBeal.

Our pedagogical goal is for students to understand that cultural beliefs and values are both socially constructed via symbolic practices, and lived and felt, to use Raymond Williams' terminology. We begin with the assumption that it is a necessity for students who want to fully participate in contemporary media culture to recognize that their thoughts are culturally shaped and historically situated. Gaining a recognition and understanding of ideology is pivotal to critical thought or questioning on the part of students. However, as Judith Williamson argues, "It is not enough just to analyze the media ... unless you can find an analogous situation in their own experience, and make it problematic for them — they will never really grasp the ideological relations between 'text' and 'reader'" (54). Teaching students to critique representations need not mean dismissing the experiential pleasures students take from popular culture. "Human beings need systems of representations in order to interpret or 'make sense' of the conditions of their experience," Stuart Hall writes, and we stress that one of the primary ways that we come to self-identify is through the use we make of images ("Signification," 105). Relatedly, our purpose as feminist teachers is not to "recruit" students to feminism or liberate our students from false consciousness. Following a critical pedagogic approach, we envision the classroom as a participatory forum for recognizing and illuminating students' experiences as women and as audience members. The goal of teaching, we believe, should be to encourage students to critically engage with complex ideas.

Drawing from coursework and assignments designed for our media studies courses, we discuss a range of teaching strategies that are especially applicable to the "postfeminist" age. We take as our premise that common sense understandings of gender and feminism are formed through culture, including media representations. We have become interested in Ally McBeal because she has become an icon of postfeminism and because she is extremely popular with our female students. Furthermore, the program *Ally McBeal* is itself on the way to becoming what Suzanna Walters terms "a symptomatic text," or a film or television program that becomes important to theorists, critics and audiences because it is part of a broader discourse about feminism and women (6). As *Entertainment Weekly* suggests, *Ally McBeal* is nothing short of "a Rorschach test, and what's being tested is the viewer's ideas of sex, power, and young womanhood" (Malanowski, 31). By critically analyzing *Ally McBeal* and the considerable extratextual discourse that surrounds its lead female character (and the actress Calista Flockhart who plays her) we encourage students to reflect on the conservative presumption that "feminism is dead." By exploring the extent to which young women have forged positive identifications with Ally McBeal, we also encourage our students to consider what makes this particular character pleasurable and why she resonates at a specific historical juncture. We believe that the theoretical sophistication now applied to the study of female audiences has much use value in the classroom, in terms of teaching students to unravel for themselves the cultural politics and the experiential pleasures of those media representations they find most compelling. We stress, along with John Fiske, that "pleasure requires a sense of control over meanings and an active participation in the cultural process" (19). In what follows, we define the theoretical and pedagogical issues that orient our work, and sketch out a range of teaching strategies.

Ally McBeal and the "Postfeminist" Challenge

As teachers of media studies at public universities, we are concerned with the "postfeminist" challenge of teaching critical perspectives on female representation at a historical moment when feminism is seen as a suspicious relic from a bygone era. Walters defines "postfeminism" as the commonsensical misperception that the movement for women's equality has already been achieved (119). Complementing this gross misperception, say feminist critics, is a conservative backlash against women and feminism that has also manifested in cultural tropes. The symbols of postfeminism range from the demonization of single career women in Hollywood films, to the call for pre-feminist traditional family values, to the perpetuation of sexist beauty-body ideals in advertising, to the media construction of feminists as militant, angry, humorless, unattractive and sexually undesirable in media representations.[4] These messages are sustained, contends Walters, by the ideologically contradictory image of a failed feminist movement "responsible for the sad plight of millions of unhappy and unsatisfied women who, thinking they could have it all, have clearly 'gone too far' and jeopardized their chances at achieving the much valorized American Dream" (119). In other words, the failure of feminism is constructed and negotiated across a range of visual sites, from advertisements to digital media to Hollywood films and television programming to representational themes (which cut across cultural venues) of body and star. These sites are linked together through clusters of meaning that together construct seemingly coherent and commonsensical ideas about contemporary feminism, and obscure the contradictions inherent to postfeminist claims. This process is not conspiratorial, but rather socially produced within and across multiple social and visual contexts. What is most significant, we believe, are the contradictions that lie beneath the seams. As Janice Radway stresses, "no ideology is a simple, uniform, organic thing. It secures the consciousness it manages to create only through a congeries of varied and related practices. Those practices, while related, are also autonomously and internally organized" ("Ideological Seams," 108). While these patterns may not be consciously recognized by students, they often underlie nonresponsiveness to feminist criticisms of female representation and contemporary visual culture.

For example, Susan Douglas argues that the "I'm Not a Feminist, But" phenomenon — or the tendency of young women to support the concept of equality for women but shun the label "feminist"— stems from the media's vilification of feminists as the antithesis of what is acceptable and, perhaps more importantly, desirable in women. Certainly, we have found that students often arrive in class predisposed to reject the relevance of feminism through preconceived notions of what feminism actually means. Such predisposition is compounded not by a rejection of critical thinking — most students are able to see the extent to which women are still maligned by the media — but rather by the presumption that feminist interpretations of media representations require rejecting the pleasures of femininity and popular media. In other words, the reluctance to adopt a feminist subject position in the classroom, or more accurately, the cultural meanings and baggage associated with that position, can make students wary of critical analytical tools that carry a feminist label.

In the late 1990s, the popular television character Ally McBeal emerged as a media-appointed icon of postfemininity, providing a useful context for translating feminist cultural studies to the classroom. In turn, the media spotlight that coincided with the successful Fox series provides a context for showing how the media itself constructs the myth of feminism's death. Radical feminist tenets that were controversial in the media of the 1970s are today summarily dismissed as extreme and dated. More sophisticated feminisms that attempt to account for pleasure, contradiction, and difference are also frequently oversimplified and negated. For example, a 1998 *Time* magazine cover displayed the heads of famous feminist icons Susan B. Anthony, Betty Friedan, and Gloria Steinem as black and white Paleolithic craniums softly glowing against a dark background, alongside the full color headshot of Ally McBeal (Calista Flockhart). The cover text asks: "IS FEMINISM DEAD?" while the visual juxtapositions assure the reader that it must be so. Inside, the accompanying article explains that feminists are viewed as "man hating," and that developments in feminist thought that do account for the contradictions of gender and the pleasures of popular culture have "evolved into the silly." This media obituary encourages readers to believe that feminism is no longer a useful concept, as "today's young chic feminist thinkers" care only about "Their bodies! Themselves!" (Bellafante, 54). The cover was yet another example of the ideological reification suggested by Walters' analysis of postfeminism: "This discourse, like so many others before it, has declared the movement (predictably if illogically) dead, victorious, and ultimately failed" (119). The man-hating militancy of feminism is predictably professed, while feminism's attempt to account for the pleasures of femininity and popular culture is dismissed. In other words, feminists who step outside the media's own negative construction of what a feminist must be are trivialized. And symbolizing this new twist on postfeminism is the disembodied head of Ally McBeal.

The intersection between postfeminist discourse and the popularity of

Ally McBeal opened up new possibilities for educators interested in critical pedagogy and student audience identifications. *Ally McBeal* was an undisputed success, its resonance attributed to the enthusiastic response from young (18 to 34-year-old) female viewers. Hyped by the Fox network as "one of the most compelling and sensitive portrayals of a woman ever rendered by a man," the program articulates many of the contradictory ideological assumptions that fall under the rubric of postfeminism. As a Harvard-educated lawyer Ally McBeal is extraordinarily successful, but she is not a self-defined feminist, and she takes her equality as a woman (as symbolized by her firm's unisex bathroom) for granted. While unmarried and independent, she pines over her unsuccessful romantic life and fantasizes frequently about her biological clock. She is often unhappy, beset with personal problems that define her life, usurp her professional responsibilities, and bring her to a therapist's office. Ally is also positioned at the center of feminist debates over manipulation and agency in the context of dominant beauty and body norms. These debates have seeped into the media, generally minus feminist explanations, where Flockhart, who is a size one and exercises regularly, garnered attention for an alleged eating disorder. Her character's habit of wearing short miniskirts was also widely noted by media commentators, often with the effect of implying that feminist stances on sexual objectification are unreasonable or unwarranted.

It would be easy to dismiss Ally McBeal as a postfeminist television character who sends young women the wrong message. However, as critical educators, we need to recognize that doing so can work in concert with the media's construction of feminism, as well as with students' often predisposed dismissal of feminist tools. A simple dismissal also overlooks the ideological contradictions negotiated by the program. Ally may look like a child and act like a grown-up, to paraphrase *Harper's Bazaar,* but she is also "a nymphet with gravitas and a law degree, and she's been known to kick-ass [literally] in the courtroom" (Kuczynski, 503). She is a contrary and confused character, which perhaps helps account for her enormous popularity among college-aged women. Ally moves with fluidity between feminism and postfeminism in storylines that address what it means to be a twenty-something professional woman and that touch on the politics of class, race, gender, and sexual expectations. Indeed, Ally is arguably popular precisely because she symbolizes and embodies the many contradictions that linger in the wake of feminism's so-called death. Ally McBeal personifies these contradictions, and as such she may, to use Radway's words, provide an "interstice in the social fabric" through which young women can reflect on the "reality of their social situation" in ways that do not work completely against their own interests" ("Ideological Seams" 97).

Female students, in particular, are often aware of the huge dissonance between postfeminist claims and real-life gender dynamics in the family and the workplace. They are attuned to the sexist and unattainable beauty and body ideals put forward by advertisers and our commercially sponsored visual culture, but they also feel the very real pressures and pleasures of participation in that same beauty culture. They know that women are equal in the official rhetoric of the workplace and that women have entered the professions; and yet, the continual sexual objectification of women in the media sends a dramatically different message about femininity and about female worth. Female students especially identify with Ally because she personifies contradictions that may be rooted in mythical anti-feminist claims, but that nonetheless speak to the experience of young women on the brink of adulthood. Students see her character as very realistic because of Ally's often contradictory beliefs, behaviors, experiences and assumptions. A critical discussion of Ally McBeal provides the cultural tools, Radway suggests, for these young women to assess "their material situation and to express their discontent with it"; as such both the television program and character can serve as a site through which "resistance and discontent might be developed into a more deliberate opposition to dominance" ("Ideological Seams," 97). By addressing and unpacking the reasons why students find *Ally McBeal* compelling, they might better understand the complexities and contradictions of their own experience.

Our pedagogical engagement with *Ally McBeal* is also attuned to the tendency of students to initially reject the critical dimensions of popular cultural forms that they find personally pleasurable and entertaining. Although students are frequently able to recognize the basis of feminist critiques of visual culture, they may nonetheless respond by stating that cultural sites such as television are "just entertainment." Furthermore, students may resist or outwardly reject feminist theories of culture because they believe that any attempt to situate the origins and effects of visual representations ideologically and historically constitutes an assertion of propaganda or conspiracy. Students who adopt this position can find it difficult to examine their own relationship with media. As Williamson says about her experience of teaching media studies, "Ideology is always what other people think, and the only possible explanation for why they believe such 'lies' or 'propaganda' is that they are stupid" (56).

We believe that typical responses such as "just entertainment and "lies or propaganda" are rooted in students' investment in the visceral experience of pleasurable identifications. Alongside media criticism we need to stress the extent to which the "the cultural imaginary," as Arina Warner argues, "contributes as fundamentally to cultural character as do a culture's laws, economy and political arrangements" (19). And yet, at the same time, we are likely asking too much if we expect our students to distance themselves completely from the symbols and discourses through which they construct a sense of self. Responses to visual culture can be both critical and pleasurable, and students know experientially what Fiske states theoretically: "That meanings and pleasures are difficult "to possess exclusively" (18). There is also pleasure in critique, and this should be emphasized. Although pleasure itself is a site of critical contestation, the negative pleasures associated with the male gaze can also be, Bergstrom and Doane argue, "a flag to rally around, offering the promise of a visual empowerment of women" (8). The exhortation of "just entertainment" exemplifies the importance of teaching feminist theories about visual culture in relation to the social dimensions of audience reception such as pleasurable identifications.

We also, however, wish to emphasize the extent to which ways of thinking about gender (and about feminism), and the pleasures obtained from visual culture, are socially constructed via symbolic practices, including media representations. We have found that critical engagement with this dynamic can also be fostered through (rather than against) an invested engagement in visual media culture. In other words, students are better poised to formulate a critical perspective that is relevant to their social position when doing so does not necessitate an enlightened rejection of everything the media has to offer. The contradictory aspects of visual media culture emphasized by cultural studies provides a model for dismantling the either-or binary between feminist criticism and fan responses,[5] and within the classroom, between critical engagement and the easy pleasures of "just entertainment."

Toward that end, we have found that it can be useful to analyze a particular series or persona, such as *Ally McBeal,* during each critical phase of a media studies course. This recurring discussion enables students to work through critical perspectives with a familiar example. It also encourages students to understand that one has critical and pleasurable responses to visual representations at once, or what Douglas describes as a love-hate relationship with the media. In other words, to understand that there are not only multiple pleasures, but contradictory aspects involved in negotiating the relationship between a text such as *Ally McBeal* and social experience; this experiential understanding might lead to a more active role in constructing meanings. Fiske observes that "pleasure results from a particular relationship between meanings and power" (19), and we encourage students to take pleasure seriously. However, we also cultivate the pleasure in critique, and do not attempt to make these processes mutually exclusive.

Adopting a critical analysis can broadly enable students to reconsider the meaning of feminism and its applicability to their social experience.

Finally, although we have students read from the critical cultural canon, we also have them read from a variety of popular sources, such as popular magazines, alternative newspapers, and current fiction. Interdisciplinary means more than Freud and Marx, Butler and Foucault, or Hall and Radway. For us, it means finding a broad range of materials that resonate with students and that can be used as evidence or as examples. We search for readings in communication, feminist criticism, sociology, and even legal studies textbooks to find accessible examples of critical theory put into practice. For example, a brief article on the interrelations of perceptions of real life female lawyers and images of female lawyers on television can be compelling. A brief sociology article with statistics on the changing measurements of Miss America can be useful for discussing cultural constructions of beauty and taste without sliding into the frequently dead end debates about the objectification of women in the mass media (Wiseman et al.). Having students read *Time* magazine's account of postfeminism can be a useful exercise in showing how commonsense understandings of feminism and postfeminism are constructed and defined visually and discursively. Incorporating fan responses to *Ally McBeal* posted on the Internet into class discussions can provide another layer of evidence when analyzing audience negotiations and identifications. Less conventional readings and assignments generally resonate with students in ways that theoretical texts alone do not; as such they help illuminate the relationship between visual representations and everyday experience.

Drawing from course work and assignments we next propose to share a range of teaching strategies for teaching critical analysis of mass media and popular culture in the age of postfeminism. Like Elizabeth Ellsworth, we emphasize "strategies in context," in which the classroom is taken as "the site of dispersed, shifting, and contradictory contexts of knowing, that coalesce differently in different moments" ("Why Doesn't This," 114). We offer ideas originating in several teaching contexts: introductory and advanced classes in media studies; production (photography and video) classes; and general education courses for communication and noncommunication majors. The strategies we present will vary according to course level; however, they can be translated into any class incorporating a critical analysis of the mass media.

Pedagogical Strategy One: Ideological Pressures

Since many students are already quite savvy to the goals of advertisers, we have found that a useful way to explain the concept of ideology is to assess the relationship between political economic factors, social pressures, and *Ally McBeal*. This can be done by having students analyze the opening sequence to the program alongside its idealized construction of femininity — and the construction of the imagined audience — demonstrated by the program's advertisements. The contrasts and continuities between the opening sequence and the advertisements are useful starting points for examining the extent to which Ally's character is partly shaped by the ideological construction of femininity and feminism preferred by advertisers.

The opening sequence features brief vignettes from the program accompanied by the theme song, "Searching My Soul," which is sung by *Ally McBeal*'s resident chanteuse, Vonda Shepard. "Searching My Soul" conjures up a message of female independence and self-esteem as well as a liberal feminist emphasis on gender equality in the professional workplace, a goal that is presented here as taken for granted, and already achieved. The opening vignettes depict Ally McBeal seated between male colleagues at a board meeting, as well as scenes of her law firm's unisex bathroom, private moments with her friend and roommate Renee, and background shots that depict her smiling, walking, and interacting at her office. The advertisements immediately following the theme song on one episode pitched beauty and personal hygiene products (Maybelline mascara, L'Oreal hair color, Listerine mouthwash), an upscale pet food, Diet Dr. Pepper, and a luxury car. Students working in groups or in class discussion discern from these advertisements, and ones like them, that the program's advertisers were interested in reaching a primarily young, upscale, female audience (whilst not excluding males), that is single and that has (or will have) the disposable income required to purchase the particular consumer items advertised. Students can be encouraged to detect and work through the dissonance between Ally's assertiveness and independence (again, symbolized most vividly by the unisex bathroom) and the conventional gender roles and beauty norms proscribed by the advertisements. The contradictions that become apparent between codes of professionalism, on the one hand, and codes of beauty on the other, are well exemplified by these examples.

From here, students are more predisposed to acknowledge these ideological incongruencies as they negotiate them regularly in their daily life experience. "When two such practices intersect," Radway writes, "their point of connection is often characterized by a seam, their joining is imperfect. Ideology is, finally, the product of a set of imperfectly joined practices; some are congruent, while others are contradictory and even mutually interactive" ("Ideological Seams," 109). Once students begin to recognize these contradictions, they are more apt to understand the contradictory nature of ideology, for ideology, as Stuart Hall stresses, is a function of the social acceptance of a discourse as coherent and, thus, as natural, universal, and inevitable ("Culture").

Another exercise that is useful for illuminating the nature of ideology involves the detection of gender stereotypes. While early feminist discussion of stereotyping stopped short of illuminating the complex process of visual representation or its equally complex ideological effects, exercises related to gender stereotyping can be an introduction to more sophisticated and illuminating concepts. As Walters explains, "The ideological effectiveness of stereotypes is based on the experience of them as not only 'erroneous' or 'false,' but rather as structurally reinforced ideological forms of repression" (42). For example, the juxtaposition between the image of professionalism and female strength conveyed by the opening sequence and a selection of clips from an episode dealing with a murder case reveals the contradictory aspects of *Ally McBeal*'s already equal, postfeminist status. In the clips, Ally responds in a less than professional way to the prospect of taking an accused murderer as a client. She faints at the crime scene, cowers behind her male colleague, and nibbles on his shoulder during a client interview. The humor hinges on the reappearance of traditional and clearly delineated gender roles that directly contradict the message of workplace equality presumed by the opening sequence.

After students have identified traditional gender stereotypes, the ideological construction of gender can be pursued in a more complex manner. They are able to understand, as Walters further contends, that "to argue for less stereotyped images avoids an attack on the deep structures of the signifying practices that produce such images in the first place" (42). Positive imaging does not account for the complexity of understanding power relations or the processes of signification. Clips from other episodes (including ones where Ally fantasizes about having a husband and a suburban home and hallucinates a dancing baby) are useful for illuminating how traditional ideologies of gender coexist with and contradict Ally's sometime assertiveness, the implicit liberal feminism of the opening sequence, and other sequences from the same episodes. This exercise can be coupled with a discussion of the social construction of gender, illuminated by feminist theories of popular culture that show how representations of women in the media intersect with both an ideological struggle to define women's proper and desired roles and with the process of gender socialization. At this point, a discussion of postfeminism can be introduced with the purpose of familiarizing students with the various cultural manifestations of conservative ideological pressures.

The extent to which *Ally McBeal* wavers between femininity and feminism is not new to popular culture; however, her resonance among undergraduate students provides a useful context for discussing the ideological forces and stakes inherent to such fluctuation.[6] It is important to explain that televisual texts like *Ally McBeal* are popular precisely because there are multiple ideological perspectives. The potential for the "multiplicity of meanings," in Fiske's words, "is both complex and subtle and has a powerful effect on the audience" (14). And yet, we do not want to suggest that the textual potential for multiple readings means that there are no points of determination. "An ambiguous TV program," Justin Lewis reminds us, "can be just as manipulative as an unambiguous one, it simply moves in multifarious ways" (205). Students already relate to *Ally McBeal;* by showing how gender is itself constructed and contested on the program, we can begin to explore the larger contradictions that contribute to their identifications.

Pedagogical Strategy Two: Sexual Objectification and Female Agency

The perpetuation of female sexual objectification under postfeminism is another useful issue to explore within the context of *Ally McBeal*. We take advantage of the many resources available for introducing students to concepts such as the male gaze, body and beauty ideals, and the internalization of female sexual objectification: Laura Mulvey's work on the male gaze of Hollywood films, John Berger's important analysis of gendered ways of seeing, Sut Jhally's video discussion of the critical distinction between subjects (male) and objects (female) constructed by visual representations, and Jean Kilbourne's feminist critique of the increasingly thin and sexualized female representations in advertising and other commercial visual contexts. We also address Susan Douglas's argument that the gradual incorporation of certain feminist principles into the mass media (such as equal pay for equal work and female entry into formerly male professions) has intersected with a tacit acceptance of the continued, even accelerated, objectification of women in media imagery. In other words, female independence and entry into the male professions has been rendered less threatening by the media-promoted presumption that women are still sexualized objects of male desire. Females in the media, even successful career women such as Ally McBeal, are concerned above all with their weight and their appearance as judged from an internalized male perspective. The casting of feminists as undesirable and unattractive works hand in hand with this contradiction, says Douglas, legitimating the presumption that strong, successful, sexual, and attractive women cannot be also feminists. While we are interested in helping students develop critically informed perspectives on sexual objectification, we also wish to address this either-or positioning between feminine desirability and feminist agency, and its relationship to the myth of postfeminism. Unless we do this, it is very hard to break down students' defenses against feminist criticism.

Ally McBeal is well-suited for exploring these issues—in terms of not only the subject matter addressed on the program, but the extratextual discourse that circulates around it—both helping to define the visual iconography of postfeminism. Extratextual discourses about Ally McBeal and Calista Flockhart focused on issues of body and style. Numerous national publications, from *Time* to *TV Guide* to *Harper's Bazaar,* printed features on *Ally McBeal* noting Ally's penchant for miniskirts and her slender girlish figure, and these issues are also self-consciously emphasized and addressed on the program, as in one episode when Ally goes to jail for wearing clothing inappropriate for the courtroom. Together, extra and intratextual examples address important issues that can lead to productive discussion regarding the relations between feminism, beauty ideals, sexual objectification, and social experience. One such issue is the extent to which Ally's character embodies the trend toward unrealistic and often dangerous body sizes in advertising and other visual venues—a trend critics link to both the version of femininity preferred by advertisers and to the cultural backlash against women prompted by the professional gains that women have made. Female students are aware of the pressure to live up to sexual and beauty ideals; reading critical literature helps them see the extent to which economic and ideological pressures underlie these ideals.

Discussing *Ally McBeal* within this context can open up space to consider the linkages between such pressures and dieting pressures, including potentially deadly eating disorders. As Fiske notes, "Social experience is much like a text: its meanings depend upon the discourses that are brought to bear upon it" (15). Examining how discourses about gender and sexuality, and weight and body are constructed across different cultural sites including television programs, gossip columns, and magazine advertising can be very persuasive in demonstrating that there are connections between mass media and daily life behaviors such as obsessive dieting and compulsive exercising.

Jean Kilbourne and others argue that the plummeting weight of fashion models has contributed to a contemporary cultural climate in which eating disorders among young women and girls are on the rise. But Ally McBeal is no dupe; she is more complex and assertive than the unreasonably thin, one-dimensional women shown in many advertisements. Because she does possess a strong sense of self and a degree of agency, she provides a useful forum for considering the effects of these media-constructed beauty and body ideals, as well as the political implications of such media images. Students are able to recognize the extent to which Ally embodies dominant (and dangerous) ideals rooted in the internalization of commercial and patriarchal norms. Media discourse surrounding actress Calista Flockhart's rumored eating disorder also resonates strongly with female students. We incorporate this discourse into our class discussions as a means to address the pressures facing twenty-something female consumers of visual culture, the contradictions of postfeminism, and the trivialization of eating disorders by the media. For example, *The Tonight Show* spoofed Flockhart's rumored condition, showing a TV dinner with a single carrot and a single pea, dubbed "The *Ally McBeal* TV dinner." The extent to which the commercial media both pressures women to meet impossible requirements of female attractiveness, while simultaneously trivializing and blaming women for "female" eating habits, angers students, many of whom experience similar anxieties about food, and some of whom have undoubtedly grappled with devastating eating disorders.

Students are often able to see the extent to which women, perhaps including themselves, internalize the male gaze as well as cultural constructions of female beauty. On the other hand, the intersecting pressures and pleasures of self-adornment, making one's self sexually attractive and participating in beauty culture are very strong among undergraduate females. Many students—like many feminists who advocate a "pro-sex" approach to female pleasure and sexuality—do not wish to conform to what they perceive as a 1970s feminism's rigid rules regarding fashion, sexuality, and style. The image of the unfashionable, unwashed, unattractive feminist stereotype with hairy legs, wearing a shapeless flannel shirt or a burlap sack, holds strong in their minds. It is important to address and legitimate these concerns and their links to feminism in the popular imagination, for if we do not, students are not apt to see the extent to which the either-or binary separating feminism from femininity and pleasure is itself an ideological construct. We are interested in showing students that they can be both feminist and fashionable; that critiquing the sexual objectification of women in the media need not lead to the wholesale rejection of socially conditioned pleasures and desires. One way of doing this is to explore the possibility that, as Radway argues, the "patriarchal surface of these texts conceals a womanly subtext and that, as a consequence, female audiences are capable of interpreting these forms against the grain" ("Ideological Seams," 98). Another way is to discuss the extent to which mutually exclusive categories are ideological, not essential. We believe that "ideological seams," to use Radway's terminology, can be unraveled without wholly discrediting the importance of popular visual culture in the lives of women, including students.

In this sense, we cannot discount recent feminist attention to the possibilities of appropriating and refashioning dominant constructs of beauty and body in ways that grant more agency to female subjects.[7]

Ally McBeal often grappled with precisely such possibilities, offering a starting point from which to grapple with the options available to students who wish to reject sexual objectification but are not prepared to conform to what they see as the alternative — the ugly feminist stereotype. In one episode, for example, Ally's law firm has agreed to represent a female client who is the boss at a manufacturing plant, where she supervises mostly male employees. The woman — who is set up as the archetypal karate chopping, non-smiling, angry feminist — is suing a Howard Stern-like radio talk show host on the basis that his broadcasts contribute to sexual harassment in the workplace by sexually objectifying and degrading women. The firm wins the suit — which is handled by Nelle, a female attorney who often handles gender discrimination cases— but drops it before losing in appeal. Ally McBeal, who was opposed to the case and is appalled by the way it was handled by her female colleague, goes on the radio program as the counterpoint to the feminist discourse that has been established previously by the program. Ally is extremely friendly and flirtatious, despite the degrading sexual comments repeatedly made by the host, and when he asks her why she wears her skirts so short, she smiles and explains that men are always trying to undress her with their eyes anyway.

This clip can be easily dismissed as an anti-feminist containment of the feminist critique of sexual objectification expressed earlier on the program. In this sense, it offers another example for demonstrating competing ideologies. However, the clip can also be productively used to open up discussions about perceptions of feminism in relation to feminism and style. The juxtaposition between the client and Ally can be deconstructed to illuminate the extent to which binary opposites (feminist = sexually undesirable, angry political subject) and (postfeminist = sexually desirable, accommodating sexual object) get constructed in ways that orient audience identifications and encourage the acceptance of anti-feminist ideologies.

Another episode that illuminates and partly subverts this binary is pedagogically useful in similar ways. Ally is taken to task by a male judge for her miniskirts, which he deems to be too short (and thus inappropriate and unprofessional). Ally defies his dress code proscriptions and arrives in court the next day wearing an even shorter skirt. When she is subsequently put in jail for contempt of court, her colleagues come to her defense, and Nelle — an attractive and intelligent lawyer whom the other women in the firm either envy or despise — explains Ally's dilemma. In a forceful subversion of either-or, feminist-postfeminist categories, Nelle implores the judge to consider the contradictions facing women in the 1990s: constantly told that their worth hinges on being beautiful and sexually attractive by mass media images, yet considered incompetent and intellectually inferior if they are sexual and attractive. To demonstrate the contradiction and its unfairness, Nelle unravels her tight bun, removes her glasses and takes off her boxy jacket, instantly transforming herself from the serious professional into an icon of female desirability. The incident subverts perceptions of Nelle, and provides a forum for moving beyond preconceived notions of feminist agency and feminine desirability to examine the casting of these subject positions as mutually exclusive. For example, one of our students took from the episode the valorization of her belief that it was "up to men to change their way of looking at women, not up to women to walk around as asexualized beings, covering themselves up."

Pedagogical Strategy Three: Audience Identifications

The final pedagogical strategy we wish to share focuses on the critical analysis of audience identifications. Alexander Doty asserts that "the most slippery and elusive terrain for mass culture continues to be negotiated within audience and reception theory ... it seems an almost impossible task to conduct reception studies that capture the complexity of those moments in which audiences meet mass cultural texts ("There's Something," 71). Our goal is to capture that complexity by exploring with our students why they are drawn to *Ally McBeal,* and to make connections between their pleasures and the contradictions facing women at today's postfeminist juncture. The components of our teaching that address difficult concepts such as the cultural construction of female beauty are most credible when developed by students through experiential means. By drawing out the already existing experiences and competencies of our students and validating the duality of their critical-fan engagement, we have found that critical and feminist frameworks can be made more immediate and more relevant.

One way to encourage students to consider the relationship between the non-conscious mind and the ideologies that circulate through media representations is to have them make connections to personal experiences. However, it should be noted that there are also pitfalls in asking students to find the missing link between personal experience and theoretical ideas. Revealing personal information may be an unbalancing and inappropriate intrusion, especially in large groups. In this sense, *Ally McBeal* can provide a safe venue for exploring personal experiences that resonate with students, without asking that students disclose those experiences to the class. Unstable notions of subjectivity are important in critiques that conceptualize the individual relationally as in other than an oppressive dyad with the media or with patriarchy. It is also important to remember, Susan Bordo suggests, that the celebration of unstable subjectivity and relational power might mean losing sight of the understanding that even constructed entities such as gender, class, and race can be hierarchical. Although our goal may be to have students recognize that what they see as reality is always changing and evolving, we also stress that subjectivity is emergent in time and place. Like discourse, subjectivity is constructed across multiple media and cultural sites.

We believe that it is vital to develop pedagogical strategies that encourage students to question their assumptions about media culture and subjectivity without asking them to dismantle their entire belief systems. While we want students to develop a self-reflexive self-consciousness about their consumption of media representations, we do not make the unreasonable request that they lose themselves in the process. And yet, we are also committed to encouraging students to consider that their cultural identifications and interpretations are not individual or arbitrary, but grounded in history, social experience, and culture. There are connections, we stress, between the postmodern insights of identity and a politically grounded materialist feminism.[8] A focus on language, ideology, and discourse does not have to erase the material conditions of women's lives even as it problematizes constructions of subjectivity. "Sexuality and femininity are great battlegrounds today," Elayne Rapping argues, and political debates which are associated with the social construction of gender include family values, abortion rights, affirmative action, domestic and sexual violence, gay and lesbian rights, welfare legislation, and single motherhood (*Looking Glass World,* 138). Although it can be overwhelming to students to consider that there might be linkages between feminism in the media and feminist issues in politics, an acknowledgment of these connections can be another way to explore social experience without asking students to self-disclose.

Teaching students about audience issues in the concrete rather than the abstract — that is, when the identifications forged by students themselves are under exploration — requires sensitivity and caution. We try to take difficult concepts regarding the social construction of reality and the relationship between ideology, social experience, and power structures and make them accessible, useful, and safe for students by stressing connections between pleasurable student readings and critical interpretive frameworks. Our students were often able to recognize that they identified with *Ally McBeal* precisely because of the contradictions that Ally embodies. Student audience members, of course, bring a range of information and experience to bear on the meanings they construct when viewing a film or watching a television program. The repertoire of interpretive strategies and extratextual knowledges (or cultural competencies) that individuals bring to viewing, Jacqueline Bobo states, "has a major impact on how viewers construct responses" (*Black Women*, 102). A validation of student individuality, creativity, and tenacity in interpreting the meaning of *Ally McBeal* can be addressed alongside critical insight into how the reworking of signifying practices might be linked to the tangible practices of daily life experiences. By this time the students are ready to engage in this discussion — not that their views of feminism have necessarily changed — but because they do have an investment in the representation of women, and of Ally McBeal and what she is said to represent.

Media constructions of racial, class, and sexual differences among women can also be explored within this context. Just as the postfeminist erasure of gender inequalities is symbolized by the firm's unisex bathroom, *Ally McBeal* constructs a multicultural world in which these differences no longer matter. Renee, Ally's best friend, is a successful black professional, as is Ally's love interest, Jesse; Elaine, Ally's working class secretary, socializes easily and regularly with her bosses; and Ling Wu, a Chinese American, dates Ally's boss and was made partner in the firm. The program also flirts with lesbianism in recurring scenes that sexualize female friendships.

Creator, executive producer and writer David E. Kelley said that differences are purposefully ignored on *Ally McBeal*: "In my naive dream, I wish that the world could be like this. Since Ally lives in a fanciful and whimsical world, there is not going to be any racial differences or tensions. All people are one under the sun" (quoted in Braxton, 28). In the classroom, this post-segregationist, post-prejudicial world can be deconstructed to show how inequalities are masked by *Ally McBeal's* assimilationist ideology. Although Kelley argues that "race not being an issue makes it an issue," this nonissue approach means that there is no presentation or discussion of race, or, for that matter, of class or sexual discrimination on the program. These erasures can be examined through the ideological pressures rooted in advertising and television's historical avoidance of topics that disturb or alienate white, middle class, heterosexual consumers. Furthermore, the construction of an already achieved multiculturalism co-exists with stereotypes that can be analyzed to probe the subtle reinforcement of a contemporary white, middle class, heterosexual norm. Renee, for instance, exhibits the "primitive" sexuality often ascribed to black women by the media; the one working class character, Elaine, is loud and tacky; and Ling is cast as the archetypal Asian dragon lady (complete with dragon-like sounds), a sexual manipulator who is highly assertive, but unlikeable, part of the team yet clearly an "other." Despite *Ally McBeal's* playful engagement with lesbianism, there are no "out" characters.

Examining these constructions of "other" women can help students begin to understand that *Ally McBeal*'s easy celebration of visibility and assimilation diffuses the representational history of groups previously invisible in or pathologized by the media. Likewise, it can help students begin to unpack their deep investments in the ideologies of individualism and equality. Having been introduced to the notion that gender is constructed in complicated and multifarious ways, they can begin to see that race, class, sexuality, and multiculturalism are also socially formed. While our goal is to explore the ways in which identities and beliefs emerge in relation to media, we also stress the importance of negotiated and oppositional readings grounded in social experience. Just as feminist cultural scholars have looked at how racial, class and sexual differences can lead to differing interpretations and audience identifications, we need to recognize that our students are also diverse, and that they can and do make different sense of *Ally McBeal*. We ask students to move beyond what Fiske calls "the easy pleasure of the recognition of the familiar and its adequacy" (12) to recognize in *Ally McBeal* a Rorschach test of their own race, class, and sexual identifications.

Black women often strongly identify with Renee's affluence and professional success in ways that reflect their historical exclusion from the American Dream. Such responses can highlight the process of audience identification and provoke rewarding dialogue about the politics of inclusion and exclusion. Asian women often see in Ling a subversion of traditional gender roles and a pleasurable rebuke of the stereotypically passive, nurturing, accommodating Asian woman. Their response can be discussed as an example of the ways in which underrepresented audiences negotiate the terrain of media imagines, accepting empowering aspects of stereotypical images while rejecting others. Black male students in our classes have read Ally's interracial love relationship through a history of lynching as the punishment for looking at white women, complicating feminist theories of sexual objectification and the male gaze. Students have also brought class issues to the forefront in their readings, providing an opportunity to discuss the material and educational advantages enjoyed by the people on *Ally McBeal*, as well as the ways in which class resentments can be articulated to the symbol of the career woman. By emphasizing negotiated readings, we can include the full range of our students in a critical analysis, while also demonstrating in concrete ways how social experience informs our engagement with media texts.

Scenes showing the easy coupling of Ally and Renee — lounging around the house, talking about sex, cuddling in bed, and gazing at one another in the bathroom mirror — can also be explored to discuss oppositional and against-the-grain readings of their friendship. Although invariably some will argue that we are reading too much into it, most students can understand why and how the codes of female friendship might be read as lesbian relationships. We also draw from readings and videos tracing the history of gay and lesbian portrayals and audience responses to provide students with a broader context for understanding that same-sex friendship can be seen through the lens of a history of representational inequality. Because pleasure, Fiske argues, "results from a particular relationship between meanings and power" (19), we emphasize not only the pleasure in constructing against-the-grain readings, but also the interplay among popular culture, social experience, and social institutions.

Having been introduced to ideological incongruencies in television programming, students are also prepared to examine ideological discontinuities between female characters on *Ally McBeal* who might pretend to be lesbians and the social experience of gays and lesbians who historically have pretended to be heterosexuals. Such culturally loaded issues can be discussed in terms of ideological pressures, negotiated readings, and cultural competencies rooted in social difference. For instance, an overt lesbian reading can be examined within the context of a scene where Ally reaches orgasmic pleasure while showing her female colleague how to appreciate a cup of espresso, or one where she kisses a woman to scare away an unwanted male suitor. We want students to be comfortable with the notion of an oppositional reading which is facilitated by the program's playfulness with lesbianism and sexual fluidity; however, we also want students to understand that oppositional readings are not the same as representational equality. In other words, it does still matter that there are no lesbian or gay characters on the program. Understanding difference, Angela McRobbie argues, is not just a celebration of difference, but also "a rigorous thinking through of what 'living with difference' might entail" (*Postmodernism* 63).

Conclusion

We believe that teaching about the contradictions of visual cultural can often become itself a site for the struggle over feminism waged in theoretical, political, experiential, and symbolic contexts. The television character Ally McBeal presented a useful cultural phenomena for critical educators interested in teaching students who are both wary of feminism and deeply immersed in and engaged with visual culture. Instead of dismissing Ally McBeal as anti-feminist or oversimplifying her media classification as post-feminist, we hoped that students might use their identifications with Ally McBeal, and their awareness of the contradictions she represents, to imagine themselves as feminists in new and significant ways. Social selves, McRobbie reminds us, are "fragile, fragmented identities formed in discourse and history and open to change, transformation and realignment" (*Postmodernism*, 192). Of course, the popularity of a program like *Ally McBeal* cannot be fully explained by a focus on gender, but must also be considered in terms of the politics of sexuality, class, race, and professionalism. *Ally McBeal* is ideologically liminal; the character's appeal among female students, in particular, is rooted in her ability to hook up with a range of cultural coordinates and ideologies. The issues raised by the *Ally McBeal* phenomenon reverberate through and cut across popularized and academic understandings of feminism, including student perceptions. We have appropriated these contradictions and ambiguities to forge connections between feminist theories and social experience in the classroom. By fully engaging with those media representations students find most pleasurable and compelling, we can move beyond an abstract understanding of media criticism to the terrain on which those representations are lived and felt. In doing so, we ask students to situate themselves, in Stuart Hall's words, in "an identity that knows where it comes from, where home is, but also lives in the symbolic" ("Ethnicity," 20).

Notes

1. The bibliography on critical pedagogy is extensive; see Paolo Friere, *Pedagogy of the Oppressed* (New York: Continuum, 1989); Henry Giroux and Peter McLaren, eds. *Between Borders: Pedagogy and the Politics of Cultural Studies* (New York: Routledge, 1994).

2. For useful overviews see: Gail Dines and Jean Humez, eds. *Gender, Race and Class in Media* (Thousand Oaks, CA: Sage, 1995); Suzanna Danuta Walters, *Material Girls: Making Sense of Feminist Cultural Theory* (Berkeley: University of California Press, 1995).

3. For comprehensive discussions see: Cathy Schwichtenberg, "Feminist Cultural Studies," *Critical Studies in Mass Communication* 6:2 (1989), 202–208; and Elizabeth Long, "Feminism and Cultural Studies," *Critical Studies in Mass Communication* 6:1 (1989), 427–35.

4. For more detailed analyses see: Susan Faludi, *Backlash: The Undeclared War Against American Women* (New York: Crown, 1991); and Susan Douglas, *Where the Girls Are: Growing up Female with the Mass Media* (New York: Times Books, 1995).

5. There are a number of noteworthy perspectives on this binarism; see Angela McRobbie, *Postmodernism and Popular Culture* (London: Routledge, 1994); Leslie Roman, Linda K. Christian-Smith, and Elizabeth Ellsworth, eds. *Becoming Feminine: The Politics of Popular Culture* (London: The Falmer Press, 1988); and Tricia Rose, *Black Noise: Rap Music and Black Culture in Contemporary America* (Middletown: Wesleyan University Press, 1994).

6. For an excellent commentary see Douglas.

7. For a more detailed analysis see McRobbie, *Postmodernism*.

8. These connections are well explicated in Rosemary Hennessey, *Materialist Feminism and the Politics of Discourse* (New York: Routledge, 1993).

Bibliography

Bellafante, Gina. "Feminism: It's All About Me!" *Time* 29 June, 1998: 54–62.

Berger, John. *Ways of Seeing*. New York: Penguin, 1977.

Bergstrom, Janet, and Mary Ann Doane. "The Female Spectator: Contexts and Direction." *Camera Obscura* 20–21 (1989): 5–27.

Bobo, Jacqueline. "'The Color Purple': Black Women as Cultural Readers." *Female Spectators: Looking at Film and Television.* Edited by Deidre Pribram. London: Verso, 1988. 90–109.

_____. *Black Women As Cultural Readers.* New York: Columbia University Press, 1995.

Bordo, Susan. "'Material Girl': The Effacements of Postmodern Culture." *The Madonna Connection: Representational Politics, Subcultural Identities and Cultural Theory.* Edited by Cathy Schwichtenberg. Boulder, CO: Westview Press, 1993.

Braxton, Greg. "In Ally's Romance, Race a Nonissue." *The Daily Hampshire Gazette,* Feb. 15, 1999: 28.

Dines, Gail, and Jean Humez, eds. *Gender, Race and Class in Media.* Thousand Oaks, CA: Sage, 1995.

Doty, Alexander. *Making Things Perfectly Queer: Interpreting Mass Culture.* Minneapolis: University of Minnesota Press, 1993.

Douglas, Susan. *Where the Girls Are: Growing Up Female with the Mass Media.* New York: New York Times Books, 1995.

Ellsworth, Elizabeth. "Illicit Pleasures: Feminist Spectators and Personal Best." *Wide Angle* 8.2 (1986): 45–56. Report in *Issues in Feminist Film Criticism.* Edited by Patricia Erens. Bloomington: Indiana University Press, 1990. 183–196.

_____. "Why Doesn't This Feel Empowering?" in Carmen Luke and Jennifer Gore, eds. *Feminisms and Critical Pedagogy.* New York: Routledge, 1989. 90–119.

Faludi, Susan. *Backlash: The Undeclared War Against American Women.* New York: Crown, 1991.

Fiske, John. *Television Culture.* London: Metheun, 1987.

Friere, Paolo. *Pedagogy of the Oppressed.* New York: Continuum, 1989.

Hall, Stuart. "Signification, Representation, Ideology: Althusser and the Post-Structuralist Debates." *Critical Studies in Mass Communication* 2 (1985): 91–114.

_____. "Culture, the Media, and the 'Ideological Effect.'" *Mass Communication and Society.* Edited by Jim Curran, et al. London: Methuen, 1977. 315–348.

_____. "Ethnicity: Identity and Difference." *Radical America* 23.4 (1991): 9–20.

Hennessy, Rosemary. *Materialist Feminism and the Politics of Discourse.* New York: Routledge, 1993.

Jhally, Sut. *Dreamworlds II: Sex/Power/Desire in Music Video.* Videocassette. Media Education Foundation, 1997.

Kilbourne, Jean. *Slim Hopes.* Videocassette. Media Education Foundation, 1995.

Kuczynski, Alex "Calista Comes Clean." *Harper's Bazaar* Sept. 1998: 502+.

Lewis, Justin. *The Ideological Octopus: An Exploration of Television and Its Audience.* New York: Routledge, 1991.

Long, Elizabeth. "Feminism and Cultural Studies." *Critical Studies in Mass Communication* 6.1 (1989): 427–35.

McRobbie, Angela. *Postmodernism and Popular Culture.* London: Routledge, 1994.

Malanowski, Jamie. "Calista Flockhart." *Entertainment Weekly,* Dec. 25, 1999: 30–31.

Mulvey, Laura. "Visual Pleasure and the Narrative Cinema." *Screen* 16.3 (1975): 6–18.

Radway, Janice. "Identifying Ideological Seams: Mass Culture, Analytical Method, and Political Practice." *Communication* 9 (1986): 93–123.

Rapping, Elayne. *The Looking Glass World of Nonfiction TV.* Boston: South End Press, 1987.

Roman, Leslie, Linda K. Christian-Smith, and Elizabeth Ellsworth, eds. *Becoming Feminine: The Politics of Popular Culture.* London: The Falmer Press, 1988.

Rose, Tricia. *Black Noise: Rap Music and Black Culture in Contemporary America.* Middletown: Wesleyan University Press, 1994.

Schwichtenberg, Cathy. "Feminist Cultural Studies." *Critical Studies in Mass Communication* 6.2 (1989): 202–208.

_____, ed. *The Madonna Connection: Representational Politics, Subcultural Identities and Cultural Theory.* Boulder, CO: Westview Press, 1993.

Walters, Suzanna Danuta. *Material Girls: Making Sense of Feminist Cultural Theory.* Berkeley: University Of California Press, 1995.

Warner, Arina. *Six Myths of Our Time.* New York: Vintage Books, 1994.

Williams, Raymond. *Marxism and Literature.* Oxford: Oxford University Press, 1977.

Williamson, Judith. "How Does Girl Number Twenty Understand Ideology?" *Exposure* 28.1/2 (1991): 51–56.

Wiseman, C. V., et al. "Cultural Expectations of Thinness in Women: An Update." *International Journal of Eating Disorders* 11 (1992): 85–89.

7

In Ms. McBeal's Defense: Assessing *Ally McBeal* as a Feminist Text

Amanda D. Lotz

At the time of its 1997 debut *Ally McBeal* inspired uncommon popular and academic debate. Few other shows at the time came close to equaling the column space devoted to Ms. McBeal and her colleagues, and the lack of unanimity of critical opinion made it a particularly compelling phenomenon. *Ally McBeal* served as a catalyst for discussions of feminism and femininity in addition to the more conventional reviews commonly written by television critics. The character of Ally, embodied in the gamine frame of actress Calista Flockhart, debuted to a society unprepared for the divergence she provided from the female characters who preceded her. The disjuncture of her character relative to those in series who most recently had been hailed as feminist, such as *Murphy Brown, Roseanne,* and *Designing Women,* led to speculation and pontification over what McBeal's presence and popularity indicated about women's gains and feminism's status.

Debut reviews of *Ally McBeal* were generally laudatory and emphasized the series' play with fantasy through digital graphic insertions, although critics were notably ambivalent about the title character. James Collins summed up many critics' uncertainty by acknowledging that their concern resulted from her predicaments seeming false because she had not yet earned the audience's sympathy (Collins, 117). Six months into the first season, reviews shifted to address the emerging debate in opinions about the series, a split that seemed a function of naysayers who sought a continuation of the role model trajectory of working women characters and proponents who either identified with the characters or were entranced by the series' whimsy.[1]

It is impossible to know whether viewers would have recognized *Ally*

McBeal's contribution to contemporary deliberations about dominant social scripts related to gender norms if the press had not explicitly identified her as the "new face of feminism." Television critics writing in newspapers and magazines acknowledged Ally as the latest in a series of remarkable female characters such as Ann Marie of *That Girl*, Mary Richards of *The Mary Tyler Moore Show*, and Murphy Brown (Chambers, "*Ally McBeal*;" Stark; Grossberger; Jefferson; Dowd). Despite the series' drama-comedy blend and ensemble emphasis, critics connected Ally to the trajectory of "new woman" stories that had built narratives around single working women in situation comedies. Curiously, only one mentioned the series and character that offered the greatest similarity, the title character of *The Days and Nights of Molly Dodd* (NBC, 1987–1988; Lifetime, 1989–1991) (Svetkey, 22). Molly Dodd's likeness was so distinct that popular criticism of Ally McBeal virtually repeated what had been written about Dodd ten years earlier (see Wilson, 110–114).

The mainstream press framed the popular discussion about the show and determined the primary analytical lens for considering the series in its initial reviews. The question of feminism in relation to *Ally McBeal* would arguably become over-determined during the summer between its first and second seasons when a poorly researched and arbitrarily informed article on the state of contemporary feminism by Gina Bellafante appeared in *Time* and used Ally's head as the current embodiment of feminism (a legacy that also included Susan B. Anthony, Betty Friedan, and Gloria Steinem) (Bellafante, 54–60). From that point on, the character, the series, and even Flockhart became central to questions about the emergence of a new generation of women and the status of feminism in U.S. society. In many accounts, invoking *Ally McBeal* became a shorthand for the coterminous rise of female-centered although ambiguously feminist content emerging in various media, including the novel *Bridget Jones's Diary*, music acts ranging from the Lilith Fair tour to the Spice Girls, as well as television series *Sex and the City* and *Buffy the Vampire Slayer* (Parker, Williamson, Stack).

The arbitrary and undefined use of prefixes before the term feminist in reviews and commentary exacerbated uncertainty about *Ally McBeal*'s relationship to feminism.

> I'm not ready for the post-post-post feminist [Katz, 36].
>
> Ally McBeal has become an icon of New Feminism [Scruggs, 1B].
>
> Ally is the quintessential postfeminist. She has all the professional advantages Mary [Richards, of *The Mary Tyler Moore Show*] never had, but unlike her more traditionally feminist sitcom sister, she doesn't want to make it on her own [Chambers, "How," 58].

[Ally McBeal is] a poster girl for postmodern feminism [Schneider, 92].

A groundbreaking postfeminist television anthem for the New Woman of the '90s. [Svetkey, 22].

Ally is a heady, seductive brew of feminist and anti-feminist ideals [Heywood, B9].

[Ally McBeal is] savvy yet vulnerable, fallible yet likable, feminist yet not.... These feminine virtues are accompanied by feminine weaknesses—by the painstaking vulnerability that has become the trademark of television's postfeminists [Shalit, 30].

Alternately, commentators discussed the cultural impact or significance of the show in terms of these variously labeled feminisms.

The most remarkable postfeminist trend is not about women. It's about men. The idea that women should mimic men is now dead. Now men mimic women [Dowd, C5].

Ally has struck a nerve with twentysomething women who feel both excited and confused by the choices bestowed upon them by the feminist movement [Chambers, 58].

The show is important not so much for what its lead character says or does, but for what the program itself attempts and symbolizes. This is a drama about a woman, and such excursions have been surprisingly rare in the history of prime-time television [Stark, 13].

The use of jargon rather than clearly defined articulations of feminism by these articles also obscured the adjustments in social attitudes toward the term "feminist" and what have traditionally been considered feminist ideals.

One of the greatest challenges facing feminism is the frequent misrepresentation of its goals and foundations by mainstream media outlets that provide the forum through which most people encounter descriptions of or commentary about feminism. Articles such as Bellafante's become authoritative to the general populace, despite the fact that few if any feminists would agree that feminism is any of the things Bellafante proposes (see NOW). Judy Mann notes of the *Time* article, "A hefty fifty percent of those from the ages eighteen to thirty-four told the pollsters in the *Time*/CNN survey that they share 'feminist' values, by which they generally mean they want a world in which they can choose to be anything—the President or a mother, or both" (E03). Yet these same respondents do not consider themselves feminists. This inconsistency makes clear that the ideals of feminism are alive and thriving, but that considerable uncertainty surrounds the label, even as just plain "feminism."

The frequent use of the term feminism with various prefixes may have left readers confused about the precise argument commentators were making, but certainly buoyed viewers' recognition that the series was dealing with gender issues in a significant way. *Ally McBeal* conformed to the various "new woman" codes that had become dominant in representing women since *The Mary Tyler Moore Show*. Its female characters are uniformly single, possess upwardly mobile, highly professionalized careers, and live without connection to family in a major city.[2] Perhaps it was this adherence to the "new woman" symbolic code that prevented many from recognizing the series' departure. Ally and her female colleagues inaugurate characters that might be named "new, new women" as a result of their divergence from the contexts that defined their predecessors.

In this article I address the finite text of five full seasons of *Ally McBeal* and the contribution the series made to the circulation of feminist discourses and ideas. Ultimately, I argue that the series did offer significant feminist innovation and may be the prototypic example of a postfeminist series— at least as in evidence by 2005. I do not use postfeminist as synonymous with anti-feminist or after feminism, although these uses are suggested by some journalistic and academic criticism of the series (Kim; Vavrus; Shalit). Rather, I find postfeminist the best descriptor of this series because of the theoretical innovation postfeminism provides and because it draws attention to the contextual breaks that series such as *Ally McBeal* typify.

Despite the copious attention to the series and its feminist or anti-feminist attributes, many assessments neglected the series' significance by failing to consider a triumvirate of contextual variances that made *Ally McBeal* fundamentally unlike the predecessors with which critics commonly compared it. Reviews of the series indicate that many believed *Ally McBeal* signified changes in social formations and gender norms, although assessments rarely attended to the complexity with which the series was enmeshed with other socio-historical changes. The series introduced a considerable break from previous female-centered series as a result of its late 1990s historical context, its characters' post–Baby Boom, post-second-wave generational context, and its representational context as one of many coterminous female-centered dramas on U.S. television. Even though many critics immediately connected Ally and her colleagues with a legacy of other female characters, few acknowledged the fundamental difference in the context of this series and many others emerging in subsequent seasons. Additionally, many reviews considered only the series' first few seasons, which provides a significant limitation because of the radical variation of the show from season to season during its five-year run.

The divergence of the series' historical, generational, and representational contexts necessitates a different critical and analytical frame for evaluating the series relative to those of previous eras. In some ways the features interrelate in a manner making them seem indistinct, yet three discrete phenomena exist. First, the socio-cultural context of life in America in the late 1990s provided clear differentiation from the early 1970s in which audiences greeted previous "new woman" series such as *The Mary Tyler Moore Show* and even the late 1980s and early 1990s of series such as *Murphy Brown*. The Mary Tyler Moore Show could not have explored sexual harassment law in the same manner available to *Ally McBeal* (particularly because it had not yet been named), and the significance of a single woman with a career varies vastly because of changes in cultural norms. Some of the concerns critics had of the series resulted from their expectation that a feminist character of the 1990s would embody the same form as a feminist character of the 1970s, but that this historical difference would require the 1990s character to be a hyper-embodiment of the 1970s character. Mary Richards personified 1970s feminism and Murphy Brown then earned her feminist distinction by enhancing Mary's professionalism. By this logic, a 1990s feminist character would then need to embody professionalism even more than Murphy, and clearly, this was not the case with Ally. This expectation is an outcome of logic rooted in the role model framework that was common in media criticism during second-wave feminism and provided valuable tools in that context. If career women were "feminist" representations in the 1970s, then the default critical mode suggested that the more career-oriented the character, the more feminist she is. But the cultural meaning of a woman with a career varies significantly in 2000 from its meaning in the early 1970s.

The variation in generational context is likely even more significant to delimiting the range of stories available to *Ally McBeal*. All of the female television characters that drew feminist accolades as new women prior to *Ally McBeal*'s arrival belonged to the Baby Boom generation and were consequently in their teens and twenties during the era in which second-wave feminism advocated social change.[3] Baby Boom characters would have grown up experiencing sexism that seems unimaginable now and fought to gain access to the male-dominated professional workforce. The characters of *Ally McBeal* and other contemporary series such as *Sex and the City* belong to another generation, whose identity (both fictional and in reality) is very much defined by experiencing the gains of second-wave activists' efforts. Sexism certainly has not been eradicated for these women, but the emphasis second-wave activists placed on opening the public sphere to women meant that access to education and professional careers were far less contested.

The narrative of *Ally McBeal* consequently exists in a cultural milieu modified from that of its second-wave precursors, and its characters possess a worldview variant from those who preceded them. Cultural events and experiences bind writers to contexts that become inscribed in the series' stories. Ally's generation was raised with both Disney fairy tales and second-wave feminism without much mainstream attention to their incompatibility. The varied generational context of the characters in *Ally McBeal* does not explain away the flightiness and apolitical tendencies many feminist critics have emphasized, but it is an important feature in understanding the series and likely why it captivated such sizable audiences of Ally's generational cohort.

Finally, the representational context in which *Ally McBeal* circulates, particularly by its third season, requires an analytical frame unlike those used previously. The late 1990s and early years of the twenty-first century provided an unprecedented proliferation of female characters in central dramatic roles. Where one or two series became feminist touchstones in previous eras (and they were most often situation comedies), *Ally McBeal* shared television schedules with more than twenty dramatic series featuring a central female protagonist. Before this era, a paucity of fully developed female characters bore the burden of representing all working women and circulated in a socio-historical context more hostile to women choosing professional careers. In an environment in which a comparatively vast plurality of single, professional female characters exists, each one need not appear as a role model for all women, nor must she conform to the limited possibilities afforded previous characters.

These contextual features become critical to developing a sophisticated analysis of the series and its contribution to gender scripts and feminist discourses. Indeed, a very different understanding of the show can be advanced if its context is not considered. Many acknowledged that the series included a spark of something truly significant, but the conventional frame of analysis failed those who sought to identify the variation the series provided.

Explaining Postfeminism

It is impossible to know what journalists such as Katz, Chambers, Schneider, and Shalit meant in referencing *Ally McBeal* as a post-post-post feminist, postfeminist, or postmodern feminist show. Articles such as these never explain their terms or their prefixes, and explanation is vital because feminist media scholars have used postfeminist to describe contradictory ideological positions (See Lotz, "Postfeminist," 111–115). Most academic scholarship prior to the mid–1990s (and by contextual clues, likely the journalists quoted here) used postfeminist as equivalent to anti-feminist, or as a descriptor indicating an era when feminism is no longer needed: a literal after feminism (Faludi; Press; Dow; Modleski; Kim; Vavrus). In national contexts outside of the U.S., some feminist scholars have used postfeminism to demarcate expansion and adjustments in theory since the height of the second wave. This use is as "feminist" and equally as activist as previous versions of feminism, but takes into account postmodern and post-structuralist deconstruction of women as a singular category in an attempt to address the varied relations to power women experience based on other aspects of their subjectivity. This theorization of postfeminism also incorporates activist structures characteristic of new social movements (see Lotz, "Communicating"; Brooks; McRobbie; Gamble; Moseley and Read; Arthurs).

Elsewhere, I extrapolated from postfeminist theory to delimit four attributes of postfeminist media content, including narratives that explore the diverse relations to power women inhabit, depictions of varied feminist solutions and loose organizations of activism, texts that deconstruct binary categories of gender and sexuality, and the depiction of situations illustrating the contemporary struggles faced by women and feminists (Lotz, "Postfeminist," 116–117). Postfeminist theory remains in the process of development, so that these may not be the only attributes to characterize postfeminist media forms. This understanding of postfeminism relies on a more sophisticated theoretical framework than its anti-feminist denotation and is useful for explaining a period of ideological transformation. Such a perspective also aids in demarcating the contextual breaks that distinguish a show such as *Ally McBeal* from many of its predecessors.

The attributes of postfeminist media forms listed above are best explained through example, requiring a closer look at the text of *Ally McBeal*. The series exhibits characteristics of postfeminism in various ways: through its ensemble of female characters with diverse perspectives, by exploring contemporary legal issues affecting women — such as sexual harassment — as complex sites for the expression of cultural expectations of gender roles and power, by raising the possibility of non-binary understandings of categories such as gender and sexuality, and by depicting a postfeminist perspective on the contemporary dilemmas women experience. *Ally McBeal*'s success in drawing the desired audience and its instigation of cultural discussion about its representations of characters and issues further illustrate the importance of critically assessing the series in relation to postfeminist ideas. I am not arguing that the series stands as some ideal embodiment of feminism or postfeminism that indicates women's gains or an equitable society. *Ally McBeal* is a complex and contradictory text of great richness and depth. Limitations and moments of conservative ideology most certainly exist in *Ally McBeal*, but a text without such features is unnecessary nor even ideal.

Ally McBeal *as a Postfeminist Text*

In May of 2002 David E. Kelley completed Ally's journey, making it possible to review a finite story and consider the series in a comprehensive manner. A complete narrative enables analysis that can assess the validity of various arguments about the character and the series as indicative of a feminist evolution or a retrograde containment of second-wave activism. Perhaps early critics were too quick in their evaluation or maybe Kelley preordained the series' conclusion by the end of the first season. Many critics sought for Kelley to offer more evidence of a feminist evolution in seasons two and three, rather than Ally's downward spiral of near hysteria. But critics must not forget the delayed gratification necessary in serialized television; audiences likely would have bored quickly had Ally earlier exhibited the certainty she found in the series' last season.

Even with the closure a series finale provides, *Ally McBeal* remains a complicated text to consider. The tone and constant variation of the series account for much of the extreme disparity in evaluations. *Ally McBeal* may have had the unusual attribute of being fairly single-authored — with creator and executive producer Kelley writing most episodes — but the uncertain tone Kelley gave the series undermined the uniformity such authorship might suggest. Narratives often slipped unpredictably from realistic melodrama to comedy and fantasy sequences, which made varied interpretations freely possible — including the possibility that the dramatic and comedic depictions of characters were parodic and critical of the very concepts they explored. Although television theorists generally acknowledge the polysemic possibilities of television texts, *Ally McBeal* took this potential further and seemed to *encourage* multiple readings. The nagging uncertainty of whether various characters and situations were being posed as parody or with literal seriousness did the most to advance this ambiguous tone and inspire bipolar critical reactions.

The lack of a dependable central character through which the audience could gauge the series' message and ideology exacerbated uncertainty. Martha Nochimson argues, "Structurally, each *Ally* episode began as if it were going to be a conventionally plot-driven show, only to be derailed when the humor on the show, with its intensity of radical and abrupt slippages, refused to resolve conflict to the expected single perspective point of view ... words and situations turned representation wrong side out and back again so that it was impossible to attain any kind of seamless view" (27). Despite affording McBeal title character status, the narrative positioned John Cage as the moral center of the story for the first four seasons, but the character's eccentricities and oddities served to discredit him as well. In the final season, Kelley reintroduced McBeal with a certain maturity that she had previously lacked; although she had always been, as Cage remarked in the finale, "the soul of this place" (5–22, "Bygones").[4]

In addition to the complex tone of the series, the season-to-season variation makes it difficult to speak of *Ally McBeal* in generalities. Substantial cast changes altered the dynamics of this character-driven series and even episodic organization varied in each of the five seasons. Season one featured episodes organized with two primary plots (one court case, one personal dilemma) and characters Ally, Billy, Georgia, Elaine, Renee, Richard, Whipper and John. Nelle and Ling were added in the second season, while Whipper became a secondary character. The dual plot structure continued initially, but courtroom stories began to dwindle as the romance between Ally and Billy rekindled. The series changed considerably in season four as a result of the departure of Billy, Georgia, Whipper, and Renee, and new romances between Ally and Larry Paul, John and Melanie West, and the triangle of attraction among Richard, Ling, and Jackson Duper became central serial narratives. In its final season the series returned to a more balanced court-personal split, however, the constantly changing cast made the season highly variable. The point of this summary is to acknowledge from the outset the impossibility of clearly demarcating a singular entity of what the series *Ally McBeal* ever was.

Negotiation of Different Perspectives Among a Female Ensemble

Ally McBeal features an uncommon majority of women, with as many as six regular and one recurring female characters who exhibit varied and divergent identities. The prevalence of female characters and narrative focus on them creates an atmosphere ripe for the exploration of the diverse perspectives among women. Notably, despite the range of ethnic subjectivities evident at a visual level, the series does not differentiate among its female characters by socio-economic status, ethnicity, or sexuality, but through variant opinions and political outlooks.

In addition to its sizable female cast, the series' frequent use of topic material emphasizing gender issues makes it a nearly exemplary series for examining heterogeneous constructs of women and their concerns. Almost without exception, the firm accepts cases affecting women or cases specifically salient to the private sphere: a space often occupied by women. These stories deal with prostitution, sex-based discrimination, sexual harassment, and questions of family or relationships, which led Brenda Cooper to argue that the series consequently "privileges women and their ways of experiencing a patriarchal world, thus creating a feminine spectatorship for viewers" (420). The legal storyline in each episode allows the series to match the examination of an issue inflected by gender politics with character-driven personal plots, which further makes the episodic text a combination of strategies and genres. Issue-oriented legal plots are significant because of how they twist and recast common feminist issues. Through the development of often-exaggerated circumstances, the series reveals women to be positioned discrepantly in relation to power and laws, despite legal presumptions that define women uniformly.

When an episode places these female characters in the context of an event or issue, they react distinctively, which illustrates the diverse perspectives among them. The range of viewpoints on issues or events provided by the female ensemble is just one way that *Ally McBeal* explores differences among women and thus produces an implicit postfeminist discourse. An example of disparate female and feminist perspectives in the negotiation of personal issues appeared in an early episode following the arrest of partner John Cage for soliciting a prostitute (1–02, "Compromising Positions"). This episode presents the characters debating the ethics of dating behavior and whether it is more honest for John to solicit a prostitute than to buy a woman a few drinks to convince her to come home with him if all he seeks is a sexual partner. John tries to present his action as less exploitative and consequently female-friendly if not feminist. Ally, however, views the gender power dynamics differently and reprimands him. John's reasoning clearly dismays Georgia, but does not move her to action, and Elaine and many of the other female support staff indicate approval. The series revisits this issue and offers yet another lens through which the audience can consider the power dynamics and implications of prostitution in the third season when Nelle, who is dating John, learns of the past arrest (3–09, "Out in the Cold"). Nelle offers a feminist examination of the issue and tries to rectify her personal politics in favor of legalizing prostitution with the feelings of disappointment she experiences when learning of John's past. The episodes provide competing views on prostitution, each presenting itself as endeavoring to be feminist, yet the series never gives sex workers a voice. The complex construction of prostitution reflects the divergent feminist positions for and against its legalization, a plurality indicative of the diversity of feminist perspectives.

Ally McBeal depicts female characters responding in diverse and discrepant ways to both legal and personal dilemmas. By featuring so many women in primary roles, the series can regularly depict women as a group composed of varied outlooks in a manner unavailable in series with just one or two female characters whose primary narrative function is as contrast to the perspective of male characters. The varied perspectives the female characters exhibit and their participation in issue debate represent women as complexly configured, which is characteristic of postfeminist approaches. The series foregrounds the diversity and complexity among women rather than portraying the women as similar in belief, yet in contradiction to their male co-workers. Importantly, despite their contradictory outlooks, deep bonds underlie the relationships among the women. Nochimson argues that, "Looking at Ally as a role model was inappropriate in a show in which the feminism was located not in Ally, but between characters, in new relational paradigms" (29). Some critical debate exists on this point as others have made much of "cat fight" scenes in which the women squabble with digital graphics of feline heads superimposed on their bodies (Vavrus, 420; Shugart, Waggoner, and O'Brien Hallstein, 205). Such scenes require close and contextualized analyses. Kelley has a history of explicitly responding to critics in his series' texts, and the "cat fight" scenes also might be seen as a reflexive awareness of the criticism of women's depictions in a parodic way, rather than the literal interpretation others have taken.[5]

A more persuasive criticism of the limitation of the series in this area can be made of the series' inattention to how ethnicity, class, and sexual identity contribute to the characters' varying subjectivities. Although the series was cast with atypical inclusion of African Americans and even an Asian American actor, Kelley intentionally chose a "colorblind" approach that never commented on the experiences of racism the characters would likely encounter, particularly when Ally dated a black man in much of the second season (Braxton, F1). The series' discussion of gay rights and inclusion of gay characters was also limited. The show represented lesbians and gay men in occasional episodes, but offered an ambiguous ideological position. An exceptionally stereotypical lesbian character, Margaret Camero, appears in two different episodes, first as an opponent's witness and later in search of representation (2–19, "Let's Dance;" 2–23, "I Know Him by Heart"). Camero's portrayal might be best understood as parodic, with the text criticizing stereotypes of lesbians, particularly as articulated in text by homophobe Richard. Admittedly, the depiction easily can be interpreted without recognizing the parody, in which case, the text reinforces some lesbian stereotypes. Ideally, a postfeminist text would engage critique of identity difference more fully (perhaps this was most evident in the Lifetime series *Any Day Now*, 1998–2002), but *Ally McBeal* does move toward a postfeminist standard through its multivocality.[6]

Critiquing Legal Solutions and Liberal Feminist Answers

Ally McBeal exhibits the second attribute of postfeminist discourse, depicting varied feminist solutions and loose organizations of activism, through its interrogation of gender issues in a way that illustrates the inadequacy of legal standards that uniformly apply laws to all women when their relation to power varies greatly. The series' critique of legal solutions that are the outcome of second-wave liberal feminist perspectives also evinces the second postfeminist attribute. The courtroom forum creates an environment for political discussion that might otherwise appear out of context in a fictional television series and provides the characters with a space for speeches about contemporary issues. Kelley consistently focuses on gender-inflected topics in the *Ally McBeal* courtroom, unlike other series— even his own — that interrogate a broader range of politics. The legal situations in *Ally McBeal* offer characteristics of postfeminism through their challenging of traditional liberal feminist positions and solutions to inequality, examination of the legal effects of sexual harassment laws, and illustration of discrepancies among women despite uniform legal definitions of women.

Cases related to sexual harassment provide numerous examples of the series' engagement with and negotiation of feminist politics. In most all cases, the firm wins either the case or its attempt not to have a case dismissed and is on the side that arguably possesses the most feminist credibility (although some situations appear deliberately convoluted and complex). The series' pilot begins with Ally as a victim of unwanted groping by a fellow attorney, which leads her to join Cage, Fish & Associates (1–01, "Pilot"). In another episode, the secretarial staff files a sexual harassment suit against the firm because male ogling of a female mail clerk creates a sexually charged workplace (1–08, "Drawing the Lines"). Although the staff organizes and plans a walkout, the collective action is undercut when the narrative reveals the suit is an attempt by Elaine to get the lawyers' attention because she feels excluded from their social relationships. Another case involves a woman suing her employer, whom she has never met, for harassment. She argues that not sleeping with him prevented her promotion, despite the fact this employer never made such a requirement evident (1–18, "The Playing Field").

Throughout the series, the legal cases became increasingly outrageous, as when Ling attempts to sue a Howard Stern-esque "shock jock" because of the environment created in her workplace by the broadcast of his show (2–02, "They Eat Horses, Don't They"). She also tries to sue an employee for harassment because she believes he had sexual thoughts about her, a case she loses (2–06, "You Never Can Tell"). The program also examines the merits of corporate attempts to avoid harassment claims, as the firm represents a couple fired for violating their company's "date and tell" office policy by not disclosing their relationship (2–14, "Pyramids on the Nile"). In the final harassment case of season two, the firm represents an employer sued by a female worker who claims the employer's "Beach Day" policy of allowing workers to wear bathing suits to work is a form of sexual harassment (2–20, "Only the Lonely").

The law governing sexual harassment continued to be tested in season three, first with a case in which the firm represents a woman and her employer who are sued by other female employees because the defendant contributes to the creation of a sexually charged environment by wearing suggestive clothing and flirting with male co-workers (3–02, "Buried Pleasures"). The firm next represents a magazine editor who sues her employees for sexual harassment after they circulate pamphlets calling her "the nymph" and organize a "blue flu" that results in late publication of the magazine and her consequent firing (3–06, "Changes"). In a rare situation, the firm does not win its case.

In season four the series continued to enact the sexual harassment debate, but with stories that ultimately took a feminist stance despite contradictory and complicated rhetoric. This season emphasized women accused of sexual harassment, in which Cage, Fish took a radical feminist approach in many defenses and argued women as different from men (4–02, "Girls' Night Out"; 4–07, "Love on Holiday"; and 4–21, "Queen Bee"). In season five, new firm member Jenny Shaw represents Raymond Milbury, who is sued by an opposing counsel for sexual harassment and features much of the chauvinism of Richard without the incompetence to undercut it (5–04, "Fear of Flirting"). The jury finds against Raymond, affirming his behavior as that of a sexist boor, but orders only $.75 be paid in damages in recognition that it was asked to apply sexual harassment law beyond its boundaries.

The continuing and often extreme reworking of potential sexual harassment litigation chronicled above illustrates how behavior leading to the creation of sexual harassment laws can become trivialized, but the dialogue in these episodes offers additional political engagement with the issue. Analysis of this aspect of the representation of sexual harassment is challenging because of the conflicted and contradictory positions presented and the text's refusal to support a single coherent perspective. For instance, although Richard and Billy present chauvinist polemics in defending clients, they often do so either in the process of arguing for a clearly aggrieved woman or in a way that can be interpreted as illustrating their incompetence as lawyers. In the first situation, the text often reaches what can be argued as a feminist end, but does so by a questionably feminist means. For example, Richard succeeds in winning an evidentiary hearing for a woman filing a sexual harassment suit with the following speech:

Women are victims. They need special help. When you look at the evolution of the sexual harassment laws, what we're really saying is that women should qualify under the Federal Disabilities Act. They are less able. They cannot cope with romance in the workplace. They cannot contend with having to do a job and have a man smile at them [1–18, "The Playing Field"].

Billy makes a similar speech in a firm conference meeting, arguing:

We're talking about sexual harassment law, Ally; let's not expect it to make sense. We just have to assume that if any woman anywhere at anytime feels the slightest twinge of hypersensitivity, and she can link it to anything remotely sexual, she has a cause of action. The courts will protect her, which is good, because as a matter of law, women need protection [3–02, "Buried Pleasures"].

In another episode he tells the client he represents, who is suing for sexual harassment, that sexual harassment is a "stupid law that works as an equalizer for weak women" (3–06, "Changes").

Leslie Heywood argues that this sort of dialogue "neutralizes the feminist critique of larger issues by making the ideas behind that critique sound silly" (Heywood, B9). Arguably this does occur. At the same time, however, the series repeatedly examines an important feminist issue and opens for cultural debate the myriad ways sexism circulates within society. Ally, Georgia, and Nelle obviously disdain the above speeches; and because the series lacks a reliable central character, the text does not make a preferred position evident. In these scenes and the earlier situation noted with John Cage, a feminist perspective develops through what Cooper terms "the comic spectacle of maleness." She contends, "Many of the series' plots are developed through exaggerated and humorous depictions of chauvinist attitudes and behaviors, and through scenes that overtly question male sexuality," and notes that, "Men's justification for sexually objectifying women is a frequent target of ridicule" (425–6). Very different interpretations of the series are possible depending on the complexity with which critics approach rhetorical, ideological, and narrative analysis. Consequently, I do not suggest that my interpretation is the only one available, but it is as practicable as the anti-feminist interpretations others have suggested (Kim; Vavrus; Shalit).

Although the series' exploration of sexual harassment law was highly varied, episodes such as the one involving the shock jock illustrate the feminist potential of the series. Some of the extreme situations that the text raised implicitly query the boundaries of sexual harassment and do not criticize the existence of sexual harassment codes so much as illustrate the difficulty of defining their boundaries. A conservative analysis of the series' representation of sexual harassment reads the difficulty in determining parameters as arguing that because a line cannot be drawn, no sexual harassment laws should exist. Yet, the text does not support this position above others, especially since the series depicts both Ally and Georgia benefiting from laws that help women combat workplace power inequities displayed through harassment and discrimination. Feminist interpretations use the series' representation of the difficulty in determining the extent of sexual harassment code application as evidence of how widespread and culturally ingrained many sexist practices are in a way that illustrates the need for continued feminist activism. Criticism of the ambiguity of sexual harassment laws, then, is not necessarily an anti-feminist position. In many cases *Ally McBeal* illustrates the inadequacy of current law and the constraints of using a legal system that attempts uniform application. Such an interpretation exposes the limited utility of legal solutions and identifies a need for continued cultural and social examination to understand the formation and transmission of inequity and bias.

The construction of sex-based legal issues and solutions in *Ally McBeal* is characteristic of postfeminism in various ways. First, it expands from individualistic liberal feminist approaches to combating sex oppression. In some cases, second-wave feminists encouraged women to use self-help strategies or consciousness-raising to help them overcome experiences of harassment or discrimination by learning to feel better about themselves, but *Ally McBeal* does not impose individualistic solutions on victims of sex-based injustice. In other situations, liberal feminists believed that enacting legal protection would eliminate problems such as harassment and discrimination. The series' critique of sexual harassment laws illustrates the limitations of legal remedies and the depths of sex-based prejudice. The variety of situations the series poses for examining sexual harassment also depicts how workplace power can result from factors other than gender and the very different relations to power women can inhabit.

Deconstructing Gender

The third attribute of postfeminist discourse, the deconstruction of distinct binary categories of gender and sexuality, plays a central role in postfeminist theories, but is much less discernable in contemporary television series. Likewise, it is less evident than other attributes in *Ally McBeal*, but arguably the occasional utterances the series provides are more substantial than in any other series airing on U.S. broadcast networks at the time. In *Ally McBeal*, the deconstruction of binaries appears in episodes exploring transvestite, transsexual, and bisexual characters.

The series offers little critique of gender classifications, such as male and female, and even tends to reinforce essentialist understandings, as when

Ally differentiates behavior as distinctly "male" or Richard and Billy criticize how "women" act. However, the wide range of circumstances through which the series examines sexual harassment law can be seen as a deconstruction of gender in the determination of workplace power. Cases exploring the type of femininity displayed by a female employer who either harasses or is harassed by a male employee illustrate the complex ways individuals embody their gender classification and power.

The series also featured two plotlines dealing with transvestite or transsexual characters. In the first, Ally represents a transvestite prostitute and comes to understand the complexity of his perception of gender identity and the reason he does not wish her to use a psychiatric defense (1–10, "Boy to the World"). The characters establish a connection in an unusually melodramatic episode that concludes with the firm hiring Stephanie/Steven as support staff. In its final scene, however, the episode takes Ally to the location of his murder, which suggests the series could not sustain its initial support of gender play. In a more extended series of episodes in the fourth season, firm member Mark Albert begins dating and falling in love with a woman who reveals herself as a pre-op transsexual (4–02, "Girls' Night Out;" 4–03, "Two's a Crowd;" 4–04, "Without a Net;" 4–07, "Love on Holiday;" 4–12, "Hats Off to Larry"). The episodes depict Mark's struggle with his emotional attachment to the woman, but culturally ingrained revulsion of her transsexuality, which Richard and Nelle exacerbate by making homophobic comments. In a depiction similar to Ally's dealing with her bisexual suitor (discussed below), Mark ultimately rejects Cindy, but the text wavers in its support for his decision. Cindy returns to the firm for representation a few episodes after the breakup because she has found a man who accepts her difference and wishes to marry her. The firm fights against the prohibition of same-sex marriage but fails out of judicial limitations. Richard then marries the couple in a legally insignificant but symbolically meaningful gesture.

Ally McBeal is slightly more flexible in its depiction of categories of sexuality, although not nearly enough to present an organized deconstruction of sexual identity. The series raises the existence of bisexuality — a possibility rarely addressed by U.S. television, but does so in a way as multivalent as the depiction of the Margaret Camero character. When Ally learns that a suitor who otherwise seems perfect is bisexual, she is overwhelmed by homophobic images and dismisses him, although the text suggests she is wrong to do so (3–13, "Pursuit of Happiness"). Additionally, in an episode in which Ally and Ling kiss, both admit enjoying the experience, but also contend that they do not find it as satisfying as kissing a man (3–02, "Buried Pleasures"). Here, the exploration and curiosity the characters experience is never acknowledged as bisexual behavior and the characters repeatedly affirm that they are heterosexual and want to be so, but also admit they are curious and even have an urge to kiss each other. The characters are confused about the implications of their desires on their sexuality, so they overdetermine their heterosexuality in dialogue, while their actions (kissing each other, pretending to be a lesbian couple) illustrate the mutability of sexual identity and how it can be performed on a continuum.[7] Despite these few narrative moments, the series' construction of gender and sexuality categories remains less deconstructed than might be expected of a postfeminist text, but suggests a loosening of binary norms.

Ally's Search for Mr. Right

The representation of career women struggling with their expectations of and options for romantic partnership and their consequent anxiety are important to consider in relation to feminism because feminists have worked to give women the option of a career. Additionally, feminists have fought cultural myths suggesting that finding a husband is the most defining accomplishment of a woman's life. *Ally McBeal*'s female characters are part of the generation first receiving the benefits secured by second-wave feminist activism throughout their lives. The new career possibilities afforded them consequently force many of the characters to reconcile the independence provided by their career success with their desire for romantic relationships. For many, the challenge comes not in finding a relationship, but in finding the right one.

The depiction of women struggling to have both career and family can be viewed as an example of the fourth attribute of postfeminist discourse because this depiction raises and examines struggles faced by women within the contemporary cultural milieu in which some feminist gains have been achieved but most relations of power remain structured by patriarchy. Popular media often give voice to such concerns as well as to contradictions in cultural expectations. Anxiety about finding the right partner appears in a preponderant manner in *Ally McBeal* and several other series airing coterminously. Ally's unsuccessful attempts to find a suitable mate structure the series' initial seasons (although both John and Richard pursue a similar goal with less narrative emphasis) and her expressions of the lack of fulfillment she finds in her professional success and work-dominated life drew considerable feminist ire and suggestion of the anti-feminist ideology of the series (Kim; Vavrus; Shugart, Waggoner, and O'Brien Hallstein).

In the past, some feminists may have categorically criticized the expression of such personal concerns as anti-feminist or as a reactionary attempt to contain feminist gains. Admittedly, one can interpret this depiction of anxiety to suggest that successful professional women cannot find the relationships they desire because of their careers— and this interpretation is evident in many of the journalistic criticisms of *Ally McBeal*. In contrast, the text constructs this issue with more complexity than this interpretation recognizes and Ally's career is by no means clearly the cause of her uncertainties about her personal life. Additionally, aspects of postfeminism make the expression of such personal anxieties acceptable and open up personal aspects of women's lives for consideration. It is also important to consider how the ongoing narrative of serial television prevents a conclusion or an answer to the characters' concerns and instead depicts the characters in a continuous process of negotiating contradictory personal desires until the series' conclusion. Importantly, *Ally McBeal* did not end with Ally's wedding, but with a character who had grown comfortable inside her own skin, who no longer pined for her life to match a culturally imposed social script, and the character's recognition that the journey is as important as the destination and that hindsight revealed the times that challenged her as highly satisfying.

Ally McBeal's main contribution to a cultural negotiation of career and family is its ambivalence: it recognizes the career gains the character achieves as an advance, but simultaneously depicts uncertainty about how to evaluate this success compared with other desires. In this ambivalence the series accepts the multiple plans, choices, and goals women may have in a way that corresponds to developments evident in postfeminism as a feminist theory that specifically embraces differences among women and that provides for discrepancy among equally feminist perspectives on issues.

Feminists of all kinds have placed the importance for women to have choices at the center of their theoretical and activist concerns and the multiplicity of characters in the late 1990s enable the depiction of characters making varied choices without suggesting containment. If a female character chooses to emphasize her personal life and is consequently categorically denounced as anti-feminist — even when many other representations exist — feminism has provided her very little choice at all. Significant anxiety and frustration result from the continued adherence to binaries of femininity and feminism established during the second-wave battle against the limited gender roles available to women at that time. These stories in *Ally McBeal* indicate an organic emergence of unspoken cultural undercurrents and it remains possible that its texts and the characters' dilemmas have connected with viewers in such a way to help initiate such organization-based change. At the minimum, the series initiated a dialogue that encouraged a reconsideration of the status of feminism on various personal and political fronts.

Conclusion

Finding the feminist (or even postfeminist in my terms) potential of *Ally McBeal* unquestionably requires considering the series through a different frame than has traditionally been used to gauge feminist, "new women," or empowered female television characters and their texts. The various discrepancies in context operating in the case of *Ally McBeal* justify the need for an adjusted frame, and the developing terrain of postfeminist theory lends itself to understanding the variation of this series. Further, the exceptional degree to which the series resonated with the female audiences who viewed *Ally McBeal* in nearly record numbers— particularly in early seasons— requires consideration that moves beyond assumptions of false consciousness. This series unquestionably touched a cultural nerve that was clearly exposed yet uncommented upon by the late 1990s.

The uncertain questions that remain relate to what the legacy of *Ally McBeal* will be. Will the cultural debate that embroiled the series force other character innovations with postfeminist attributes into ignominy because of analysis lacking context? Can we develop critical tools that acknowledge the complicated status of female characters in the twenty-first century? Will the journalistic debates and anti-feminist co-optation of weak analyses such as Bellafante's scare Hollywood's creative minds from offering other contestable and innovative images or encourage them to expand the trail Kelley initiated? Can we develop more sophisticated analyses and understandings of female characters that deviate from "role model" standards and yet reach audience members? And now that such a range of post–Baby Boom characters exist, how will they continue to redefine the issues facing women?

In the nearly ten years since *Ally McBeal*'s debut, few series have offered the consistent and sophisticated storytelling about women's lives after the intervention of second-wave activism and the related challenges. Most series do not comment on the challenges that result for women who live in a culture in which some feminist gains have been achieved but much of patriarchy remains firmly entrenched. Stories depicting the new options available to women may now circulate in series featuring tough career women and women involved in more equitable romantic relationships, but most assume these gains without dealing with the complexity of residual sexism and patriarchal power. The engagement, uncertainty, and ambivalence of *Ally McBeal* with a society in change allowed the innovation and novelty of the series that has yet to be replicated or extended. Although new series tell stories about women that draw critics and viewers (for example *Desperate Housewives* and *Grey's Anatomy* of late), no subsequent series has utilized postfeminist strategies to engage and interrogate gender relations in contemporary society in the way endeavored and achieved by *Ally McBeal*.

Notes

1. Throughout the series' run, a substantial number of negative reviews were based on the series' deviation from "reality" (real lawyers don't wear short skirts, have so much time to talk, act that way in court). While such arguments make fine special interest pieces, most television critics realize that adherence to "reality" is not an imperative in evaluating fictional storytelling. Additionally, because of my focus on feminism and gender, I am not able to devote space to assessing Kelley's "colorblind" approach to the series. Critique of the series' implicit and explicit racism is important and complicated, but beyond the scope of this article.

2. Georgia initially provides an exception, but she later separates from Billy and then becomes a widow.

3. A similar divergence can be argued of *Xena: Warrior Princess*, which began in 1995, and *Buffy the Vampire Slayer*, which began five months before *Ally McBeal*. Discussion of generation is irrelevant in *Xena*'s case because of its fantastic mythical setting, but I would argue *Buffy the Vampire Slayer* faces challenges similar to *Ally McBeal* in deviating from the Baby Boom generation setting.

4. In the final season Ally displayed considerable new maturity as a mentor to youthful doppelganger Jenny, was promoted to firm partner in John's absence, purchased a house, became the mother of a 10-year-old girl conceived from an egg Ally had donated during law school, and spent much less time pining for love.

5. For example, Kelley responded explicitly to critics such as Bellafante with a storyline in which McBeal is asked to be a role model — but only if she makes some changes in her appearance.

6. Like nearly all U.S. television series, socio-economic class does not emerge as a factor in characters' subjectivity, although it is likely to have considerable effect in contributing to varied outlooks among women.

7. For a more thorough assessment of how television depicts bisexuality and its appeals of lesbian chic characters see Clark.

Works Cited

Arthurs, Jane. "*Sex and the City* and Consumer Culture: Remediating Postfeminist Drama." *Feminist Media Studies* 3.1 (2003): 83–98.

Bellafante, Gina. "Feminism: It's All About Me!" *Time,* 29 June 1998: 54–60.

Braxton, Greg. "Colorblind or Just Plain Blind? 'Race Not Being an Issue Makes It an Issue,' Says David E. Kelley of an Unspoken Topic on *Ally McBeal*. But Others Say He's Being Irresponsible." *Los Angeles Times,* 9 February 1991: F1.

Brooks, Ann. *Postfeminisms: Feminism, Cultural Theory, and Cultural Forms.* New York: Routledge, 1997.

Chambers, Veronica. "*Ally McBeal*." *Newsweek,* 13 October 1997: 71.

_____. "How Would Ally Do It?" *Newsweek,* 2 March 1998: 58–61.

Clark, Danae. "Commodity Lesbianism." *Camera Obscura* 25 (1991).

Collins, James. "Ally McBeal." *Time,* 10 November 1997: 117.

Cooper, Brenda. "Unapologetic Women, 'Comic Men' and Feminine Spectatorship in David E. Kelley's *Ally McBeal*." *Critical Studies in Media Communication* 18.4 (2001): 416–435.

Dow, Bonnie. *Prime-Time Feminism: Television, Media Culture, and the Women's Movement Since 1970.* Philadelphia: University of Pennsylvania Press, 1996.

Dowd, Maureen. "Ally McBeal Is a Unisex Role Model." *The New York Times,* 15 April 1998: C5.

Faludi, Susan. *Backlash: The Undeclared War Against American Women.* New York: Crown, 1991.

Gamble, Sarah, ed. *The Routledge Critical Dictionary of Feminism and Postfeminism.* New York: Routledge, 2000.

Grossberger, Lewis. "Ally's No. 1 Ally." *MEDIAWEEK,* 16 February 1998: 38.

Heywood, Leslie. "Hitting a Cultural Nerve: Another Season of *Ally McBeal.*" *Chronicle of Higher Education,* 4 September 1998: B9.

Jefferson, Margo. "You Want to Slap Ally McBeal, But Do You Like Her?" *The New York Times,* 18 March 1998: E2.

Katz, Alyssa. "*Ally McBeal.*" *The Nation,* 15 December 1997: 36–39.

Kim, L. S. "*Sex and the Single Girl* in Postfeminism: The F Word on Television." *Television & New Media* 2.4 (2001): 319–334.

Lotz, Amanda D. "Postfeminist Television Criticism: Rehabilitating Critical Terms and Identifying Postfeminist Attributes." *Feminist Media Studies* 1.1 (2001): 105–121.

_____. "Communicating Third-Wave Feminism and New Social Movements: Challenges for the Next Century of Feminist Endeavor." *Women and Language* 26.1 (2003): 2–9.

_____. *Redesigning Women: Television After the Network Era.* Urbana-Champaign: University of Illinois Press, 2006.

McRobbie, Angela. *Postmodernism and Popular Culture.* New York: Routledge, 1994.

Mann, Judy. "An Unfair Assessment of Feminism." *The Washington Post,* 26 June 1998: E03.

Modleski, Tania. *Feminism Without Women: Culture and Criticism in a "Postfeminist" Age.* New York: Routledge, 1991.

Moseley, Rachael, and Jacinda Read. "'Having it *Ally*': Popular Television (Post-) Feminism." *Feminist Media Studies* 2.2 (2002): 231–249.

Nochimson, Martha P. "*Ally McBeal:* Brightness Falls from the Air." *Film Quarterly* 53.3 (2000): 25–32.

NOW. "NOW Issues Friendly Advice for *Time* Magazine." National Organization for Women, June 1998. 3 July 2002. *http://www.now.org/press/06–98/time.html.*

Parker, Kathleen. "Feminism Isn't Dead, Just Bored and Confused." *Orlando Sentinel,* 27 June 1998: 15A.

Press, Andrea L. *Women Watching Television: Gender, Class and Generation in the American Television Experience.* Philadelphia: University of Pennsylvania Press, 1991.

Schneider, Karen S. "Everybody's Picking on Calista Flockhart's Weight." *People Weekly,* 9 November 1998: 92.

Scruggs, Afi-Odella E. "Miniskirt Feminism Baffles Veterans." *The Plain Dealer,* 21 October 1998: 1B.

Shalit, Ruth. "Canny and Lacy." *The New Republic,* 6 April 1998: 27–33.

Shugart, Helene A., Catherine Egley Waggoner, and D. Lynn O'Brien Hallstein. "Mediating Third-Wave Feminism: Appropriation as Postmodern Media Practice." *Critical Studies in Media Communication* 18.2 (2001): 194–210.

Stack, Teresa. "Fiction Is Not a Feminist Issue." *Pittsburgh Post-Gazette,* 18 July 1998: A13.

Stark, Steven D. "Ally McBeal." *The New Republic,* 29 December 1997: 13–15.

Svetkey, Benjamin. "Everything You Love or Hate About *Ally McBeal.*" *Entertainment Weekly* 30 January 1998: 20–26.

Vavrus, Mary Douglas. "Putting Ally on Trial: Contesting Postfeminism in Popular Culture." *Women's Studies in Communication* 23.3 (2000): 413–428.

Williamson, Linda. "Let's Get Real on *Ally McBeal.*" *Toronto Sun,* 2 July 1998: 15.

Wilson, Pamela. "Upscale Feminine Angst: *Molly Dodd,* the Lifetime Cable Network and Gender Marketing." *Camera Obscura* [special volume on "Lifetime: A Cable Network for Women," edited by Julie D'Acci] 33–34 (1994): 102–131.

8

Worshipping at the Altar of Barry White: *Ally McBeal* and Racial and Sexual Politics in Crisis

Jennifer Harris

"You're not who you are, you're only what other people think you are. Fishism."

— Richard Fish

If, as Toni Morrison asserts in *Playing in the Dark: Whiteness and the Literary Imagination,* the American Africanist presence has had a "dark, abiding, signing" influence on the concerns of the traditional American literary canon (5) then it should also hold that this same presence has equally affected mainstream popular culture in ways that are likewise as pervasive and unacknowledged.[1] Of all of the established popular culture forms—music and music video, film, books, television, magazines—it is the television medium of the series that best offers the opportunity for an extended and developed visual and audio narrative of American culture. Yet, dependent upon what Morrison terms the "economy of stereotype" (67) to introduce characters, establish scenarios, and advance plots, television is often the most conservative of media even as given shows proffer themselves or are interpreted as groundbreaking. One series, the David E. Kelley production *Ally McBeal* (1997–2002), exemplifies this dynamic. Recognized as innovative in its representation of single, contemporary working women — notably the eponymous character — and in its witty externalization of the characters' unspoken and subconscious perceptions and desires, the show nevertheless employs a series of superficially benign, but in fact racially charged, images and devices in devising and sustaining its fictional world. In fact, I argue, tropes of blackness are omnipresent in *Ally McBeal*. They haunt and shape the internal world of particular white characters, inform the representations of African Americans, inescapably shape the soundtrack, and define the construction of white masculinity. Identifying these tropes and they ways they are deployed exposes how the show is dependent upon the subordination of race and racial difference, calling into question the discourse of liberal pluralism that *Ally McBeal* might otherwise be seen to promote. However unintentionally, we can read in the series the tendency of white cultural forms to draw upon particular constructions, appropriations, eroticizations, and fetishizations of blackness, following the work of Morrison, bell hooks and others.

With the debut of *Ally McBeal* it was evident narrative devices would be of key importance. The most obvious—and most remarked upon—is the visualization of characters' internal imaginings. Unlike the isolated dream sequences often utilized in television series to demonstrate the subconscious desires, fears, or imaginings of characters, the visualizations in Kelley's series are integrated into everyday scenes. They are sometimes literal visions for the characters—as is the case of the dancing baby famously seen by Ally McBeal (played by Calista Flockhart)—or sometimes visual representations of emotions, as when characters who suddenly feel insecure are represented on a smaller scale than the furniture or individuals around them. The literal visions can be uncontrollable, or a character might deliberately try to invoke one, as is the case of John Cage (played by Peter MacNicol) and his relationship with singer and composer Barry White. Those with more than a passing familiarity with the series are aware of White's importance to *Ally McBeal*. That White, who is African American, is for many viewers inseparable from the landscape of the show, despite his having appeared in only one episode ("Those Lips, That Hand") is noteworthy, particularly given the predominantly white universe of the program. However, these viewers are not misreading the show: Barry White is in fact fundamental to *Ally McBeal*, as the ideational and musical intersect in its construction. That he is most closely associated with the white character John Cage is likewise telling. While Cage is an intelligent and kind but fundamentally insecure lawyer who frequently stutters when embarrassed, the very real White is known for his R&B compositions and the deep voice with which he performs them. White is most renowned, however, for the success of his music as the very crucial background track of many a real-life seduction. Therefore, that Cage "taps into" the power of Barry White when he wishes to seduce, whether it be a woman or a courtroom, is not necessarily inappropriate. Staring into himself whether literally (as in the case of a mirror) or figuratively via introspective reflection, Cage ritualistically summons "Barry" as he calls him, the opening words and bars of "You're My First, My Last, My Everything" signaling his triumph, at which point he begins a carefully choreographed yet comical dance.

Barry White is Cage's inspiration because for Cage he represents what the latter has been unable to attain: sexual prowess, popularity with women, remarkable stature, and undeniable masculinity. He is a figure drawn from popular culture by the writers of the show, and recycled in the popular culture of Cage & Fish, the law firm that is the setting of *Ally McBeal,* further enshrining his iconic status as a performer who enables other men to perform (albeit in a different arena). However, to read the relationship John Cage is represented as having with the *image* of Barry White as simply one of admiration is to ignore the way utilizing that image resonates in relation to race, sexuality, and privilege, particularly given the history of black-white relations in the United States. As Stuart Hall writes of black people and to black people:

> [P]opular culture, commodified and stereotyped as it often is, is not at all, as we sometimes think of it, the arena where we find who we really are, the truth of our experience. It is an area that is profoundly mythic. It is a theater of popular desires, a theater of popular fantasies. It is where we discover and play with the identifications of ourselves, where we are imagined, where we are represented, not only to the audiences out there who do not get the message, but to ourselves for the first time. As Freud said, sex (and representation) mainly takes place in the head [32].

In the case of Barry White and John Cage, there are two levels of the imagined and the represented operating. There is the fictive level of the character John Cage drawing upon the popular musician Barry White; and there is the reality of David E. Kelley and his writers imagining a white, male, upwardly mobile and successful lawyer with his own firm and all of the privileges these things accrue and represent in American society, who nonetheless has to turn to a prominent figure of black masculinity to enhance his own self-image and sexuality. Given the history of utilizing black people as signifiers to represent the mythic desires and fantasies of whites that Hall references above, it is, at this point, also impossible not to think of the tradition in America of white men with economic privilege appropriating the bodies and contributions of black men and women. The use by Cage of "Barry-White-as-black-signifier-of-sexual-potency" is, therefore, not merely an assertion of White's power, but also a representation of a historical tendency by white Americans to invest images of African Americans with particular power or meanings. Chief among these meanings that African Americans have come to signify in the white imagination — and I will demonstrate, in *Ally McBeal* — is a hyper-sexuality.

The process by which blackness accrued connotations of licentiousness has been well-documented. Briefly, the encounter of Europeans with indigenous Africans whose geography and cultures often favored less clothing, differing attitudes towards sex and sexuality, and in some instances polygamy, led to voyeuristic surmises about the sexual appetite and mores of the "dark other." The conditions of enslavement of African people in the Americas advanced the opportunity for racist suppositions, as those enslaved were denied privacy, suitable clothing, encouraged to "breed," and, in the case of women, subject to sexual abuses which they were then accused of inviting.[2] While black women were commonly understood as always sexually available (rather than rarely in a position to resist), black men were read as rapacious sexual predators, "bucks" whose sexual prowess was a threat to white femininity, or rather to white male possession of white women. Eldridge Cleaver, in the 1968 classic *Soul on Ice*,[3] wrote that black men embodied a hyper-masculinity that white men both envied and feared. The logical extension of envying black men the sexuality one imagines they possess is the desire to appropriate that power for one's self. The history of lynching black men in response to unfounded charges of the rape of a white woman is a way of claiming that power. The life of the black male victim and the sexual potency he represents is transferred to the white male lynchers who, in a horribly macabre but symbolically appropriate gesture, often removed the genitals of their victim. Lest we think these were isolated incidents, it is worth remembering the statistics: 113 blacks were reported lynched in 1892; 161 in 1892; 118 in 1893, and so on (Bennett, Jr., 508–509).[4] It is noteworthy that this ritual functioned to reinforce bonds between white men, as surviving photos demonstrate. That sexualized black bodies also functioned as places where white men could meet safely and engage in homoerotic rituals (including the gang rape of women) demonstrates that white men additionally conceived of black bodies as contrivances enabling the development and cementing of their own relations.[5]

Obviously, John Cage is doing nothing so horrific. And unlike his colleague, Billy Thomas (played by Gil Bellows), whose personal crisis leads him to exercise an excess of chauvinism, literally embodied by the pack of "Robert Palmer girls" he hires to accompany him,[6] Cage does not fall into the more overt trappings of white masculine power. But neither is he divorced from the white male tradition of envy and appropriation. Indeed, he embodies the historic American paradigm whereby white masculinity is produced through appropriations of blackness. In this paradigm, sexuality is displaced onto African Americans (as well as Latina and Latino populations), then reappropriated through a series of strategies which nevertheless reify the "blackness" of sexuality — as well as the "sexuality" of "blackness," a process bell hooks has written about at length.[7] Despite his ingenious courtroom strategies and rhetorical and verbal excellence (stuttering aside) Cage is dependent upon the power that he accrues through his relationship with the image of Barry White in his construction of self. In the episode "Car Wash" which opened the third season of the series, Cage loses his ability to "channel" what he describes as his "inner Barry White," and is left without confidence personally as well as sexually. This loss is represented as a source of concern for Cage and those around him, rather than a moment for examining why he relies on an external yet inaccessible figure for sexual invigoration. Why he identifies his "inner" sexual being as black, as evident in his naming and imagining of it as "Barry White," is also never addressed within the show, precisely because it doesn't have to be: the supposition that African Americans are inherently sexual and cool, and that middle- and upper-class white people aren't, is understood as a cliché in North American society, rather than a stereotype. It is this same understanding that obscures the inherent homoerotics of the identification as well, for if what White represents is an effortless or natural sexuality, then it is logical that he becomes the fountain from which other men can draw, without drawing attention to how that might trouble certain assumptions of heterosexuality. However, instead of considering the ways in which Cage's fantasy of Barry White might unsettle beliefs about the source and operating of white masculine power, the idea that a white man might turn to a black man for sexual inspiration is represented in *Ally McBeal* as idiosyncratic and a site of humor. When his co-workers surprise him with an actual live performance by Barry White, Cage is transfixed in a state of joy, waving his arms in a fashion suggesting worship, while the other characters and the audience cannot help but be swept away by the humor resulting from his unabashed pleasure ("Those Lips, That Hand"). Clearly, when John Cage dances his "Barry White dance" we are meant to feel amused, uplifted, and vicariously happy.

Indeed, this sense of uplift is key to the use of Barry White and his music as well as the other 1970s recording artists who appear in the series. In the third season, Al Green appears, serenading Ally McBeal at every turn ("Seeing Green"). Despite her active fantasy life, she admits that he is the one fantasy she can't control. Later in that season, Gloria Gaynor "stalks" Ally singing her classic disco tune "I Will Survive" in an episode of the same name. Al Green, now an ordained minister, sings of sexuality and seduction like White, but he also sings of love, sorrow, and loss. Gaynor's featured song is one of empowerment and survival. Not coincidentally, while these are certainly universal themes, they also exemplify the legacy of suffering and survival to which African Americans have a special claim within the nation. With the exception of Barry Manilow (whom Miss McBeal tries to punch in "Reaching Out"), these are the preeminent performers whom characters' subconsciouses conjure. All have a certain nostalgic appeal for those in the age range of the ensemble cast and, no doubt, David E. Kelley himself. The past they cumulatively musically invoke is a personal one, with personal resonance and triumphs, rather than a collective experience. For a white audience, they need not invoke a racially specific past or history either, though it is improbable that an African American audience might see them outside of that context of black musical production and activity. Their music is also, within the context of mainstream popular culture, perceived and reproduced as apolitical, lacking the racial politics that characterized the work of some other African American musicians (Marvin Gaye, Stevie Wonder) popular during the 1970s. As Herman Gray observes of early television, "Culturally, because blackness served whiteness in this way, the reigning perspective of this world was always staged from a white subject position" (75). Here, the reigning subject position is that of Ally McBeal.[8]

This evacuation of a historical past in favor of privileging a personal one is in keeping with the tenor of the show, where the racially diverse — and often charged — atmosphere of Boston is replaced with a sanitized vision of quaint buildings and charmingly winding clean streets. In the Boston of *Ally McBeal,* characters often walk home alone late at night on streets populated with well-dressed and usually white individuals and lovers and, occasionally, a homeless person figured as harmless. This is not the same space Kelley represents in his other Fox series, *Boston Public,* where we see examples of contemporary black culture as well as the frictions that sometimes result within the context of an urban multi-cultural and class-stratified milieu. In *Ally McBeal* while class conflict may exist on a personal level, any racial friction is non-existent. Instead, the black performers whom characters imagine fulfill the role of nurturer and reassurer, another historically resonant association with blackness by white America. That this is accomplished through music is crucial, given the importance of black music as a psychic support and source of revitalization in America across race. After all, African American music has long defined the shape, if not actually constituting the core, of American popular music, as well as providing a constant musical-cultural refrain. This definitional role is apparent in *Ally McBeal,* as the in-house musician at the bar downstairs from the law office where the majority of the show is set is Vonda Shepard (as herself), a white singer whose blues-y vocal stylings are indebted to African American musical forms. Her singing dominates the soundtrack of the show, weaving in and out of various scenes set nowhere near the bar. The three black women who form her back-up group are the Ikettes, named after Ike Turner's back-up singers.[9] Not only do they sing back-up for Shepard, they also provide back-up for any character who wishes to climb onto the stage and sing. The continuous presence of the Ikettes to provide "backup" is indicative of the way in which the African American musical presence is necessary and yet simultaneously marginalized on a greater American stage. However, the presence of black back-up singers supporting predominantly white artists is not original to *Ally McBeal,* but in fact is part of a larger and longer trend of utilizing black voices to support white stars and lend credibility and depth to their endeavor, without offering similar credit to those supporting voices.[10] Appropriate to a show so much about the individual who relies upon the "other" for self-definition, is Morrison's observation: "the subject of the dream is the dreamer."

While blackness and black voices provide a refrain for the emotional trajectory of the show and its characters, it would have been notable had Kelley's series otherwise featured an all-white ensemble cast. The question "why no black *Friends*" was repeated throughout the late 1990s, as most larger ensemble casts came to include a non-white character (though not necessarily in a principal role).[11] While minority characters do not exactly abound in *Ally McBeal,* they are present, and their personalities and the situations in which they are placed forward the supposition that ideologies of race are fundamental to the show's construction. From the series' launch, the ensemble cast featured Lisa Nicole Carson as Renee Raddick, public defender and roommate to Ally McBeal. The African American character of Renee manages to escape the common trope of having a non-white character act as ancillary to the lead, as she is a public defender who frequently confronts the lawyers of Cage & Fish in the courtroom and carries her own story lines. Nevertheless, she often acts as a foil to Ally, whether in matters of conscience or opinion and is regularly bested in the courtroom by her roommate or her roommate's colleagues. Furthermore, just as Barry White does to John Cage, Renee represents an overt, assertive sexuality that makes that of her friend pale in comparison. She is sexually aggressive, and uses her voluptuous persona to make John Cage uncomfortable. While we are not privy to her sexual history, the audience does witness her overt performance of sexuality, and hear the assertion of the law office's self-proclaimed slut, Elaine Vassal, that "Renee's a bigger tramp then me." Whether or not this is true of the character is irrelevant; what is interesting is that the audience, and her fellow characters, *perceive* her to be highly sexual.

In an episode from the first season titled "The Inmates" we encounter these assumptions directly. Renee invites a male lawyer, played by Isaiah

Washington, to ask her out, dances suggestively with him, grabs his buttocks, and invites him home. When he does not acquiesce with her request to "slow down," she slaps him, he reciprocates, and she knocks him unconscious utilizing skills learned in kick-boxing class. A trial for assault results, and while the end result affirms that "no means no" (how could it do otherwise on this show?), the narrative nevertheless affirms Renee's partial responsibility for the situation due to her manner. In a revealing and insightful conversation with her roommate, Renee admits that she locates her self-esteem in her sexuality ("The Inmates"). However, never addressed or acknowledged is the way in which her position as a black woman results in her racial inscription as sexually available in the American context. Nor are the difficulties of negotiating a predominantly white professional world as an African American woman addressed, though plots involving both Ally and her colleague Georgia Thomas (played by Courtney Thorne-Smith) address sexual harassment. Instead, Renee's identification of her self-esteem with her sexuality is represented as simply one more quirk exhibited by an eclectic cast of characters. Her racial presence remains consistently unacknowledged by the scripts while it is simultaneously utilized by the framework of the series as a form of discursive shorthand: Ally, who is the core of the show, cannot be racist because she has a best friend who happens to be African American. Renee's blackness therefore functions as a reassuring subtext, and yet is a nonexistent subject, exemplifying one of the primary tensions of the program. Midway during season four of the series, another African American actress, Regina Hall of *Scary Movie* fame, appears on one episode. She is the nemesis of several of the program's main characters. Due to her popularity with fans, she is brought back as a regular during the shows fifth and final season as the character Corretta. Like the other African American female character, Renee, she is attractive, however, she lacks the overt sexual prowess of Renee. The character of Corretta is more subdued, humorous and is racially conscious as her name would symbolize.

In 1998 Lucy Liu joined the cast of *Ally McBeal* as Ling Woo, the fierce best friend of the equally fierce Nelle Porter (Portia de Rossi). Like the character of Renee, Ling's race is never the focus of an episode or discussion on screen, though the racialization of the character is so evident to viewers as to have generated significant public commentary.[12] The characterization of Ling evokes a legacy of American racial stereotypes of Asian women, particularly the ways in which they have been sexualized. According to Laura Hyun Yi Kang this sexual stereotyping is embodied in two primary forms: "the Dragon Lady represents a special Asian mix of sexual perversity, moral depravity, and drive for domination [while] the submissive Lotus Blossom projects a more welcoming image of exotic differences and erotic possibilities" (72).

A hybrid of these two types, Ling is a seductive temptress who both pun-ishes and pleasures men, sometimes at once. Moreover, it is not an Asian man who is her primary sexual partner in the series, but the wealthy and often offensive Richard Fish. This pairing with a white man may seem ini-tially progressive in terms of representing interracial relations as accept-able, until one confronts the history that in American television or film Asian women are *never* paired in heterosexual relations with Asian men, and instead inevitably serve as partners to white men, thereby enhancing their "virility" (Kang, 72). Ling engages in a game of withholding sex and then performing an erotic otherness for the satisfaction of Richard, an approach that both differs from and complements the licentiousness asso-ciated with Renee. For Renee, sex is most often represented in terms of physical desire; for Ling it is represented in terms of the struggle for power and mastery. This is the crux of the "Dragon Lady" persona — intelligent, dangerous, ambitious, and vain. While *Ally McBeal* does provide opportu-nities for Liu's character to demonstrate moments of complexity, more often it relies on the economy of stereotype to advance the plot or create humor, rather than undermine that stereotype. As Asian American actress Amy Hill comments, "[Ling] could be terrifying in the hands of a lesser actor, simply because it could be 'stereotypical' if played without the depth and complexity that [Liu] provides" (Lee, 1999).

With Liu and Carson as part of the ensemble cast, *Ally McBeal* sur-vived the NAACP's 1999 criticism of the national networks and their "white-washed" fall line-up. However, in 2001, Kelley introduced the third non-white actor to join the ensemble's increasingly shifting secondary cast, Taye Diggs. Diggs was, at that point, best known to mainstream moviego-ers as Angela Basset's love interest in *How Stella Got Her Groove Back.* There he played an irrepressible and desirable "colonial-other" who is a source of sexual and spiritual regeneration for an older, bourgeois African American woman. On *Ally McBeal* he assumed the role of Jackson Duper, an ambi-tious lawyer who has previously bedded Ling, and with whom Renee goes to bed with on the first date. From the beginning his sexuality, and its impact on those around him, is crucial in defining his personal interactions and the situations in which he finds himself, particularly as he lacks the defining quirks that the other male ensemble characters often exhibit (a fondness for "wattle," eccentric gadgets, an in-office dentist chair).[13] Rather, Jackson Duper's oddity is the sexual response he incites in those around him. Larry Paul (played by Robert Downey, Jr.) is openly hostile when confronted with Jackson's well-muscled physique and the pride with which he carries him-self:

JACKSON: Is there a problem, Larry?

LARRY: No, I just like to pull torso flexes at night, Jackson.

JACKSON: Oh do you?

LARRY: Yes, I do.

JACKSON: Are you making fun of me, Larry?

LARRY: No, the truth is I've been trying to work on my posture and I'm admiring yours. If I could just learn to walk like that.

Larry's response reveals a combination of envy coated with disdain. His remark about Jackson's self-confident and self-possessed walk invokes John Cage's admiration of Barry White's stature, while simultaneously refusing to recognize his own envy and desire, manifested as disdain. Finally, there is an uncomfortable edge in Larry's closing remark alluding to the self-confident and "natural" movement associated with young African American men.[14] Larry's hostility suggests that Jackson is out of place or that, at the very least, his style is out of place in a corporate environment. Nor is the girlfriend of Larry Paul, Ally McBeal, completely comfortable with the firm's new hire, though she often expresses animosity to new recruits. However, her behavior, like Larry's, expresses both desire and suppression of that desire. In a notable hallucination she mistakes tall, African American Jackson, for shorter, white Larry and kisses him passionately. Her excuse — that she thought he was someone else — does not ring true for the recipient of her kisses who is most definitely not interested. Jackson's relationship with her roommate, Renee, means that Ally has more opportunities to "accidentally" sexually engage with him. When Ally wakes up in the middle of the night and finds the remote control for the television missing, she decides to search in the tangle of sheets in Renee's bed, where Renee and Jackson are sleeping. Groping under the covers for the remote, Ally in fact gropes Jackson, as their following public exchange details:

JACKSON: First you're kissing me.

ALLY: I thought you were him.

JACKSON: Then you climb into bed.

ALLY: I thought you were her.

JACKSON: And your hands were all up on my privates.

ALLY: Well, because I thought it was the remote control.

LARRY: Hold on.

JACKSON: Felt like the remote, did it?

ALLY: Yes, it did feel like the remote control, hard, plastic.

RENEE: Excuse me?

JACKSON: Oh, please, don't flatter yourself.

LARRY: Excuse me too. You had your hand on his....

JACKSON: Remote.

RENEE: Hard plastic?

JACKSON: Men have it when they're sleeping.

LARRY: Remotes?

JACKSON: No, erections, and it had nothing to do with her thin little hand.

ALLY: Oh, well isn't that the remote calling the wrist skinny.

JACKSON: What?

While *Ally McBeal*'s resident chauvinist, Richard Fish (played by Greg Germann), frequently refers to his "dumb-stick" (his euphemism intended to explain how men's sexual urges rule them), it is notable that it is the highly sexualized character Jackson Duper whose erect phallus is groped, imagined, and described for the viewer as a source of humor. Unlike the other male characters, Duper is frequently featured less than fully clothed, something with which Diggs was rumored to be dissatisfied, and may have eventually influenced his leaving the show.[15] The sexualization of Jackson Duper through costuming — or rather lack thereof — and the response of female characters (discussed more fully below) is completed in this comparison of his erect penis to a television remote control: Ally describes it as hard and plastic; remotes are also generally black, and always "on." What happens in this scene is a verbal complement to Robert Mapplethorpe's (in)famous photo *Man in a Polyester Suit* (1980)[16]: it answers the unasked question which is nevertheless foregrounded (through the process of ongoing sexualization); the black phallus aggressively enters the public domain as a source of conversation; and this public revealing exposes the individual both literally and metaphorically. That Jackson is also the character whose private parts get the most sexual action from the female characters featured on the show indicates the degree to which his undeniably racialized sexuality is a key component of his characterization.

Ling, Renee, and Ally may have first-hand private knowledge of Jackson, but it is Elaine Vassal (played by Jane Krakowski) who exhibits the most blatant physical desire for the firm's new lawyer. She is, most literally, the racialized gaze fixed upon Jackson Duper, reducing him to his body and in turn reduced to her desire. While a metaphorical (and cartoon animated) tongue may roll when Ally spots a handsome man (or her male co-workers become fixated on an office delivery woman), Elaine's response exudes actual physicality: she sweats profusely from every pore when confronted with Jackson. Yet the desire she exhibits is not only *not* innocent, but the attribution of that desire to her by the writers is also of interest. Elaine, as the only non-lawyer in the ensemble cast, is the lower-class female other. She exhibits the stereotypical markers imagined as the property of lower-class women: Elaine's cologne is too strong, her hair flips too obvious, her clothes are too revealing ("moderately slutty" she states); she describes herself as constantly "in heat," and she is a believer in infomercials. That her last name is a synonym for "servant" further reifies her position in relation to the other characters. In their introduction to *White Trash*, Matt Wray and Annalee Newitz write about the "racing" of lower-class whites as a race apart from their more financially well-off counterparts. Like the process of displacement that occurs with sexuality and African Americans, lower-class whites are also cited as repositories of undesirable physical and carnal behaviors that more privileged whites do not wish to own. Sweating is among them, as it violates polite norms. Elaine's sweating when confronted with Jackson is so profuse as to leave her drenched. It is as if the longing of the other female onlookers, those of a higher class status, has been displaced onto Elaine, their metaphorical sweat literally expunged through her body as actual moisture. Humorous and disturbing, this soaking body registers the writers' understanding of the sexuality of both Jackson and Elaine.

Given the factors cited above — the association of African Americans and lower-class whites with sexuality, the reliance upon these associations as a source of humor, the ways in which African American musical traditions resonate, the setting of Boston — it is of significant interest that blackness, and race in general, are not ever subjects of discussion on *Ally McBeal*. It is particularly noticeable because race is one of the few forms of difference and discrimination *not* addressed in any episode. We view episodes of gender discrimination frequently, that being the premise upon which Ally left her previous job to work at Cage & Fish. But racial discrimination is absent. In *Ally McBeal* discrimination is something that most often happens to white or nearly white people, whether on the grounds of gender, sexuality, beauty, weight, mental health, class, or hipness. We watch episodes that demonstrate the prejudice against older women dating younger men ("I Want Love"); the overweight ("The Promise"); transvestites ("The Oddball Parade"); transgendered people ("Girls' Night Out"); bisexuals ("Pursuit of Loneliness," though Ally is unable to overcome her prejudice); prostitutes ("Boy to the World"); the mentally ill ("Mr. Bo"); religious difference ("It's My Party"); and people with Tourette's Syndrome ("Reason to Believe"). There is even an episode where a waiter fired for being straight sues for wrongful termination on the grounds of discrimination ("The Inmates"). Many of these themes are treated more than once in the series. With the exception of Ally's inability to overcome her prejudice against dating bisexual men (though she has no problems with the possibility of bisexual women, as she flirts with it herself in kissing Ling, Georgia, and Elaine), each of the other prejudices is represented as groundless, and the humanist discourse of the show moves beyond simply preaching tolerance to urge understanding, acceptance, and often, empathy. The underlying message of *Ally McBeal* appears to be that despite our differences we are all people, a humanism of the heart that, while well-intentioned, does serve to undermine the specificities and complexities of various forms of oppression.

Given this discourse of liberal humanism, where all of the differences cited above can be addressed and resolved via an extension of the "heart," it is all the more remarkable that race does not signal similar possibilities, whether for rupture, bridging, or — most relevant — reflection. Instead, any inference of racial difference is displaced onto subjects that are more manageable in an American context. Richard Fish, a staunch supporter of patriarchy, has a recently deceased uncle who is introduced as a bigot. While the immediate conclusion might be that his uncle is racist, it is revealed that his uncle in fact hated short people. After concluding his uncle's eulogy, Richard leaves the stage to the choir who break into Randy Newman's "Short People" which includes a list of the shortcomings of those Richard Fish refers to as the "vertically challenged." A humorous and uplifting moment for those witnessing the funeral, as well as those watching the show, it is impossible not to consider whether or not a parallel situation would have been constructed if, indeed, his uncle had hated African Americans, Latinas or Latinos, Jews, Asians, South Asians, or First Nations people. While not all discussions of difference are fodder for humor — though a fair number are the subject of office jokes — the reality is that race, one of the most fundamental markers of difference and sites of contestation defining the United States, is possibly still too hot a topic. Alternately, it is also possible that it is considered too overdone, though given the multitude of racial and ethnic groupings still underrepresented in television that seems impossible. Instead, race is sublimated into other discussions of difference, always a present but never addressed signifier in the humanist discourse of *Ally McBeal.*

In an odd twist, the closest the series ever comes to addressing race is through the interracial relationship of Dr. Greg Butters (played by Jesse L. Martin) and Ally, a relationship where race is never mentioned or apparently considered — the ultimate marker of liberalism, of course, being the ability to not "see" or consider race. In the episode "Happy Birthday Baby" Greg takes the stage at the downstairs bar after work to serenade Ally on her birthday. Renee is so moved by the quality of his voice that she spontaneously joins him onstage in a steamy Motown-styled duet. It is one of the rare moments in the show where you see African American characters genuinely enjoying — reveling in, even — each other's company. This disturbs Ally to the point where she leaves the bar during the song, convinced that the two are interested in each other. That this vision of black pleasure disrupts Ally to the point where she considers ending her relationship with Greg suggests that the character and the writers are able to recognize the possibility of racial difference as a potential topic needing to be addressed, even if they are unable to articulate it in any meaningful way.[17] Ally has very little to fear in the way of betrayal from her best friend and her boyfriend, which suggests that her insecurity is rooted elsewhere. And while the character possesses numerous insecurities, her faith in her best friend remains constant throughout the show with this exception, suggesting that it is precisely the issue they are not discussing — the dynamics of interracial relations — that is the real source of her palatable anxiety.

Whether the end result of evacuating race from a show in which tropes of blackness are so prevalent is intentional or not is ultimately irrelevant. What is relevant is the way that blackness continues to resonate throughout *Ally McBeal* in ways that reflect its influence and construction in the shaping of popular culture. Historically, television shows that have been stylistically innovative have offered significant potential for addressing or even representing historical ruptures or differences. *Northern Exposure* used its own version of magical realism to represent alternative world views, and to create a space where a multi-ethnic community might collide, but could also collectively progress. Likewise, for a brief moment in 1998, *Maximum Bob,* a short-lived network show (based on an Elmore Leonard novel), also offered possibilities for addressing racial tension and histories in the American South through the use of tropes of story-telling and the fantastic. So it would follow that *Ally McBeal,* a show in part about struggling with the definition of self and the ethical relation of that self to others, would offer the same opportunities to, and considerations of, its African American characters. What the show in fact demonstrates is the failure of these ethical relations and the ability to ever really "see" the racial other. Instead, the white characters continue to understand non-whites in ways that support the way in which they understand the world in order to maintain their own identities. When, in season five, John Cage takes a hiatus from practicing law to retreat to Mexico and "find himself," it is notable that where he ends up is not in Mexico at all, but as a mariachi player in a Boston restaurant that represents the white fantasy of Mexico. Garbed in a Disneyland version of a Mexican costume, Cage admits that for him, the real Mexico could not compete with his fantasy of it, and so he returns to Boston to engage with the ahistorical, romanticized fantasy version ("Love Is All Around," part 1). Just as John cannot engage with the reality of Mexico and therefore dismisses it, *Ally McBeal* understands race as unimportant in human relations. People are, as the discourse of the show stresses, individuals first and foremost to be judged on individual merits. Historically where this logic fails is in the limited extension of individuality. The individual has the potential to step outside of the group, but it is only in that act of stepping out that the individual comes into existence. This is in contrast to what it might mean to recognize the group itself as composed of individuals. It smacks of the pseudo-liberal assertion that "I don't think of you as *x*" (*x* being the qualifier that identifies one as outside of the norm). It is precisely that act of *not thinking*, of seeing the other only as she or he intersects with or reflects the self, that lets the greater patterns of race and its uses remain unacknowledged. In the world of mainstream television fiction this reflection of the (white) self is evident in the lack of representations of non-white supporting cast members with friends of their own racial group. Furthermore, in recent years, as mainstream shows featuring protagonists in their thirties frequently introduce famous senior actors in guest-starring roles as their parents, it is notable that non-white characters are consistently the least likely to be the focus of this kind of episode. This is consistent in *Ally McBeal*, as Ally, Richard, Nelle, and Jenny (Julianne Nicholson) all have one or more parents appear. The creation of external and extended family units for white characters and not for non-white characters makes it easier to "not think of" Renee and Jackson as African American, or Ling as Asian American,[18] and to avoid placing them within an "explicit" (as opposed to implicit) racial context. Whether this constitutes an elision, or rather a lack of character development, the end result is to reinscribe whiteness as normative and prevailing. It is also this evasion of race that manages to mark the world of *Ally McBeal* and its inhabitants as colorblind, a goal often represented by liberals as desirable (akin to "I don't think of you as..."). How valuable is being colorblind, however, in a world where racial inequities still define, to a certain extent, key social attitudes and realities? Unless being colorblind is to sustain the fiction of white liberalism and the creation of an independent self, which is, in part, the project of *Ally McBeal* as the title character struggles towards self-definition. Kelley relies on the audience's faith in her as a fundamentally good, albeit occasionally misguided or annoying, person as she negotiates her individual relations with others based on their differences, similarities, and congruities. And it is because of this inherent fundamental goodness that she is ultimately able to overcome any ignorances, prejudices, or biases she might initially possess. So perhaps, then, it is appropriate that race is the most notable division never addressed in this series. After all, if anything in the US has continued to undermine the liberal fantasy of the individual liberated from prejudice by the power of the heart, it has been the ongoing challenges posed to that vision by non-white peoples who insist on asserting their ongoing experiences of the realities of race.

Notes

1. Morrison writes: "I use [Africanist] as a term for the denotative and connotative blackness that African peoples have come to signify, as well as the entire range of views, assumptions, readings, and misreadings that accompany Eurocentric learning about these people" (6–7).

2. *c.f.* Deborah White, *Ar'n't I a Woman?: Female Slaves in the Plantation South.*

3. Eldridge Cleaver, *Soul on Ice* (New York: McGraw Hill, 1968).

4. These are simply reported numbers. No doubt there were significant numbers of unreported lynchings as well.

5. James Baldwin's short story "Going to Meet the Man" is a powerful rendering of how this power works. Likewise, David Marriot's reading of Baldwin's story provides a more extensive analysis of how these encounters I cite function within the spectacle and psychology of lynching (Marriot, 15–19).

6. In a popular 1990s video series, the musician Robert Palmer was backed by a number of white female models with identical hair, make-up, and clothing. The women managed to move to Palmer's songs in a manner that was both robotic and sensual. The most famous of these videos was "Addicted to Love," from the 1992 album of the same name (Island Records).

7. See *Black Looks,* particularly hooks's essay "Madonna" (157–164). For a historical analysis of how this process has occurred historically, see Sander Gilman "Black Bodies, White Bodies: Toward an Iconography of Female Sexuality in Late Nineteenth-Century Art, Medicine, and Literature."

8. McBeal's middle-class whiteness is likewise a crucial unacknowledged subtext in the discussions of bourgeois feminism and the program. See Mosely and Read.

9. The composition of this group shifts occasionally. Performers include: Sy Smith, Vatrena King, Renee Goldsberry, Cynthia Calhoun, and Melanie Taylor. There appears to be no actual relation between their members and Ike Turner, who has since been eclipsed by his more famous ex-wife, Tina, whose print and filmic biography has forever marked Ike Turner as physically and sexually abusive.

10. This is so pervasive as to be unremarkable. Popular mainstream acts like Madonna, Michael Bolton, John Cougar Mellencamp, and the Eurythmics are just a few who have engaged in this practice. Sandra Bernhard's 1990 film *Without You I'm Nothing* is an interesting reworking of this scenario (directed by John Boscovich).

11. *Friends,* 1994–2004, creator, David Crane.

12. Including articles in *The New York Times* (Dec. 24, 2000), *The Village Voice* (December 1–9, 1999), and *The Seattle Weekly* (August 24–30, 2000), and others.

13. In the universe of *Ally McBeal,* "wattle" is a term for the skin on the neck between a woman's chin and collarbone that becomes less firm as she ages.

14. Even as this itself can be an example of physical performativity. See E. Patrick Johnson (7–47).

15. I would like to thank Elwood Watson for directing me to a source for this: http:/www.eon-line.com/Gossip/Awful/Archive2001/010607.html.

16. *Man in a Polyester Suit* (1980) is a photograph of a suited man cropped to reveal only his torso. From his undone fly protrudes a large, black penis. I identify the penis as black rather than the man, because a) this is the only indication of race, and b) the photo is set up to work in this way. In this instance, the man is literally embodied by the penis.

17. I am aware that I am assuming here that the majority of, if not all, the writers on the program are white. David E. Kelley certainly is, as is, I believe, the co-author of this episode, Thomas Schlamme. According to the NAACP "a recent survey showed that among the 839 writers currently employed on prime-time television shows, only 55 are African American, 11 are Latino, and three are Asian American. None are Native American" (Nov. 3, 1999).

18. While Ling Woo's sister, Leigh (Lydia Look), does appear in an episode it is notable that she is present more as a prop (both physically and in terms of the narrative) than a character. Like the man in Mapplethorpe's photo, Leigh is reduced to her breasts, or in this case, her breast implants.

Works Cited

Baldwin, James. *Going to Meet the Man.* London: Michael Joseph, 1965.

Cleaver, Eldridge. *Soul on Ice.* New York: McGraw-Hill, 1968.

Gilman, Sander. "Black Bodies, White Bodies: Toward an Iconography of Female Sexuality in Late Nineteenth-Century Art, Medicine, and Literature." *Critical Inquiry* 12, 1985. 204–242.

Gray, Herman. *Watching Race: Television and the Struggle for "Blackness."* Minneapolis: University of Minnesota Press, 1995.

Hall, Stuart. "What Is This 'Black' in Black Popular Culture?" *Black Popular Culture.* Edited by Gina Dent. Seattle: Bay Press, 1992. 21–33.

Hemphill, Essex. *Ceremonies: Prose and Poetry.* New York: Plume, 1992.

hooks, bell. *Black Looks: Race and Representation.* Cambridge, MA: South End Press,1992.

Johnson, E. Patrick. *Appropriating Blackness: Performance and the Politics of Authenticity.* Durham: Duke University Press, 2003.

Kang, Laura Hyun Yi. *Compositional Subjects: Enfiguring Asian/American Women.* Durham, NC: Duke University Press, 2002.

Lee, Chisun. "The Ling Thing." *The Village Voice,* December 1–7, 1999.

Marriot, David. *On Black Men.* New York: Columbia University Press, 2000.

Morrison, Toni. *Playing in the Dark: Whiteness and the Literary Imagination.* New York: Vintage, 1993.

Moseley, Rachel, and Jacinda Read. "'Having It *Ally*': Popular Television (Post-)Feminism. *Feminist Media Studies* 2.2, 2002. 231–249.

"NAACP Announces Hearings on TV Diversity: Possible Boycott and Demonstrations." National Association for the Advancement of Colored People (NAACP) Press Release, November 3, 1999.

"NAACP Blasts TV Networks' Fall Season Whitewash." National Association for the Advancement of Colored People (NAACP) Press Release, July 12, 1999.

White, Deborah. *Ar'n't I a Woman?: Female Slaves in the Plantation South.* New York: Norton, 1999.

Wray, Matt, and Annalee Newitz, eds. *White Trash: Race and Class in America.* New York: Routledge, 1997.

9

The Angler, Fish, and Fishisms: Universal Themes and Contemporary Issues in a Popular Television Series

Twyla Gibson

One of the challenges in understanding the popularity of a television series involves recognizing how it represents both universal themes and contemporary issues in a way that strikes an emotional chord with viewers and captures the public imagination. When David E. Kelley's situation comedy *Ally McBeal* premiered on Fox television on September 15, 1997, it garnered widespread attention and high ratings for its portrayal of the trials of public and private life. Shows pivoted around a major trial handled by the Boston law firm Cage & Fish. Scenes of the public trial were juxtaposed with scenes of the personal and private travails of the characters associated with the firm. As the hour progressed, it became clear that there were a number of resonances between the legal and personal cases. When the final show aired on May 20, 2002, over 10 million viewers watched the series finale.[1] These numbers testify to the broad appeal of the show and to the impact this comedy had on North American audiences. What attracted viewers to *Ally McBeal?* How did the show achieve its emotional effects?

In this inquiry, I look at the way *Ally McBeal* represented both timeless themes and current issues. I focus, in particular, on the character Richard Fish (Greg Germann) as a classic case of the angler, as the voice of the oral tradition in popular culture, as the fictional embodiment of thoughts and feelings that lurk below the surface, and as a characterization of masculine bewilderment in the face of changing sex and gender roles in North American society.

The approach combines philosophical techniques with current research on sex and gender issues—both in the workplace and at home. I use the classical categories of philosophical analysis to classify Fish as the angler in the system of definitions set out in Plato's *Sophist.* I use these sequences of ideas to show how Fish fits into the definition of the fisherman — an acquisitive lawyer who uses either the force of his position or the power of persuasion to lure clients into the firm. I bring these associations together with research on contemporary sex and gender issues to analyze the role Fish played in the emotional dynamics of the series.

To set the stage, I begin with the philosophical definitions set forth in Plato's *Sophist.* In this classic play, the actor in the leading role, called the Stranger, guides the other characters in the dialogue as they search through a number of sequences of classifications that make up the different strands of the complex definition of art (*techne,* craft, skill technique, expertise, profession). The search involves successive attempts to distinguish the statesman and genuine philosopher from crass imitators—known as the Sophists. The point of the investigation is to discover criteria for differentiating the authentic person from those with only a pretense to authenticity. Aristotle, in the *Metaphysics* (987b), refers to these classifications as the "universal definitions"—for they address timeless types, themes, and ideas that translate across languages, cultures, and traditions. Since the universals are unchanging categories, this ancient method may be brought forward to our own time. Since Plato's definitions relate to statesmen, legislators, lawyers, and orators in Greek culture, this makes the classifications relevant to an analysis of attorney Richard Fish. Finally, since Sophists were notorious for the high fees they charged and for the money, gifts, and other favors they demanded for their professional services, this makes the classic definitions even more apropos to our examination of Fish.

Before embarking on the investigation however, a brief description of Plato's procedure for applying the definitions is in order. The platonic classifications were divided into sequences of opposite topics arranged hierarchically, moving from general to specific. Each stage in the sequence was separated into two major parallel groupings, one for visible images and things and another for abstract and intelligible ideas. In this system, visible things and abstract ideas had the same name, and they were matched in a one-to-one correspondence based on principles of analogy, polarity, and symmetry. The procedure for searching through the definitions entailed first distinguishing a unified class, then dividing it in two polar topics. However, since each of the resulting two classes contained both a visible thing and an abstract idea, which both had the same name, each division actually generated twin sets of twins. So in all cases, a division of a unified class produced two contrary classifications, each of which was divided into a pair (*Sophist,* 266d). After each division, one pair was identified and then set aside, and the procedure concentrated on the other twin, subdividing it further in the same manner. Though it sounds complicated in theory, it is not hard to understand in practice.

The Universal Theme: Definition of the Angler

Let us choose as the starting point Richard Fish's last name. The name, Fish, links this character to a whole range of ideas surrounding fish, water, and fishing — and to the universal theme of the "angler." Fish and fishermen are associative clusters, complex notions around which a large number of meanings have gathered over time. They have a universal quality because they have meant similar things to so many people throughout history, and this constancy, familiarity, and repetition makes meanings communicable across a range of media, languages, and cultures. It is the "quality of repetition that is essential to the universal in all of its contexts."[2] So beginning with Fish's family name, we turn to the first and simplest definition in the classifications presented in Plato's *Sophist,* that of the angler. According to the Stranger, the angler is familiar to all of us" (*Sophist,* 218e).

In a conversation with John Cage (Peter MacNicol) in the premiere episode of the television series, Fish points out that he is the "shark" in the Cage & Fish partnership.[3] Fish consistently uses fish and water metaphors to describe himself, his ethics, and the depths of his emotional life. Here, in describing his professional role, he presents himself as a predatory sort of fish, a shark. In depicting his emotional life in a later episode, he draws an analogy to a different kind of fish. Referring to his capacity for feelings and relationships, Fish says to Ling (Lucy Liu): "We're emotional guppies, eventually we'll always reunite at the shallow end of the pool" ("The Obstacle Course"). That he presents himself as a person with little emotional depth is confirmed in the following typical comment, "If I had feelings, that remark would hurt" ("In Dreams"). In our own language, just as in Plato's system, there is a sensible and tangible sort of shark that stalks the ocean and a corresponding type of fish in the realm of ideas. As an idea, the term "shark" is associated with rapacious and crafty types who prey upon others through usury, trickery, or some other devious means. Similarly, the guppy that inhabits the shallows has the same name as the guppy on the ideational level, where the emotional guppy brings to mind an immature type with little capacity for relationships involving deep feelings.

The comparison between the depth of the water and the depths of

Fish's emotions is also made apparent in a number of episodes. Consider a conversation in the show appropriately titled "Troubled Water." When Fish's girlfriend, Judge "Whipper" Cohn (Dyan Cannon), makes emotional demands on him, he tells her he prefers to "swim in the shallow end," noting that marriage — i.e., the deeper relationship — looks like too much work.

Recurring references to water often describe the size of the body (pools, seas), the quality of the liquid (dirty, murky, troubled), or to the levels (shallow, deep). The following is a typical instance:

> That was the dirtiest pool to its deepest depth, and you did it looking like you took the high road ["They Eat Horses, Don't They?"].

Fish, water, depths, drowning, swimming: These are themes that bear meanings that have persisted from Plato to our own time. Fish are creatures of the depths, representations of emotion rather than the intellect, and of that which is not conscious rather than that which is readily apparent to consciousness. Water, too, is a universal symbol for emotions; one thinks of a sea of emotions or drowning in emotion. Just as fish are contents of the visible oceans, so fish symbolize the contents of feelings and emotions in the realm of ideas. At the level of abstract ideas, we mentally separate and remove associations with particular examples, and concentrate on the general characteristics that all particular instances have in common. The professional shark as an aggressive and unscrupulous legal professional is an abstract representation of common attributes belonging to a more general pattern. Similarly, the shallow, emotional guppy is an abstraction of standard features belonging to a different sort of type. Representing human emotional contents as creatures points to an animal nature (especially to the sexual instincts), and to natural human feelings that are in tension with cultured and civilized inclinations reflecting laws, moral codes, and socialized human behavior.[4] That Richard Fish represents the "animal in the human" is confirmed by his alternative description of himself (in the series pilot) as the "ass." The ass, like the fish, is an animal that conveys meaning on two different levels simultaneously. The visible ass is a sort of donkey (*equus asinus*), a beast known for its contrary and stubborn nature. As an idea, the ass represents the obstinate or perverse sort of person who is always "horsing around." Our *Ally McBeal* character is a "smart ass," a professional "shark" (a predator), as well as an "emotional guppy" (a content of the shallows). He combines all the attributes associated with guppies, sharks and asses into one very slippery stereotype.

At the same time, Fish not only describes himself as the fish, he makes reference to the other end of the pole. He is both Fish and fisherman. At Cage & Fish, his main job is to administer the affairs of the firm. He lands new clients and keeps their business. He is responsible for hiring new associates. When it comes to the personal affairs and emotional lives of his colleagues, he plays the part of fisherman as well. Consider his advice to John Cage: He suggests that Cage use a beautiful woman "as *bait* to attract other beautiful women" ["Two's a Crowd"].

The fisherman, too, is a recurring type that appears in many different tales, stories, parables, and legends. Like fish, the fisherman works on more than one level at once. Fishermen are common figures in fairy tales, where they often illustrate that bringing the fish up to the surface is as difficult as catching it. In Ernest Hemingway's tale *The Old Man and the Sea*,[2] the main character was a fisherman. So was Captain Ahab, who went in search of the great white whale in Herman Melville's *Moby Dick*. Fishing, in these stories, suggests casting a line into the depths in order to bring contents to light. Similarly, Jesus of Nazareth was a "fisher of men" in the seas of Galilee, and the fisherman is a key figure in the legends of the Holy Grail.[5]

The alternative term for fishing is "angling." Ideas associated with angling add further dimensions of meaning to the Fish character. Angling denotes both the sport of fishing at the visible, tangible level and the pursuit of calculated means to attain an objective at the level of ideas. In terms of the sport, Richard Fish is certainly a "player," and he uses all manner of means to achieve his ends. The angler's rod and line corner space at an angle, forming a figure, and an "angle" is also a name for the barbed hook at the end of the line. In terms of ideas, the angle is the viewpoint, an approach, or a technique for accomplishing an objective — a "figuring out." Thus, Fish represents emotional contents from a certain point of view. Fish is a man with all the "angles," and his "Fishisms" can be described as "barbed" comments. As both fish and angler, our character is a kind of anglerfish (*lophlus piscatorius*), a creature with an appendage atop its head (*illicium*, Latin for "lure" or "inducement") that swings forward in front of its mouth to attract and trap prey. Anglerfish mating habits are out of the ordinary. The male angler bites through the skin of the female and the two circulatory systems join. From the moment of attachment, the male is completely dependent on the female for nourishment and protection. Fish, angler, anglerfish ... Richard Fish in the television series is more than just the actor, Greg Germann, playing the character we see on the screen. Fish stands for all the ideas that have become attached to fish, fishing, and fisherman over a long-term history of repeated usages, practices, and conventions.

Let us continue with the next stage of the classification. The Stranger asks, "Does the angler possess an art?" Does he have a "craft, technique, skill, expertise, profession or some other method that involves systematic rules? (*Sophist*, 219a-b). Fish is an attorney, but as to whether he has the art, skill, and expertise requisite to the legal profession, the jury remains out; it is not entirely clear whether Fish is fully in possession of the rules of his art. Hence we set aside this unity and proceed further with the investigation. All art, according to the Stranger, is divided into two kinds, production and acquisition. With respect to production, we are told that the thing that is brought into existence is "produced." The person who brings into existence something that did not exist before is called a "producer." These things are said to be characterized by the "power of producing." The question concerning Fish is whether he is "a man having art or not having art, but some other power?" (*Sophist*, 219a-b). Fish produces associates, clients, and money for the firm. Does he have genuine power? In the fourth season episode "Hats Off to Larry," Fish presides at the quasi-wedding of Cindy and her fiancée. He proclaims:

> Then by the powers of me, Richard Fish, rich attorney with his own firm ... I pronounce you husband and wife.

Fish's power is not vested in him by divine dispensation, even though God is still a presence. Rather, Fish relies on his own human power (at least in this instance). At the same time, our character presides at the ceremony because he has been granted this power by the wedding party at least. So his power comes from two sources, both human. Among the classifications assigned to human production, one series of the definition concerns the art of representation (*mimesis*, imitation, copy, or counterfeit). As a character in a television production, Richard Fish is a fictional "re-presentation" of an attorney that "imitates" a real-life lawyer, by way of a "copy" and a "counterfeit" that does not correspond to *any* living person. Further still, there is much that is imitative in Fish's presentation of himself even within the context of the series itself. He has established that the "shark, hammer, and ass" is a pre-agreed role that he plays for professional purposes rather than who he really is. He once stated, "You're not who you are, you're only what other people think of you. Fishism" ("In Dreams"). So even within the fictional world framed by the television screen, Fish is imitating a stereotype when he carries out his role as law partner. At another level, the actor is performing in the role of Fish. At higher levels still, Fish represents a whole range of ideas and cultural associations. So the Fish character has power on a number of different levels simultaneously.

We pause at this juncture to observe that the principles governing both the character types and the action in dramatic comedy have remained remarkably consistent over time. Television comedy production draws on the same principles that Aristophanes employed over 2,500 years ago, and viewing audiences still laugh at jokes that were considered old at the opening of *The Frogs.* Greek comedy, as both form and formula, is the basis for comedy down to our own day, and *Ally McBeal* is no exception. According to this age-old formula, the movement of comedy is from one kind of society to another. In the typical comic construction, a man is not able to come together with a woman because his desire is blocked by some opposition (usually paternal), that keeps his from participating fully in society. Near the end, some change occurs that allows the hero to come together with the woman and live happily ever after. The obstacle to the man's desire forms the action of comedy, and surmounting the barrier forms the comic resolution. Since the obstacles are usually paternal, comedy typically turns on a conflict between a son and a father. The change that lifts the obstacle and makes it possible for the man to have the woman causes a new society to take shape around him. The appearance of this new society is frequently marked by a party or festive ritual, typically a wedding, which serves as the culmination of the story.

The action of comedy in moving from one social center to another is not unlike the action of a lawsuit, in which plaintiff and defendant construct different versions of the same story, one finally being judged as real and the other as illusory. This resemblance between the structure of comedy and the structure of the court case has been recognized from ancient times.[6] In *Ally McBeal,* the contrast between the legal and private trials takes its cue from this classic formula. True to type, the public trial represents sexuality as it is policed formally by adjudication in the law courts. The private trials represent the way sexual relations are conducted informally by individuals. The juxtaposition between the legal and personal cases serves a key function. Parallelism allows the audience to imagine the dissonance between sexual relations as publicly sanctioned and officially enforced, and the practical negotiation of them in private. By dramatizing and offsetting the constraints on sexual desire implicated in the public realm and in the private sphere, *Ally McBeal* "produced" an imaginary framework for working through and coming to terms with laws, morals, and cultural norms.

Having identified the productive class, we follow the procedure, bracket production, set it aside, and move to the right side of our pairs. That is, we continue to follow the main lines of the angler definition as it concentrates on acquisition. Acquisition is divided into exchange and conquest (*Sophist,* 219b-c). Accordingly, we first focus attention on exchange. How does exchange figure in to Richard Fish's character? According to his partner, John Cage, Fish has money making and sex at his very core. Money and sex are in fact two universal forms of exchange. Of the two, Fish makes clear that money is his first priority, "Lasting happiness only comes with money. Fishism. For temporary well-being: Viagra" ("Seeing Green"). This example shows Fish conflating money and sex, so that financial assets are construed as aids to potency and power. Our fisherman sees money as a lure, indeed as bait in the competitive sexual marketplace. When he worries that Ling may prefer another man to him, he comments:

> I just hope at the end of the day, she looks at him, looks at me, and realizes I have more money ["The Getaway"].

In fact, these statements show that Fish sees relationships, even marriage, as a sort of monetary transaction. Perhaps this explains why Fish is insatiable when it comes to money making: "The good news is the firm is making money; the bad news is I can never get enough...." In his attitudes to public and private sorts of exchange, Fish embodies a viewpoint that seems quite reprehensible.

Money is in fact the major reason why Fish wanted to start the practice with John Cage. Though he may sometimes pursue his profession for other reasons, he emphasizes, "What does it all come down to? Say it with me, John: money" ("The Last Virgin"). He takes money to heart, so that when someone warns him that "they don't want to make this personal," he cries, "It's about money! It's personal!" ("Hope and Glory"). His avaricious nature is established in the pilot, when he asserts, "Make enough money, everything else will follow." As one might expect of a shark, money takes precedence over ethical and moral principles and over matters of character. Hour after hour over the course of five seasons, we learn that Fish stands for money.

In terms of the sex in the "money and sex" equation, Fish expresses definite ideas concerning sexual relations between men and women. With regard to right and wrong in the sexual arena: "Sex for men, when it's right, it's right, and when it's wrong, it's still right" ("Love Unlimited"). It is also noteworthy that Richard Fish's first name, too, is symbolic. Toward the end of the series, we meet his parents, and his mother reveals that his given name stands for the male "dumbstick," i.e., "Dick."

So Richard's name stands for the male member. We have already discerned that his last name is associated with the "animal in human nature." His given name brings additional dimensions of meaning to the notion of primitive emotional contents.

> NELLE: Just speak from that thing inside you ... the thing inside all men which makes a man a man.
>
> RICHARD: The dumbstick?
>
> NELLE: Exactly ["Just Looking"].

So "Richard" represents "the thing inside all men which makes a man a man." In other words, "Richard Fish," stands for the most basic and primitive male sexual feelings, products of instinct and nature (rather than reason and culture). When Richard Fish speaks, he gives voice to psychological impulses "inside all men" that are in conflict and tension with both official rules enforced through the law courts, and rules regulated by social customs.

Let us continue with the definition. Exchange is separated into a pair: giving and selling. Of the two, Fish would seem to be more focused on the selling rather than the giving. We have already noted that for Fish, sexual relations in the private sphere and earning power in the professional domain are tied together. In "Seeing Green," he demonstrates his feelings about this connection in a boardroom diatribe about the differences between the sexes as he sees them:

> RICHARD: Ultimately, a man will be ruled by his wants, just like women will be ruled by theirs. And what we want is sex, what they want is money.... What you all need to do is go home today and say, "Honey, give me back my penis" ["Seeing Green"].

Our character sums up his view of money as the basis of male allure and sex as the basis of female powers of attraction. Thus, in Fish's view, men must be primarily concerned with the acquisition of money because women are objects that must be purchased. In addition, he accuses his fellow males of being "whipped" and having "given away" their penises (i.e., their power). The expression "whipped" likely takes its impetus from a vulgar expression for men who are dominated by and dependent on the females to whom they are attached (very much like the male anglerfish). The occurrence of the expression "whipped," in the context of a plea for the return of the penis, confirms that the anatomical part that does the "whipping" in this conversation is the part of the female body that corresponds to the male "dumbstick."

Plato's Stranger goes on to inform us that the class related to selling is distinguished into the sort that markets their own productions and the kind that hawks the productions of others (223d). We would have to place Fish among the latter group. For in the public domain of the law firm, he most often sells the work of his colleagues rather than his own productions. To continue, selling is further subdivided into two kinds of merchandise: food for the body and food for the soul (223d). Those who deal in merchandise that nourishes the body deal with a more tangible and visible acquisition — such as money and sex. Those who deal in food for the soul offer a more subtle form of merchandise. And so we learn that goods of the soul are separated into a playful kind that is strictly for amusement or display, and a more serious kind that involves a trade in learning involving instruction and knowledge (224a–c). As a one-hour comedy-drama, *Ally McBeal* is clearly classed with the former, playful sort of goods. According to Aristotle, who developed Plato's definitions further, the difference between comedy (the playful kind that is strictly for amusement) and tragedy (the more serious kind) is that comedy represents people who are inferior to people in real life, whereas tragedy represents those who are superior (*Poetics*, 1448a1). Comic characters are either elevated or base, as it is "through vice and virtue that the characters of all men vary." Again, according to the age-old formula, audiences are more attracted to the bizarre and unusual that to mundane, ordinary people. Richard Fish is no mundane character; he is a rather extraordinary embodiment of the baser sort of character concerned with vice. His traits grossly exaggerate qualities and attitudes of the worst sort of stereotypes. So in terms of the divisions of the definition, we allocate Fish to the category of the comic rather than the tragic sort of salesman, merchandiser, and money-maker. And since money and sex are vices rather than virtues, his angling most often produces amusement rather than serious goods. In fact, Richard Fish rarely engages in serious reflection at all.

At the same time, exchanges of money and sex are not Fish's sole priorities. He is a stereotype but he is not a stock character. If Fish were merely base and despicable, viewing audiences would have no sympathy for him. Sympathy is rooted in the Greek word for emotions (*pathemata*). As the situation unfolds onscreen and our character confronts society, we sympathize with him, that is, we feel the same emotions. According to criteria developed by Aristotle, television is a medium of representation "employing the mode of enactment" to achieve its effects. It is through the enactment of strong emotions that catharsis is accomplished (Aristotle, *Poetics*, 1449b28). In another work (*Politics*, 8, 7, 1341b38), Aristotle elaborates on how representation provides a beneficial emotional outlet. He says that enactments provide a release and an amusement that relaxes and offers rest from tension. When viewers are exposed to enactments that "arouse the soul" in sympathy, they are "thrown into a state as if they had received medicinal treatment and taken a purge." Though the degree of cathartic benefit varies with each individual, all "undergo a purgation and a pleasant feeling of relief." The cathartic purgation provides harmless pleasure and relaxation. So if our fisherman were all bad, solely a representation of vice, we would not sympathize with him, feel the emotions he rouses, and experience the beneficial cathartic effects of his enactments.

How does Fish gain our sympathy? What are his virtues? One of the foregoing exchanges demonstrated that Fish stands for "fun." Playfulness, however, is not the only positive attribute he displays:

I wanted to make lots of money when we decided to create the firm, but I wanted to be surrounded by a little humanity ... to go with my money ["The Wedding"].

Fun? Friendship? Caring? Humanity? So there is more to Fish's nature than appears on the surface. This, too, is consistent with the Platonic system, where the surface only hints at what is going on at deeper levels.

We continue to divide acquisition. Leaving aside voluntary exchange involving giving or selling, we now shift attention to the class on the right hand side that entails more forceful and involuntary kinds of acquisition, that is, to conquest. Again, as we try to pry apart these classifications and slot Fish into one category or another, we find that he slips through the cracks. For Fish, sex is not just exchange. Sex entails conquest. Indeed, he implies that something is missing in sex without conquest.

In terms of the law partnership, Fish is also concerned with conquest. His goal is to win in order to collect the financial rewards for the firm — and more specifically, himself. There is, however, a subtlety here. Fish has it figured out so that everybody wins: "If we win, we're heroes, we pulled off a miracle. If we lose, the wacko goes to jail, justice is served. Win/win!" ("Happy Birthday Baby").

As Fish brings to light these thoughts and feelings, similar emotions come to the fore in viewers, and the audience experiences a purge of tension that provides a relief from conflict. When our predator says, "In every person's life there comes a time when you have to go forth and be vicious! ("Alone Again"), or when he says, "It's not just winning, it's winning ugly that matters." ("They Eat Horses, Don't They?") — viewers sympathize with him, feel these baser impulses that are undercurrents in human nature, and experience a cathartic release.

Sigmund Freud commented that "since the time of Aristotle, the purpose of drama is to arouse sympathy ... and so to purge the emotions." Freud pointed out that the "spectator is a person who experiences too little," who longs to "give way without a qualm to such suppressed impulses as a craving for freedom in religious, political, social and sexual matters, and to 'blow off steam.'" However, the viewer knows that the actual expression of these impulses in the real world would "threaten damage to his personal security." Watching a spectacle or a television program "does for adults what play does for children." By *identifying* with an actor, spectators experience an "enjoyment that is based on an illusion." Experiencing vicariously through "someone other than himself who is acting" mitigates against the threat of reprisals, which would "cancel out the enjoyment."[7] Freud maintained that we need to sympathize with an actor in order to be able to identify with him or her. So again, if Fish were an all-bad, one-dimensional character, he would not be able to work his emotional effects. So we find that when it comes to winning, Fish plays against type once again. Consider his eulogy at the funeral of his uncle:

> He said that if you're loved in the end, you win. [*choking*] He wins ["Boy to the World"].

This vignette demonstrates that Fish is not entirely a seller and a taker without the emotional capacity for giving, loving, and the expression of deep feelings.

We proceed with the divisions. Conquest is separated into fighting and hunting (219d). The court case is a sort of fight and a battle. Relations between the sexes are often described as a form of battle. Life is a kind of a battle. As it turns out, Richard Fish grew up in a battle, for his parents were perpetually fighting. He tried to avoid listening to his parents' fights by hiding out in his room. When viewers learn about his childhood, they begin to sympathize even more with his character. For how many members of the audience spent their childhoods trying to stay clear of fighting parents? In terms of the personal case, then, Fish was raised in a situation involving an acrimonious sort of exchange. With regard to the professional case, law involves a fight before a judge in a public trial. With respect to the comic formula, the action entails a fight to remove the obstacle that prevents the character from having the woman and shifting from the old to the new society. Freud pointed out that the social action of drama can "move on yet to another terrain, where it becomes *psychological* drama." In the psychological drama, the struggle "is fought out in the hero's mind itself — a struggle between different impulses." The structure of the psychological fight that is internal to the character is yet another level of action that works in tandem with the structure of the court case and the structure of comedy. The comic formula ends with the conquest of the new society over the old. The court case ends with the conquest of one side over another. The psychological drama "must have its end in the extinction, not of the hero, but of one of his impulses; it must end, that is to say, in a renunciation."[8]

We set aside fighting and move onward to hunting. Hunting, on the private level, entails a search for sexual partners, and acquisition by hunting is divided into a pair. One sort hunts for lifeless things, and the other seeks living animals (219e). Money is a lifeless thing. But the other sort of hunting that entails a search for a living animal is distinguished into land and water. When the Stranger gets to this division, he notes that the fisherman and the Sophist "part company." The Sophist goes to "land and water of another sort." The angler belongs to a different class than the Sophist, then.

As we continue with the definitions, we learn that land animals are divided into wild and tame creatures (including humans, 222b), whereas water is separated into fish and fowl. The land and water allocated to the Sophist concerns acquisition by conquest entailing a hunt through "rivers of wealth and broad meadowlands of generous youth," for the Sophist is "intending to take the animals which are in them" (222a). The land and water of the angler is of a different variety. Still, before we can place Richard Fish in a different class from the Sophist, we must examine the next set of divisions in the series. For the Stranger explains that water animals, or those that swim, are separated into winged (called fowling), and water (involved in fishing) (220a). Though our character has an interest in "rivers of wealth" and in "human animals," we find once again that he is not so easy to categorize. For Fish (our animal that swims in the shallows) has a most peculiar interest in fowl.

RICHARD: I like wattle.

MARK HENDERSON: Excuse me?

RICHARD: Neck wattle, the way it hangs. I finger it. If you like feet, you'll love wattle ["Happy Birthday, Baby"].

Wattle is a term for the loose skin on the neck of a bird, a caruncula that springs from the chin of the fowl. Loose neck skin, on the chin of a woman, is a sign that she is ... well ... no spring chicken. So Fish is attracted to older birds.

Indeed, for the first half of the television series at least, Fish expresses a clear preference for older women. Unlike the Sophist, he is not after youth. Fish's inclination to older women sets him apart from the Sophist, who appears to be a more sinister sort of character who preys upon the young with an intention to violate them. We have already confirmed that Fish pursues acquisition by the voluntary sort of exchange involved in selling. Let us now consider how he interacts with his quarry so that we may classify him as one who captures by luring or by more violent means.

When Fish goes fowling, he typically touches the bird under the chin and strokes the wattle. He attempts to perform this action in professional settings and in his personal life. For example, Janet Reno appears as herself in the series, and Fish immediately proceeds to touch her under her face. He is also aroused to playfulness and fun by the chin-skin women.

Fish attempts to win over his quarry by gently stroking them under the chin. What does this gesture represent? The division into wild and tame reminds us of the most common way to soothe and tame wild animals, or to subdue the wildness in tame animals, namely, by stroking them on the neck until they become docile and calm. This leads us to suspect that when Fish stroked a wattle, he was attempting to tame the wild animal in the woman's nature. Fish is an angler because his mode of conquest is by "force of persuasion"— wherein the fowl is a willing participant in a voluntary kind of exchange. By contrast, the Sophist pursues acquisition by violent kinds of force involving involuntary forms of acquisition and exchange.

Let us now consider the reasons underlying Fish's proclivity to fowls. Why does he try to placate and tame them? It is worth noting at this juncture that the nickname for Judge Cohn is "Whipper." We suspect then that Richard Fish may be one of those "whipped" males. Recall as well his statement concerning his parents' fights. Seeking to avoid such fights, he avoids forming a stable relationship with a woman. Fish chooses to be with women who are not his own age because age sets up a social barrier — a guardrail, as he calls it in "Silver Bells," that prevents a serious and deep attachment from forming. If a social barrier such as age were not present, he would probably manufacture some other obstacle. For Fish, by his own admission, is deeply afraid of relationships, of marriage, of ending up like his parents, in a constant fight, of being whipped. Fish's family background has further implications for our understanding of his character, for we learn that he grew up with a father who did not express his emotions, especially his feelings of love for his son.

> Men don't walk around saying "I love you" to other men. That's a gay thing. My father never had to say "I love you," he just said "Mambo Cat" ["The Getaway"].

So there are good reasons why our character is an "emotional guppy." His father never came out and told him that he loved him. Nor did his father share feelings—"stiff upper lip"— and so Fish equates "manliness" with suppression of feeling. Moreover, he is deeply anxious about his sexuality — he equates men who share feelings with homosexuals. In fact, his attitudes concerning men and feelings are so out of balance that even a conversation repudiating emotions seems to him "touchy-feely."

We learn more about Fish's relationship with his father in a subsequent episode where Fish reveals the meaning of his father's code words:

> "Mambo Cat...." My favorite pitcher for the Red Sox, Bill, uh ... "Mambo Cat." Also, to my father, it was a bonding thing. He didn't have to say, "I love you." He'd wink. He'd go, "Mambo Cat," and I got it. It was his way. I got it ["Boys' Town"].

Fish has trouble feeling deeply because he was rarely exposed to direct and profound expressions of feeling from his father. So the barrier and obstacle has a paternal origin. Fish has problems forming close attachments because he is afraid his relationships will turn out like the relationship his father had with his mother.

Let us continue with the next sequence of divisions. Fishing is partitioned further into a kind that captures the quarry with nets and another kind that takes them by striking. It is quite striking that Fish's partner is John "Cage"—a name representing an enclosure (220c). So we may anticipate that Fish's law partner provides the function "of baskets, nets, nooses, creels ... and other enclosures" (221c).

In accordance with the procedure, we set aside nets and continue on with the other side of the pair. We learn that striking includes barbing, which entails the use of barbed hooks that concentrate on the head and mouth, with the goal of drawing the captive upward from below. We have already noted that Fish's comments could be described as "barbed," and that one of his functions in the series is to bring underlying emotional contents up to the surface. A barbed comment both comes from and strikes the head and mouth and hooks the quarry, which is then "drawn from below upward with reeds and rods" (220e).

"Fishisms" appear to be just this sort of barbed line. Fishisms are wisecracks and aphorisms that presume to offer a sort of wisdom about the relations between men and women. "Quote me," Fish often says. Suppression of emotions leads to a build up of tension which erupts at unexpected moments, bringing unacknowledged emotional contents to light. A "wisecrack" parts the surface of consciousness, providing an opening for the expression and enactment of submerged impulses. Fishisms string a line that communicates complex cultural meanings in condensed form. Wisecracks, as comic devices, were as prevalent in the classical period as they are today. Fish's trademark "Fishisms" bring up base or politically incorrect male views, e.g., "always hire ugly secretaries"— and give voice to bruised feelings or unacceptable thoughts which are then quickly withdrawn. In "Bygones," the last episode of the series, we learn that Fishisms are a family inheritance passed down to our fisherman from his father (Senior Fishism: "love without sex is an empty experience"), indicating that these quips belong to a family legacy and tradition of such sayings. As the shark, the ass, the emotional guppy, and the dumbstick, Fish is the voice of a whole range of traditional views that he inherited from his paternal line.

So much for the barbed lines. We have yet to consider the rod and reel. Having separated land animals into wild and tame (which includes humans), tame animal hunting is then distinguished into the class that captures by force of persuasion and another kind that is more violent. The more violent kind includes piracy, manstealing, tyranny, and the military art. Persuasion involves popular orators, lawyers, and conversation. We are tempted to place Fish in this second class, for he does not seem to fit into the category that includes piracy, manstealing, tyranny, or military art. Our Fish character reels clients into the firm and women into his bed primarily through the force of persuasion rather than through more violent means. Yet even here, there is some ambiguity. For during the course of the series, Fish engaged in manstealing on at least two occasions when he stole new associates (and their business) from other firms.

In spite of the ambiguity, the balance seems to swing in favor of classifying Fish under the power of persuasion, and so we divide this class into private and public (222d). Private hunting is partitioned into a kind that goes for hire (involving money), and another that involves gifts (involving love). Strangely enough, we cannot firmly designate Fish to the private kind that goes for money. For it seems that Fish does not conduct many of his affairs in private — he makes jokes about cameras in his bedroom ("I Know Him by Heart"). As for the gift-giving sort, that has to do with the way that lovers hunt their intended by offering inducements. Fish certainly speaks for guarded love that requires inducements; regarding Viagra, he says, "Respect only gets you so far. True love? It needs chemicals" ["Reasons to Believe"].

Even though he may use inducements, we recall Fish's desire for a little humanity to go with his money, as well as the fun-loving aspects of his nature. Is Fish in it "for love or for money"?

In an episode titled "Boys' Town," Fish and Cage engage in a squabble that escalates to the point where their friendship and partnership are threatened. They take their problems to a psychiatrist, and during that session, Cage tries to reach out to Fish and confirm his affection for his friend. Later, Fish confesses to Cage that Cage is his best friend, adding, "I'm even more proud of that than all my money."

Cage, in turn, is moved to show Fish his secret room — a hideaway reached through a door in the unisex bathroom. As Cage points out to Fish, "You can't escape if you reveal your hideaway." Thus, John Cage manages to get past Fish's guardrail and barrier. Cage communicates that he does not consider their friendship to be what the psychiatrist called it: "pathetic" (which implies a mixture of contemptible and pitiable). By opening up and exposing the "secret place," where he goes to "hide away," he makes it possible for Richard to expose his own hidden feelings in the only way he knows how: "Mambo Cat!" The obstacle is dislodged. Cage caught Fish. This exchange between the two friends shows that Fish is not just about "sex and money." This episode marks a turning point in the emotional dynamics of the series.

At the end of the definition, the Stranger looks back over the sequence and retraces each step. He concludes that fishing strikes with a hook and draws the fish from below upward, and the nature of the operation is denoted "angling or drawing up" (221b-c).

Contemporary Issues

Ally McBeal appeared at a cultural moment when traditional sex and gender roles were being questioned and challenged. Now that we have dealt with timeless, universal themes, we must anchor the analysis in the historical context in which this show was embedded.

When the series went on the air, it had increasingly become both a man's *and* a woman's world. In the previous 20 years, the percentage of women ages 25 to 54 working outside the home had climbed from 50 percent to 76 percent. The presence of women in universities also rose dramatically during those years. Higher education had made it possible for women to increase their participation in occupations commanding prestige and earning power. In the legal profession, for example, the percentage of women lawyers and judges had doubled to 29 percent in less than 20 years. The presence of more and more women in public life, combined with their increased independence and earning power in the private sphere, had touched off major upheavals in the sexual dynamics of professional and personal relationships.[9]

These changes produced conflict, tension, and resistance. In spite of vastly increased popular support for equality between the sexes, there had been little progress toward dismantling either traditional sexual stereotypes and attitudes, or the division and segregation of occupations by sex. The judiciary and law, for example, were considered "traditional male" professions. Studies point to the resilience of barriers segregating jobs by sex. These studies also demonstrate that entrenched attitudes, expectations, and stereotypes are the major reason for the persistence of barriers, as well as the resistance encountered by those who attempt to challenge them.[10] Richard Fish embodied, expressed and gave vent to these traditional stereotypes, attitudes, and expectations. When Ally asks if Fish hired her for her looks, he points out that he had nothing else to go on, adding, "Why bite the hand that wants to touch you?" ("Mr. Bo").

The *Ally McBeal* series struck a chord at a time when women were making significant inroads in occupations that were not traditionally open to them, especially the law.[11] Between 1997 and 2001 in the United States, while the show was on air, lawyers were among the best-paid women in all job categories.[12] Since the law was not regarded as a "female" profession, women who chose to pursue legal careers faced a range of visible and invisible rules constructed around traditional "male" and "female" stereotypes. Fish was the fictional embodiment of the slimy lawyer who expressed these traditional ideas. Research has shown that women in the law encountered a number of sexual issues in the workplace.[13]

The rapid influx of record numbers of women in the conservative and traditionally male-dominated legal profession made the judiciary and the law the site of what the late media theorist Marshall McLuhan called a "break boundary." According to McLuhan, a break boundary is an area of encounter, clash, and cross-fertilization between two different systems that ultimately leads to the transformation of major aspects of social and psychic existence.[14] At the end of the twentieth century, the legal profession was the site of such an encounter. Law and the judiciary were zones of overlap between traditional attitudes and stereotypes and new, non-traditional options that were opening up for both men and women. As a real life break boundary between tradition and non-tradition, public and private, the legal profession provided an ideal imaginary situation for enacting, playing out, and giving vent to some of the tensions experienced by many television viewers at that particular cultural moment. It is therefore no surprise that Cage & Fish specialized in sexual harassment law.

Richard Fish, however, spoke for two sorts of impulses. He gave voice to a whole range of stereotypical thoughts, feelings and ideas bound up with traditional views of men, women, sex, money, and professionalism. Yet he also spoke for the impulse to challenge those traditions. Through this ambiguity, Fish represented and enacted a very complex and distinctive viewpoint. He was a classic case of "the angler," the voice of tradition, the fictional embodiment of attitudes and expectations that lurked "below the surface," and a characterization of confusion concerning changing sex and gender roles in contemporary society.

A law office staffed by young, sexually active lawyers, the judges, clients and cases—all offered fertile ground for examining sex and gender issues that North Americans were experiencing in real life. The television screen framed situations in a way that transformed their meaning by defining them as a kind of play, thereby establishing a realm of experience altogether different from the real world and actual life experience.[15] Through sympathetic engagement with the Fish character, audiences had a cathartic outlet for the release of tension. Research has shown that the way that a television program frames characters and situations influences the attitudes of those who watch.[16] Thus, *Ally McBeal* provided an imaginative construct—a forum for playing out a range of possibilities—that both mirrored conflicts and resistances in the real world, and helped to reframe some of them.

Conclusion

Was Richard Fish a Sophist or a statesman? A charlatan or a wise man? Did he practice his art for money or for love? We have seen that Fish's character spanned both sides of these classical dualities, and this ambiguity played a crucial part in the success of the show at both the imaginative and emotional levels.

Each character played a role that contributed to the overall effect of the series. "Single lawyer" Ally McBeal (Calista Flockhart) was, according to Fox television, "the spirit of the firm."[17] Ally's childhood sweetheart, Billy Thomas (Gil Bellows), was her colleague at Cage & Fish as was Georgia (Courtney Thorne-Smith), the woman who stole Billy away from her. Elaine Vassal (Jane Krakowski), the nosy legal secretary; Fish's partner, John Cage; along with a host of other characters, both regular and intermittent, all contributed something to the series. But as we have seen, Richard Fish contributed something extra. According to the comic formula as well as the criteria of the definition, Fish was the comic hero. He shaped the action of the series as he moved from sophistry to authenticity.

Ally McBeal captured a share of the popular imagination at a key cultural moment. By the time that the spirit of the show left, the spirit of the times had changed as well. Over the course of five years, Fish had assignations with several women — Judge "Whipper" Cohn, Ling, and then finally, Liza (Christina Ricci). In the series finale, court and courting came together, and the social, legal, and psychological cases merged when Fish acted as his father's attorney and proposed marriage to Liza. "The theme of the comic is the integration of society, which usually takes the form of incorporating a central character into it."[18] Fish won the sexual harassment suit for his father, thereby removing the paternal obstacle and demonstrating that he was in full possession of his "art." He married Liza — because he no longer saw her "as merely a sexual object, but as someone I can actually love" [What I'll Never Do for Love Again]. Fish was the comic hero who triumphed and won, and with the festive ritual of the wedding ceremony in the series finale, a new society crystallized around him.

It was through the juxtaposition of the trials on the public level and the trials on the private level — and Richard Fish's role as a bridge between the two — that the show achieved its emotional effect.

Notes

1. "*Ally McBeal:* Bygones," 15 August 2005. <*http://www.tv.com/episode/144967/summary.html*>.
2. Northrop Frye, The Great Code: The Bible and Literature (Toronto: Academic Press Canada, 1990), p. 48.

3. All citations from the show were obtained from *"Ally McBeal,"* TKTV, 17 August 2005 http://allymcbeal.tktv.net/.

4. Tom Chetwynd, A *Dictionary of Symbols* (London: Paladin Books, 1984), pp. 16; 151–2.

5. J.E. Cirlot, *A Dictionary of Symbols,* trans., Jack Sage (London and Henley: Routledge & Kegan Paul, 1967), pp. 106–8.

6. Northrop Frye, *Anatomy of Criticism* (Princeton: Princeton University Press, 1957), pp. 163–166.

7. Sigmund Freud, "Psychopathic Characters on the Stage," *Art and Literature,* trans. James Strachey and ed. Albert Dickson (Harmondsworth, Middlesex, England: Penguin Books, 1985), vol. 14, pp. 121–123.

8. *Ibid.,* pp. 124–125.

9. United States, Bureau of Labor Statistics, Department of Labor, *Household Data Annual Averages — Median Weekly Earnings of Full Time Wage and Salary Be Detailed Occupation and Sex,* 17 August 2005 <http://www.Stats.bls.gov/cps/cpsaat39.pdf>.

10. Ruth Milkman, *Gender at Work: The Dynamics of Job Segregation by Sex During World War II* (Urbana and Chicago: University of Chicago Press, 1987), pp. 158–160.

11. International Labor Office, Geneva, *Breaking Through the Glass Ceiling: Women in Management.* Update, 2004, 17 August 2005. <http://www.ilo.org/dyn/gender/docs/RES/292/F267981337/Breaking%20Glass%20PDF%20English.pdf>.

12. United States, Bureau of Labor Statistics, Department of Labor, *Household Data Annual Averages — Median Weekly Earnings of Full Time Wage and Salary Be Detailed Occupation and Sex,* 17 August 2005, http://www.Stats.bls.gov/cps/cpsaat39.pdf.

13. *Ibid.*

14. Marshall McLuhan, "Playboy Interview: Marshall McLuhan — A Candid Conversation with the High Priest of Popcult and Metaphysician of Media," *Playboy,* March 1969. Reprint. *Essential McLuhan,* edited by Eric McLuhan and Frank Zingrone (New York: Basic Books, 1995), p. 249.

15. Eviatar Zerubavel, *The Fine Line: Makings Distinctions in Everyday Life* (New York, Toronto: The Free Press, Macmillan, 1991), p. 11.

16. George Gerbner, Larry Gross, Michael Morgan, and Nancy Signorielli, "Growing Up With Television: The Cultivation Perspective," In, J. Bryant and D. Zillmann, editors, *Media Effects: Advances in Theory and Research* (Hillsdale, New Jersey: Lawrence Erlbaum, 1994), pp. 1–15.

17. Fox Entertainment, *Ally McBeal* 12 June 2005 http://www.foxhome.com/ally/index_frames.html.

18. Frye, *Anatomy of Criticism,* p. 43.

Bibliography

"Ally McBeal: Bygones." 15 August 2005. <http://www.tv.com/episode/144967/summary.html>.

"Ally McBeal." TKTV. 17 August 2005. <http://allymcbeal.tktv.net/>.

Chetwynd, Tom. *A Dictionary of Symbols.* London: Paladin Books, 1984.

Cirlot, J.E. *A Dictionary of Symbols.* Translated by Jack Sage. London and Henley: Routledge & Kegan Paul, 1967.

Fox Entertainment. *Ally McBeal.* 12 June 2005. <http://www.foxhome.com/ally/index_frames.html>.

Freud, Sigmund. "Psychopathic Characters on the Stage." In *Art and Literature,* translated by James Strachey, edited by Albert Dickson (Harmondsworth, Middlesex, England: Penguin Books, 1985), vol. 14, pp. 121–123.

Frye, Northrop. *Anatomy of Criticism.* Princeton, New Jersey: Princeton University Press, 1957.

_____. *The Great Code: The Bible and Literature.* Toronto: Academic Press Canada, 1990.

Gerbner, George, Larry Gross, Michael Morgan, and Nancy Signorielli. "Growing Up with Television: The Cultivation Perspective." In, Bryant, J., and D. Zillmann, editors. *Media Effects: Advances in Theory and Research.* Hillsdale, New Jersey: Lawrence Erlbaum, 1994.

International Labor Office, Geneva. *Breaking Through the Glass Ceiling: Women in Management.* Update, 2004. 17 August 2005. <http://www.ilo.org/dyn/gender/docs/RES/292/F267981337/Breaking%20Glass%20PDF%20English.pdf>.

McLuhan, Marshall. "Playboy Interview: Marshall McLuhan — A Candid Conversation with the High Priest of Popcult and Metaphysician of Media." In *Playboy* March 1969. Reprint. *Essential McLuhan,* edited by Eric McLuhan and Frank Zingrone. Basic Books: New York, 1995.

Milkman, Ruth. *Gender at Work: The Dynamics of Job Segregation by Sex During World War II.* Urbana and Chicago: University of Chicago Press, 1987.

United States, Bureau of Labor Statistics. Department of Labor. *Household Data Annual Averages— Median Weekly Earnings of Full Time Wage and Salary Be Detailed Occupation and Sex.* 17 August 2005. <http://www.Stats.bls.gov/cps/cpsaat39.pdf>.

Zerubavel, Eviatar. *The Fine Line: Makings Distinctions in Everyday Life.* New York and Toronto: The Free Press, Macmillan Inc., 1991.

10

It's More Than Just Another Silly Love Song: *Ally McBeal* Brings the Hollywood Musical to Television

Diana Sandars

Introduction

Ally McBeal begins with a deconstruction of the classical Hollywood[1] musical's utopian representation of courtship rites and love. In the first episode it is revealed that Billy has been Ally's one true love since childhood, but that by their mid-twenties the romance was over and Billy had married someone else. A later episode in the series, "The Promise," opens with Ally and Renee "breaking in" Ally's new piano with one of her favorite songs "Good Night, My Someone." At the close of the song Renee reflects that this song, taken from *The Music Man,*[2] musically describes the main female protagonist, Marian's, wish for true love as someone to take away her loneliness. The poignancy of this scene is delivered when Renee mournfully declares that it aptly describes both her and Ally's present-day situation.

In the musical, "the duet is the musical's center of gravity, its method of summarizing in a single scene the film's entire structure."[3] Ally's mournful duet with Renee adapts this trope of the classical Hollywood musical to define the central ideologies surrounding the love and relationships extolled by *Ally McBeal.* Sung at home with her best friend, this duet is positioned within a contemporary cynical perspective that critically assesses the song's romantic yearnings and the single fate that Ally rallies against. The tension that this duet sets up continues for the next three seasons of *Ally McBeal.* This scene therefore represents David E. Kelley's first direct appeal to the television spectator's knowledge of Hollywood musicals, to read Ally as a modern-day Marian, burdened with the objective of the typical musical hero: the "search for the perfect partner."[4] Ally is intelligent and entrusted with the maintenance of social and moral order in her professional life as a lawyer and a friend, and like Marian she juggles the conflicting worlds of dreams and real world demands.

Ally McBeal is unique in its formal blend of courtroom drama with the Hollywood musical and conventions borrowed from music video. These elements combine to provide the structure through which the theme of love and romance in a litigious corporate culture is examined.[5] The musical's dominant thematic concern with success and romance is shared by television drama and soap operas, enhancing the suitability of this film genre's evolution into the intimate and domestic format of broadcast television. By the late 1990s the genre hybridity and intertextual relay between media forms, which proliferated in the 1980s, restructured the creative and economic relationship between film and television as well as generic expectations and possibilities. Television series provided ironic and self-reflexive uses of classical Hollywood genres to entertain and instruct the media literate postmodern audiences of the late 1990s. This excessive formal hybridity forms the basis for *Ally McBeal*'s self-reflexive comedy, as it exaggerates these conventions to comically reveal the pleasures and ideologies they separately evoke.

Through its postmodern ironic and parodic appeals to film musical and music video literate viewers *Ally McBeal* has created a polysemic form layered by the dualities that similarly define the classical Hollywood musical. Stylistically *Ally McBeal* is dominated by the use of pop music to convey a ubiquitous love and desire expressible only through music. Dance features prominently in *Ally McBeal* as the series employs the classical Hollywood musical's primary element of dance to express euphoric and melancholic emotional states of both individual characters and the firm as a whole. *Ally McBeal*'s generic hybridity and postmodern representation of love and desire conspire to offer the promise of romantic and emotional resolution but deny the narrative form or cultural representation through which this would be achievable.

Ally McBeal perpetuates the signature musical finale of the classical Hollywood musical using its spectacular form to perpetuate the ideology conveyed in this formal structure of romantic love, social unity and dream fulfillment. Musical finales are also used by *Ally McBeal* to deconstruct these myths, reflecting on the failure of this ideology as being only momentary and not compatible with a lived reality in a 1990s corporate culture. These musical finales, instead, celebrate the bonds of friendship and collegiality as the 1990s equivalent in social aspirations to the classical Hollywood musical's aspirations of romantic love and marriage.[6] Significantly it is when the musical's stylist structure overwhelms the drama series conventions that *Ally McBeal* is at its most emotively and self-reflexively powerful.

The Mapping of the Classical Hollywood Musical onto a Soap Opera-Dramedy Television Series Format: Ally McBeal Rewrites the Romantic Ideology of the Classical Hollywood Musical

"Maybe we were meant to love each other but we weren't meant to
be together.... We were not meant to be."[7]

Through the use of its stylistic and thematic elements,[8] *Ally McBeal* reflects the superimposition of key thematic and stylistic elements of the Hollywood musical genre onto a television series. A product of television's increasing intertextuality,[9] the narrative structure of *Ally McBeal* constructs the diegesis, and most importantly the characters, as the product of competing past and present social ideologies and expectations, creating a complex format to examine, "the conventional American willingness to make courtship the paradigm of life."[10] In *Ally McBeal* it is through its unfurling that this courtship myth's continued influence on contemporary culture is revealed. The Hollywood musical's thematic concerns with success and romance are appropriated and reconfigured in *Ally McBeal,* as the conflicts between cultural expectations and individual fantasies thematically define *Ally McBeal.*[11] Romance in *Ally McBeal* is represented as indelibly linked to career and workplace culture, imbuing the term office romance with new meaning. This dominant theme is articulated through a formal blend of court case segments and musical fantasy driven segments creating a dual-focus interrelating narrative through which issues surrounding relationships and careers are explored.

Dance is the metonymical expression for the emotional landscape in *Ally McBeal* as it is used both to represent the celebration and the disillusionment with love. This key narrative device uniquely links *Ally McBeal* to the classical Hollywood musical. The supradiegetic level, a formal concept defined by Rick Altman, is unique to the musical film. In supradiegetic moments the image is subordinate to the musical soundtrack to create "a 'place' of transcendence where time stands still, where contingent concerns are stripped away to reveal the essence of things."[12] Rick Altman defines these supradiegetic moments as,

leaving normal day-to-day causality behind, the music creates a utopian space in which all singers and dancers achieve a unity unimaginable in the now superseded world of temporal, psychological causality.[13]

The mapping of the musical's style and ideology onto the stasis of the fictional world of a television series thwarts the tenability of the simple narrative resolution of the musical, while simultaneously creating a nostalgia for its tidy simplicity.

In writing on television narratives Michael Porter, et al., suggest that the importance of the story arc lies in its ability to shift viewer focus from the plot to the character through its maintenance of continuity and resistance to closure.[14] While this structure is in accordance with television series conventions, ideologically it re-engineers the musical's need for successful heterosexual coupling. In the musical, the successful coupling is achieved through a romantic fallacy dependent on "reconciling terms previously seen as mutually exclusive, ... reducing an unsatisfactory paradox to a more workable configuration, a concordance of opposites."[15] The maintenance of the musical's non-realist narrative necessitates the pretense of this tidy closure. This reconfiguration in its devotion to realism instead suggests that the search for the one complementary partner and enduring romantic relationship is never ending and ultimately unachievable. The television series' formal structure therefore dictates the romantic ideology as the search for the one true love becomes a story arc transversing several seasons without successful resolution. The mapping of the classical Hollywood musical onto a television dramedy in *Ally McBeal* results in a repeated pattern of raised expectations, of utopian heterosexual romantic fulfilment created through the use of the musical's narrative and ideological structures and the dashing of these through the soap opera-dramedy formula.

Rick Altman notes that the classical Hollywood musical's narrative closure is facilitated through the successful union of the main protagonists denoted by the film's ending at the point of coupling. Utopian in its presentation so that the permanence of true love is not questioned, the spectator is also "unable to verify whether this apparent solution is actually a workable one."[16] In the episode "Civil War," when Ally realizes that she has lost her latest love, Greg, and will never regain a romantic relationship with her "true love," Billy, the episode closes with Ally slow dancing in her pajamas alone in her lounge room with a similarly pajama-clad inflatable male doll. This cinematography evokes the Hollywood musicals duet shot[17] that is designed to maintain the ideological focus on romantic coupling by displaying the paired stars of the film. Not only is this conclusion in *Ally McBeal* contrary to the happy ending promised by the Hollywood musical, it further suggests that the promise of the musical's ideology is as hollow and artificial as the man she is dancing with. The message, that the solution of the Hollywood musical is not a workable one, recurs through the season as Ally is repeatedly framed enacting the fantasies of musicals and pop songs, dancing alone in her apartment, or with the inflatable man. The use of supradiegetic music in these scenes reflects Ally's emotional state as being trapped in heartbreak as she slow dances to songs like "Bye-Bye Love" and "Wrong Number." The dance that articulates love in the musical, in *Ally McBeal* instead cynically portrays the momentary and illusory status of this love.

The Hollywood musical implies that "the natural state of the adult human being is in the arms of an adult human being of the opposite sex."[18] *Ally McBeal* adapts this ideology, inserting the arms of platonic friendship where romance once resided. In *Ally McBeal,* as in the musical, "the duet serves the important function of crystallizing the couple's attitudes and emotions."[19] The performance of a duet is unusual in *Ally McBeal* and it is significant that it is this song she sings with Renee. In the 1990s revision, marriage brings heartache and pain as same-sex friendship provides the love, laughter and emotional support promised by the classical Hollywood musical's dominant ideology surrounding heterosexual courtship and marriage. Conversely life is celebrated for its heartbreak and disappointment rather than its optimistic, emotionally and financially harmonious resolutions.

In the world of *Ally McBeal* the happy ever after of romantic coupling eludes the main protagonists, both by choice and circumstance. In "Sex, Lies and Politics," Ally pronounces a 1990s postmodern deconstruction of this 1950s romantic myth as she declares the split between being in love and being able to live together happily ever after. Ally defines her relationship with Billy as, "He will probably always love me as I will always love him. Maybe we were meant to love each other but we weren't meant to be together ... I would never be happy with him ... we are not meant to be." This contemporary revision of the Hollywood musical's ideology dominates this episode's coda, and those of the first three seasons of *Ally McBeal,* as Renee and Ally, or other paired colleagues are depicted on the street walking home arm in arm.

The "Let's Dance" episode of *Ally McBeal* rewrites the musical's heterosexual coupling through the culture of swing dance. Ling agrees to substitute for Elaine's injured partner so that Elaine has a chance to make it through to the swing dance finals. Ling's Asian appearance and her masquerade as a man visually conspire to undermine the celebration of heterosexual romance constructed by the musical's narrative structure and dance form. Equally it reaffirms the role of costume and dance performance to construct and stabilize race and gender. While it is comedic, Ling's highly visible masquerade suggests fluidity in romance and coupling in the late 1990s as an aspect of American values not present in the classical Hollywood musical period. As the dance continues to act as a metaphor for love and desire, Elaine's ability to find success with Ling as a last-minute substitute suggests the instability of the ever-after coupling advocated by the classical Hollywood musical. Partners in the 1990s are easily interchangeable. It further suggests that the heterosexual courtship denoted by dance has been replaced by a desire for success without love and romance. Romance has been replaced by an intimacy and mutual support shared between colleagues rather than lovers. While the characters of *Ally McBeal* aim for the musical's promise of true love, the consistent relationship resolution at the end of each story arc is that your colleagues are your best friends and surrogate family, and fulfill the requirements assigned to a heterosexual relationship in the classical Hollywood musical.

The Dialogue Between the Real and the Ideal in Ally McBeal

"The fundamental configuration underlying the musical's imaginative geography: an ideal realm is never more than a dissolve away."[20]

Television's focus on character over plot and its formula of constant reconfiguration of events and dilemma rather than narrative resolution and closure,[21] is antithetical to the classical Hollywood musical's form and ideology. Television's character development as a realist device is antithetical to the musical's reliance on the discreet structure of fantasy. The musical conveys a snapshot moment of wish fulfillment, necessitating character construction only to this point of coupling and prohibiting continuous character and story development beyond this point in order to maintain the fantasy of this state beyond the closure of the narrative. Similarly, television's situation comedy "presents conflicting forces or emotions that can never be resolved."[22] In the classical Hollywood musical genre narrative progression necessitates a shift in the characters' mindset and social status as the narrative resolution is predicated upon the character's conventional and inevitable entry into coupling and marriage.[23] When integrated into *Ally McBeal*'s soap opera-dramedy format the factor of inevitability is inverted. Instead, the narrative hook offered by the element of soap opera is premised on the knowledge that it is predictable that Ally will *not* achieve the conventional romantic pairing fundamental to the Hollywood musical.

Paradoxically, Ally's character development in *Ally McBeal* is premised on her desire to live her life according to the idyllic romantic moment of the musical. Ally's ideology is reflective of the 1950s musicals where "only effort and willed self confidence could maintain the traditional ways."[24] Her repeated desperate attempts to enact this static fantasy, in opposition to the social forces that dictate her lived reality, form the unique core of her character and its development throughout the series. Therefore, Ally's character is defined by her steadfast reluctance to develop beyond this moment of adolescent fantasy. The slightest pretext prompts Ally into her inner world delusions from which she must be jolted back. Her private energy constantly overwhelms her and cripples her functioning in the real world. For this she freely admits she is "nuts." However, it is an emotional state that is ultimately romanticized, defined by John Cage as "special." The thematic structure of *Ally McBeal* perpetuates this paradox as the pop cultural promise of a never-ending utopian existence is applied to a lived reality that can never fulfil this promise.

Porter suggests that "one of the most engaging points of television drama [is] the continuous development and creation of interesting characters."[25] *Ally McBeal* employs this mechanism of audience identification through the heavy use of pop songs complemented by a narrative concern with various models of love and desire. However, the use of music to define and develop the characters of *Ally McBeal* merges both television's and the musical's use of characters. Jane Feuer argues that in the classical Hollywood musical two modes of address are employed. The audience watches the story unfold from a third person position, a typical level of identification of the classical Hollywood narrative.[26] This switches to a closer level of identification in the musical production numbers as the film audience is performed to directly, encouraging the spectorial position of participation in live entertainment rather than an outside observer.[27] *Ally McBeal* employs this dual level of identification through its use of musical production numbers within the narratives of some episodes and the use of supradiegetic musical moments.

In times of identity crisis or personal stress several *Ally McBeal* characters employ the use of theme songs as a mode of empowerment through personal fantasy. These theme songs are represented at a supradiegetic level, replicating the classical Hollywood musical's use of the supradiegetic to convey fantasy states and denote a character's inner fantasies. Ally gains a theme song after visiting her therapist, Tracey, in "The Theme of Life." When she hears her theme song it is in response to her desire for Greg Butters. Ally is visually depicted standing waiting to cross at the lights within a crowd of people. As Ally begins to dance with exuberance to the tempo of the song, the crowd around her similarly dances to its infectious beat as they cross the street. The euphoria of initial desire is as socially contagious in *Ally McBeal* as it is in the classical Hollywood musical, where "the characters break out of the normal world into a realm ... where stylization and rhythm provide a sense of community and beauty absent from the real world."[28] In *Ally McBeal* this narrative device is created from a blend of Hollywood musical and the cultural use of pop songs. A key trope signifying the Hollywood musical's realm of fantasy and whimsy, in *Ally McBeal* this textual use of theme songs at a supradiegetic level instead suggests the vulnerability of fantasy to a diegetically located harsh mundane reality.

Ally McBeal primarily reflects a cynical shift from the ideologies conveyed through the musical's production numbers in its self-reflexive use of this convention. In the musical the supradiegetic expression of romance and euphoria overwhelms the dictates of reality and is allowed to run its course. In the cynical postmodern world of *Ally McBeal* the reverse is true as these flights of fancy are condemned as character flaws. As a result, the full articulation and closure denied to the supradiegetic moments in the series symbolically reflects the closure denied to the narrative. However, through the tensions displayed by this struggle essentialist representations of normalcy[29] are explored and rendered problematic. Additionally, the personal empowerment is as momentary as the fantasy. The episode "You Never Can Tell" opens with Ally trying to dance her way to happiness through the upbeat tempo of her theme song, but her inability to transcend her despair is evident at a supradiegetic level as her song plays at a slower speed slurring the upbeat words. Ally jumps and sashays in her lounge room, desperately trying to will her frame of mind into the optimistic upbeat tempo that defines the song. Similarly, in a later episode, John stands infront of the unisex mirror willing Barry White to return to him. These moments suggest that the classical Hollywood musical's fundamental ideology, a rosy, confident, optimistic outlook on life, is not a spontaneous or inevitable state, but must be artificially conjured and is difficult to sustain.

The importance of halting fantasy's infiltration of reality is signified through the layered use of the soundtrack in *Ally McBeal*. The non-diegetic use of a sound of a needle scratching a record represents another person's intrusion into the private worlds of Ally or John. It is a non-diegetic sound that imposes itself onto the supradiegetic sound of these characters' inner worlds. The jarring of this noise creates a shift between narrational and identification modes, disrupting the realm of fantasy that song and image have colluded to construct. Instead, utopian fantasies are fleeting and always disrupted, never properly fulfilled. When depicted in *Ally McBeal*, this state is not only joltingly ruptured by the intrusion of another person, it is depicted as a state that can be easily lost and one which is the source of comedy or derision rather than celebration or admiration as defined by the classical Hollywood musical.[30] Therefore, the characters of *Ally McBeal* may aspire to the status of musical star in their fantasies but they are firmly located within the realist structures of a television series.

Due to the dominance of the realist conventions of *Ally McBeal*'s narrative and formal structure, which work to contain the disruption of the fantasy segments, *Ally McBeal* reflects the frantic will for happiness as a misguided struggle in the face of self-doubt and economically linked emotional pragmatism. This dooms the characters of *Ally McBeal* to soap opera's constant cycle of raised expectations followed by bitter disappointment, as each relationship will not last or be the one true love, while simultaneously proffering hope through the successful union of couples encountered by the firm and through transcendent musical moments. They will never find what they are looking for, even though the narrative's musical formal and thematic structures repeatedly assure that it is there, that dreams really do come true. As Martha Nochismson observes, "*Ally McBeal* laughingly refused to rescue us from a world of loneliness and impossible contradictions, while also (hilariously) troubling naturalistic narrative representation."[31]

Predominantly, the realist narrative of *Ally McBeal* is disrupted through the use of special effects that illustrate an extreme emotional reaction to a situation, providing greater emotional insight into the characters and plot, as a comparative device to the narrative production numbers of the classical Hollywood musical. John's courtroom tricks and the visualization of Ally's inner thoughts provide moments of comedy, a greater level of empathy, and in the courtroom, a bias as to the ridiculousness of the opposition's case. In the realm of expected verbal eloquence that the courtroom denotes, visual spectacle is employed as an effective counterlanguage, creating an alternative level of audience identification as well as knowing humor at understanding the pun. The public settings of the court cases in *Ally McBeal* additionally serve the soap opera narrative level, as the cases exist as metaphors or catalysts for examination of the events and relationships in the personal lives of the lawyers in the firm.[32] *Ally McBeal*'s characters are developed through the various themes of each episode that are complementarily explored through the court cases and personal life problems of the lawyers of the firm. The eloquence of the lawyers' arguments in court as they debate issues ranging from sexual discrimination, romantic fraud, and breaches of contract is juxtaposed to the emotional timbre of the pop songs which are used in other segments of the episode to succinctly redefine these intellectual issues through their emotive appeal.

The musical genre shares this soap opera thematic. As Thomas Schatz argues, the classical Hollywood musical examines the positives and negatives of the cultural ideals of sexuality and success through the construction of characters whose lifestyles are defined by personal success and familial and personal relationships.[33] He further argues that this combination will "often accent another basic generic conflict associated with those themes: the conflict between natural individual vitality and staid social decorum."[34] The culture of the Fish and Cage law firm reflects Schatz' view of the musical's celebration of success and sexuality, as the firm was founded by Richard to be a uniquely fun and profitable work culture. Unlike the other major firms it operates as a surrogate family for its lawyers. Through the court cases tried and through the courtship beliefs and practices of the lawyers themselves, love and romance is made to seem peculiar, disruptive and even dangerous.[35] This acts as wider commentary on the professionally driven society in which Ally lives, suggesting the problem created by the romantic ideologies, perpetuated by pop music, Broadway and Hollywood musicals, with which women in Ally's generation were raised.

In her courtroom arguments, Ally articulates these ideologies as though they are the product of a common nostalgic state. She is able to persuasively appeal to the jury, and assumedly the viewer, through her unashamed embodiment of these romantic fantasies, removing them from their social position as childlike and inferior to intellect and reason. Ling adopts this tactic in her closing argument in "Sex, Lies and Politics," speaking to the jury in Mandarin Chinese, in a soft moving tone, her winning argument appears in subtitles at the base of the screen: "You hear my tone; it's appropriate to feel sorry for me. As I drop to a faint whisper ... you'll feel sadness yourself." The use of this stylistic device in *Ally McBeal* reflects the coding of meaning and identification in pop songs, where "it is the sound of the voice, not the words sung, which suggest what a singer *really* [sic] means."[36] In the courtroom of *Ally McBeal,* the realm of the idealised and emotional triumph over pragmatic rational argument. Appeals to idealized and romantic states made through melancholic feminine voices form winning strategies.

The dilemma of the everyday,[37] rather than the everyday transcendence of the musical, is at the core of *Ally McBeal.* This is reconfirmed by the themes and ideologies which provide "no final closure to the series' own recurring problematic."[38] However, it is the momentary transcendence of utopian romance that makes the everyday bearable. *Ally McBeal* replicates the musical's depiction of the diegetic present as "banal, limited, ruled by necessity,"[39] which is set in opposition to a fantasized future or distant past depicted as "exciting, limitless, controlled by a romanticizing memory or tendency towards dream."[40] *Ally McBeal* declares that the potential loss of this state is something to be mourned. John informs Ally, "The world is no longer a romantic place. Some of its people still are however, and therein lies the promise. Don't let the world win, Ally McBeal." In this speech John articulates the thematic premise of *Ally McBeal*—contemporary cultural tensions between lived reality and romantic expectations espoused by classical Hollywood ideologies and perpetuated by pop music.

Music Video vs. Musical

Multiple music genres are employed in *Ally McBeal* to create a complex, emotionally governed social landscape. Individual definitions of love are represented through the songs that define each character and the romantic dilemmas in which they find themselves. The love expressed through the faith and innocence of ballads from Broadway musicals are complemented by the yearnings of disco music and juxtaposed by the pop songs from the late 1960s to the 1990s. This is constructed through *Ally McBeal*'s formal dialogue between music video and the musical's contrary formal and ideological relationships between image, song, music genre and narrative. The musical number John Cage performs with the jury in "Sex, Lies and Politics" perpetuates the narrative ideologies of the musical and its promises of the consistency of the status quo. This highlights the differences between the musical number and music video, as it is compared to Billy's performance of the Robert Palmer music video "Addicted to Love," in the third season.

Ally McBeal recreates the codes and conventions for an MTV matured audience.[41] The characters' theme songs construct the characters both within popular culture and as defined by it, while simultaneously evoking the spectator's own associations with the song and its artist. *Ally McBeal* substitutes speech for song. It is the familiarity and pattern of the melody through which narrative meaning is conveyed, rather than what is said. *Ally McBeal*'s characters, therefore, operate on a similar level to the pop stars of music video, as they evoke familiarity through the songs they perform to rather than the words they speak. The emotional state of *Ally McBeal*'s characters is conveyed not only through the theme songs they choose but also in the aural manipulation of these songs. When applied to *Ally McBeal*, it is evident that the songs chosen to define this state for John and Ally further signify this utopian space as a past adolescent romantic creation as denoted by their love songs, "We've Got It Together" and "Tell Him," as compared to Billy's rock anthem, "Addicted to Love."

In the episode "Sex, Lies and Politics," John discovers that the sequestered jury watched *The Music Man* the night before and so structures his closing around main protagonist Henry Hill's persuasive number, "Ya Got Trouble." John replicates Henry's performance as he cajoles the jury to sing with him in an agreement with his rhetoric, just as the townspeople in *The Music Man* joined Henry in his song. When employed musically, it the persuasive power of the rhetoric of love and romance that is used to sell the narrative of each episode of *Ally McBeal*. Used as lyrics rhetoric combined with the persuasive power of rhythm and melody is presented as a powerful tool of emotional and consequently thought manipulation. Its use in this scene enhances audience identification through its reference to *The Music Man* and through the adaptation of the formal structure of the integrated musical where the mundane is transformed by the impromptu break into song. John therefore shares with Astaire and Kelly the qualities of the music men whose voices easily flow into the singing of lyrics, and movements transform into entertainment spectacle, merging "this exuberant private energy with a wider community."[42] Similar to these music men and the integrated musical, John's courtroom tricks suggest that he shares the belief in the primary importance of "the show."[43] He therefore fits Schatz's definition of the archetypal music men,

> who awaken ... [their] partners to the music and gaiety all around them; they seem to generate an aura of self-contained energy that emanates from their characters and affects all with whom they come into contact.[44]

In the late 1990s context however, this personality trait is labelled strange and odd by clients and colleagues, reflecting a cultural cynicism with the classical Hollywood musical's model of romance and displays of emotional excess.

Ally McBeal's re-articulation of the classical Hollywood musical's music man and his female co-star simultaneously competes with the pop star personas created by pop songs and music video. The result of *Ally McBeal*'s engagement with music video aesthetics and cultural influence is that the aspirations of the Hollywood musical's heroine are now articulated through MTV dominant codes and conventions. The episode "The Green Monster" begins with a flashback of Ally as a child miming and dancing with her friends to the music video of Robert Palmer's rock anthem "Addicted to Love" playing on the television in her bedroom. The flashback, or video dissolve, is a key narrative device of the Hollywood musical, used to merge the real with the ideal through the use of the song to link both realms. When his marriage to Georgia is in crisis, and he is feeling emasculated by the women in his life, Billy adopts "Addicted to Love" as his theme song, drawing on the "old rock and roll truths of sex and gender — rutting, romantic men...."[45] Through the opening segment Ally and Billy are linked on a musical level as Ally worships through imitation the ideology of the song that Billy comes to personify. Billy acts out the music video to this song by dressing like Robert Palmer and hiring women identical in dress and look to the back-up singers in the video clip to follow him around. This is a disparaging adaptation of the role Rick Altman assigns to Gene Kelly as the musical star who "personifies the co-existence of man and child in the same body."[46] The youthful exuberance and spontaneity of Kelly that brought gaiety to those around him is reconfigured through Billy as petulant, selfish, overindulgence, derived at the expense of others. Billy is a perversion of the musical's music man's ideologies as he incites scorn and ridicule.

Billy shares with Ally and John the musical star's resistance to growing up and abandoning childhood beliefs,[47] but contrary to John Cage, the show Billy enacts is borne of music video's gimmickry, epitomised by his dyed blonde hair, rather than the musical's ideologies surrounding morals and romance. Instead, the parodic excess and superficiality of Billy's performance of masculine authority and desirability articulates the discourses of rock music and music video. Through their direct opposition, rock discourses challenge the musical's fantasy of desire and love, as performed by John and Ally in the courtroom and their private lives. Additionally, this use of rock music denotes another conflicting layer of ideology surrounding love and identity that competes with Hollywood musical, pop songs, and pragmatic corporate culture for meaning in the contemporary society in *Ally McBeal*. However, the disruptive potential of rock's alternative ideologies are eviscerated through its parodic employment in *Ally McBeal* to reinforce the dominant ideology constructed through pop music and the musical.

The comedy of Billy's rock persona is clearly conveyed that this identity is sustainable only through the fantasy structures of the musical, rock music and music video, but is not transferable or sustainable in a lived reality. His persona has been created within terms of high concept as his image is "connected to a concept that is marketable and exploitable,"[48] and is identifiable only through the heavily bounded confines of mimicry, a self lost in endless codes of repetition and simulation. Music video's form opposes television's realist narrative's necessity for consistent character construction, as the possibility of character in music video is determined by the lyrics, and contained by the song's length. The superficiality and formal limitations of a music video identity therefore limits the transgression and power of its discourse when enacted in a realist narrative context. If the image of Billy walking through the law office with these women trailing behind him was not ludicrous enough, the condemnation expressed by his wife and female colleagues clearly articulates that this behavior is the product of male fantasy that is ineffectual in the negotiated relationships of real life. This masculine fantasy is dismantled as socially inappropriate and abnormal, as it is eventually revealed that a brain tumor is the cause for Billy's rock fantasy inspired behavior. Rock music's masculinity therefore becomes the musical representation of pathology and terminal illness. Whereas rock's masculine fantasy is dismantled in *Ally McBeal*, the feminine fantasies of pop persist.

The Musical's Use of Dance Finales for Narration and Spectacle in Ally McBeal

"It only happens when I dance with you."[49.]

One of the most significant structural elements that *Ally McBeal* shares with the classical Hollywood musical is the use of music to provide a seamless transition into song and dance. Michael Wood further argues that this represents "the greatest achievements of the American movie musical."[50] In *Ally McBeal*, the bar, Ally's lounge room, the office, the courtroom, the streets, and the unisex toilets become the stages for performances that reflect individual desires. The highly stylized and contrived nature of these segments evokes Jane Feuer's observation that "the proscenium is reborn out of ordinary space in the classical Hollywood musical."[51] The signature musical coda of *Ally McBeal* therefore extends the structural device associated with the classical Hollywood musical's proscenium, to suggest an ideological bridge being built between the characters and a stylistic bridge between the audience and the series through the intercutting across both public and private spaces linked by Vonda Shepard's songs. This stylistic device is characteristic of the style of the musical where the diegetic and the non-diegetic soundtracks are merged[52] which "blurs the borders between the real and the ideal."[53] Through this stylistic device the diegetic events and various characters' emotions are conflated and reduced to the level of the emotional or romanticized realm of the song's narrative that governs the narrative.

The episode codas of *Ally McBeal* typically employ a melancholic use of the Hollywood musical's musical finale to elucidate the emotional ramifications of the narrative. These closing segments therefore employ a dominant structure of music video, which "cross the consumer's gaze as a series of mood states.... The moods often express a lack, an incompletion, and instability, a searching for location."[54] The particular state conveyed by these closing segments is defined by Vonda Shepard's song which non-diegetically governs these scenes and articulates the characters' inner states more poignantly than the supradiegetic use of songs. The use of aerial shots combined with the distancing of the music to the non-diegetic realm signifies a shift from the real world to the ideal.[55] It also encourages a reflective spectorial position summarizing the issues of the episode, as well as the viewer's departure from both this realm and the position of emersion that has governed the spectorial positioning throughout the episodes. Unlike the musical that provides hermetic closure, the poignancy of romance represented in *Ally McBeal* is an unresolvable dilemma. This provides a poignant romanticized closure to the episodes, providing the viewers with the feeling that they are leaving an emotionally intimate and melancholically idyllic realm, against which reality seems too sharply focused.

Just as in the musical "the production number on stage compensates for the world's drabness,"[56] so the musical numbers in the bar compensate for the drabness defined by the rational dictates of the corporate realm and by the loss of romance. By the end of season two of *Ally McBeal*, every cast member had been featured singing and dancing at the bar. The bar where Ally and her colleagues meet after work represents a realm replicating the characteristics of the classical Hollywood musical, "a world with endless pretexts for song and dance."[57] It is the site where romances are played out and friendships, birthdays and holidays are celebrated. Read in terms of the formal structure of the classical Hollywood musical the bar replaces the theater stage as the space of the proscenium in which the finale[58] that provides narrative resolution is held. It is significant that the bar where they dance and court new love interests is situated in the same building, located below their offices. This metaphorically suggests that the desires expressed on the dance floor reside below their intellectual corporate persona, as co-existing parts of the characters, but especially for Ally.

Ally McBeal uses song to articulate its narrative and thematic concerns. Songs are used non-diegetically, diegetically, but most innovatively supradiegetically. Therefore song is employed for its capacity for emotional range and manipulation experience at a broad-based popular cultural level. The power of words in song is contrasted to the power of the words used to form rational arguments and conclusions in the court cases. In the courtroom conclusions are drawn and final verdicts rendered. This contrasts significantly to the emotional ambiguity of the lawyers' private lives which are represented predominantly through pop songs, and the songs, dances and discussions in the bar scenes. The bar therefore, represents an antithetical culture to the demands of the practice of law. It is defined as a space where love and friendship are physically celebrated as spontaneous and socially participatory, unlike the practice of law where love and romance are experienced as strange, painful, dangerous, and socially threatening. Similar to a disco, the bar represents a social space defined by:

> the exhilaration of the collective experience, the inversion of social roles, the supremacy of the present, the triumph of imaginative life ... [and] the dusk to dawn alternative world of the nightclub.[59]

This is most clearly articulated through the coda of "Those Lips, That Hand" when Nelle arranges for Barry White to sing at the bar for John's birthday. In this scene John celebrates of the best of himself as he dances on stage with Barry White. His ecstasy infects his colleagues as one by one they are drawn to the stage to dance with him. This closing number continues for three minutes and adopts both the thematic resolutions and the editing style of the classical Hollywood musical's finale. A series of intercutting between the performance on stage and separately coupled members of the firm joining the performance culminates with a shot of the clapping audience. This replicates the editing of the 1930s Hollywood musicals, noted by Jane Feuer, where, "the internal audience serves a symbolic not a realistic purpose; they are the celluloid embodiment of the film audience's subjectivity."[60] This cuts to a centered medium long shot from the perspective of the internal audience to reveal of the entire cast of *Ally McBeal* lined up in two lines performing synchronized disco dancing steps. The camera pans across the cast members, intercutting with close-ups of Barry White singing behind them. This shot is overlaid with the sound of the audience clapping and cheering and the screen fades to the black before the credits, crystallizing the jubilance of the moment and creating a unity between the characters that eluded them throughout the narrative of the episode.

In the musical's finale, "the ecstatic, uplifting quality of the musical's final scene permits no doubt about the permeance both of the couple and the cultural values which the couple simultaneously guarantees and incarnates."[61] *Ally McBeal*'s manipulation of this narrative device is evident in this scene and the following episode. The coupling in this finale reinscribes the romantic coupling of the Hollywood musical to equally situate the relationships of both colleagues and lovers at the same level of social importance and desirability. Additionally, the romantic couplings conveyed in this scene are dismantled in the next and subsequent episodes. The certainty of the union depicted through the musical's finale, in *Ally McBeal,* is guaranteed only until the next episode. During the episode John had been troubled that he had never really known true love. By organizing Barry White to perform, Nelle has demonstrated that she understands John on an intimate level, suggesting her qualification to be his true love. However the romantic certainty of this scene is eviscerated in the opening of the following episode when Nelle expresses disdain at John's excitement over her gift of Barry White. Not only does this cast doubt over their potential romantic union, it also mocks Nelle's character through the Hollywood musical's suggestion that, "people who are insensitive to entertainment somehow miss out on the best part of life."[62] The tidy resolution of the Hollywood musical is deconstructed through *Ally McBeal*'s use of the television series format that permits it to reflect on the events after the musical finale, dismantling the faith constructed by the Hollywood musical that there is a "happy ever after."

Conclusion

Ally McBeal maintains the Hollywood musical's thematic focus on "romantic love and individual accomplishment, both of which confirm the premise that music, life, and love are complementary and co-equal forces."[63] The attainment of this balance forms the basis of the narrative trajectory in *Ally McBeal* as Ally struggles to fit a conception of love, marriage, and family defined by musical romances into a 1990s career oriented culture. *Ally McBeal*'s use of the Hollywood musical's stylistic and ideological elements disrupts the conventional television series codings of intimacy and "realistic" familiarity. Instead, *Ally McBeal* codes intimacy through its use of pop songs and their opposition to the distanciation created through the gimmicky moments of spectacle. Additionally, Ally's values are constituted by the classical Hollywood musical and pop songs. The belief in the ideal partner, one true love, is pitted against this social complexity and is seen to hinder her and render her an outsider in her environment. The ironic distance created by the gap by the application of the classical Hollywood musical's ideologies surrounding love and romance to the representation of the lived cynical corporate reality of professional women in the late 1990s creates a position from which these competing ideologies can be examined.

Notes

1. David Bordwell, et al., define the classical Hollywood period as Hollywood films made roughly between 1917–1960. For more information on classical Hollywood cinema see D. Bordwell, et al., *The Classical Hollywood Cinema: Film Styles and Mode of Production to 1960* (London, Melbourne and Henley: Routledge & Kegan Paul, 1985).

2. The Hollywood film version of *The Music Man* is based on Meredith Willson's 1957 Broadway musical of the same name.

3. R. Altman, *The American Film Musical* (Bloomington & Indianapolis: Indiana University Press, 1987), 37.

4. L. Braudy, *The World in a Frame: What We See in Films* (Garden City, New York: Anchor/Doubleday, 1976), 140.

5. *Ally McBeal* operates as a late 1990s successor to *L.A. Law* (1986–1994). The first series for which *Ally McBeal*'s writer/ producer, David E. Kelley, wrote, *Ally McBeal* reflects the evolution of this law genre and its themes. Consequently, *Ally McBeal* reflects the ideological filtering of the Hollywood musical through a 1980s broadcast television's obsession with the yuppie search for spiritual values. This is evident as the characters in *Ally McBeal* display many of the traits Jane Feuer identifies as yuppie guilt. "Yuppie guilt is not an aftermath of yuppie values but a constitutive part of them ... what are yuppies guilty about ... their compromised ideas, and for the women, their lost opportunities for love and children." J. Feuer, "Yuppie Envy and Yuppie Guilt: *L.A. Law* and *Thirtysomething*" in *Seeing through the Eighties: Television and Reaganism* (Durham: Duke University Press, 1995), 60.

6. The conclusion of "Forbidden Fruits," *Ally McBeal* consists of shots of John and Richard, intercut with shots of Billy and Georgia, walking home together. Ally is walking home by herself. This effectively aligns Richard and John's relationship with Billy and Georgia's marriage. This bond is perpetuated in the closure of an episode in the fourth series when Richard and John console each other over the loss of their girlfriends, through disco dancing home together through the streets to the supradiegetic sound of John's Barry White theme song. This reflects a collapse of boundaries between the classical Hollywood musical's focus on romance and community, where "friends are terrifically loyal and strangers are often supportive," as friends now additionally occupy the

position previously reserved for lovers. E. Mordden, *The Hollywood Musical* (Newton Abbot and London: David & Charles, 1982), 107.

7. Ally to Georgia about her relationship with Billy in "Those Lips That Hand," *Ally McBeal*.

8. The Hollywood musical's key stylistic trait is to convey narrative information "through music, as distinct from a movie with music in it." M. Wood, *America in the Movies* (New York: Basic Books, 1975), 152. Rick Altman's definition of a musical concurs with this definition, stating that the musical is a film "with music that emanates from ... the diegesis, the fictional world created by the film (as opposed to Hollywood's typical background music, which comes instead out of nowhere)." Adding that, "Hollywood calls everything that shows music on film a musical." R. Altman, *The American Film Musical*, 12, 13.

9. Nicholas Abercrombie notes that increasing television series are intertextual. See N. Abercrombie, *Television and Society* (Oxford and Cambridge: Polarity Press, 1996), 25. *Ally McBeal* reflects not only an intertextuality with other television forms but more significantly engages in an intertextual rely across media forms, as it engages with the Hollywood musical, pop music and music video forms. Characters in *Ally McBeal* watch news items covering their court cases, and in other episodes, Elaine produces an infomercial for her face bra, Richard and Ling watch *Chicago Hope* (another David E. Kelley series), and there is a flashback of Ally watching music videos as a child. Additionally the narrative of *Ally McBeal* merged with *The Practice* in a double episode.

10. R. Altman, *The American Film Musical*, 51. As Altman suggests the heterosexual courtship myth and its reconfiguration is at the center of the evolution and numerous sub-genres of the classical Hollywood musical genre. This contention, as noted by Lucy Fischer, is shared by J. Collins, "Toward Defining a Matrix of the Musical Comedy: The Place of the Spectator Within the Textual Mechanism,' in R. Altman, *Genre: The Musical, a Reader*, 143, L. Braudy, 141, and T. Schatz, *Hollywood Genres: Formula, Filmmaking and the Studio* (New York: Random House, 1981), 189. L. Fischer, "Shall We Dance? Women and the Musical," *Shot/Counters Hot: Film Tradition and Women's Cinema* (Princeton, New Jersey: Princeton University Press, 1989), 132.

It is important to note that the instability and subversiveness in the musical's representations of this paradigm that is developed in *Ally McBeal* has also been the subject of much academic work, notably from feminist and queer theorists. See L. Fischer, 132–171. The most recent of which is Nadine Willis' article, "'110 Per Cent Woman': The Crotch Shot in the Hollywood Musical." Willis argues, "The musical is not simply about marriage or even sex. In spite of connubial endings, couplings and marriage are essential only because they contain the excessive femininity of the musical by directing it, eventually, towards a socially acceptable arrangement." N. Willis, *Screen* 42:2 (Summer) 2001, 139. This is reflected in *Ally McBeal*'s hindrance of the musical's courtship myth that defines in the series' key narrative element created through the failure to provide a socially acceptable arrangement for excessive femininity.

11. In her article on *Ally McBeal*, Martha Nochimson similarly identifies this trait as "a remarkable, perhaps unique, vision of multiple levels of reality burgeoning in the individual universe of each of its characters." M. P. Nochimson, "Ally McBeal Brightness Falls from the Air," *Film Quarterly* 53.3 (2000), 25.

12. R. Altman, *The American Film Musical*, 66.

13. Ibid., 69.

14. M. Porter et al., 1.

15. R. Altman, *The American Film Musical*, 27.

16. Ibid., 51.

17. "Duet shot" is Rick Altman's term. Ibid., 35.

18. Ibid., 32.

19. Ibid., 37.

20. Ibid., 77.

21. J. Ellis, "Broadcast TV Narration." *Television: The Critical View*. Edited by H. Newcomb (New York & Oxford: Oxford University Press, 1987), 555 and 561.

22. J. Ellis, 563.

23. R. Altman, *The American Film Musical*, 19.

24. R. Ray, 168.

25. M. Porter et al., 6.

26. J. Feuer, "Spectators and Spectacle," 29.

27. Ibid., 29.

28. R. Altman, *The American Film Musical*, 61. Additionally Ethan Mordden argues that the theme song is a primary musical element, "developed as soon as the soundtrack had come into use in 1927." E. Mordden, 18.

29. Martha Nochimson argues this point in her article on *Ally McBeal,* assigning character complexity to a "tension between paradoxically different inner and outer realities." This is the conflict at the core of the musical genre. M. Nochimson, 25.

30. Rick Altman defines the song world as antithetical to the real world driven by dialogue and describes the shift back from the supradiegetic realm as, "an audio dissolve returns us gently to the narrative." R. Altman, *The American Film Musical,* 66.

31. M. Nochimson, 27.

32. These segments are dominated by the conventions of soap opera where the "public sphere is examined *through* the concerns of the private.... they are also orientated around *personal and emotional* life." Abercrombie further contends that in soaps, "even relationships between employer and employee are presented not so much as business, management or employee relationships but as opportunities for the development of personal issues." N. Abercrombie, 51.

33. T. Schatz, *Old Hollywood/New Hollywood: Ritual, Art and Industry* (Michigan: UMI Research Press, 1986), 88.

34. Ibid., 123.

35. In the third season David E. Kelley made office romance the focus of the series, departing from the courtroom stories. Reported by F. McKissack, "Ally Gets Jiggy," *The Progressive* 63.11 (Nov. 1999), 38.

36. S. Frith, *Music for Pleasure: Essays in the Sociology of Pop* (Cambridge: Polity Press, 1988), 154.

37. John Ellis theorizes that the television series format creates a fairly unfaltering pattern of everyday normalcy, and that, "this everyday is a dilemma between characters." J. Ellis, 564.

38. Ibid., 563.

39. R. Altman, *The American Film Musical,* 74.

40. Ibid.

41. In an article that analyzes gender roles on prime time television in the US, Jack Glascock notes that "the face of prime television is becoming increasingly more feminine" as empowered representations of women on television are created at the expense of men, to form a gendered bond with the audience." J. Glascock "Gender roles on Prime-time network television: demographics and behaviours." *Journal of Broadcasting and Electronic Media* 45.4 (2001), 658.

Ally McBeal was developed in 1996 when David E. Kelley was asked to write a series to appeal to a female audience in the demographic age group of 18–49 years old, to retain the *Melrose Place* audience in the following timeslot. Hence the series combines all of the elements demographically reported to appeal to a female audience on a thematic, stylistic and formal structure.

Additionally, the vast majority of the *Ally McBeal* target audience is the original MTV target audience, and an appeal to this audience is evident though the use of music and music video aesthetics employed by MTV in the 1980s.

42. R. Ray, *A Certain Tendency of the Hollywood Cinema, 1930–1980* (Princeton, New Jersey: Princeton University Press, 1985), 166.

43. T. Schatz, *Old Hollywood/ New Hollywood,* 91.

44. Ibid., 125.

45. S. Frith, 166.

46. R. Altman, *The American Film Musical,* 58.

47. Ibid.

48. J. Wyatt, "Construction of the Image and the High Concept Style." In *High Concept: Movies and Marketing in Hollywood* (Austin: Texas University Press, 1994), 30.

49. R. Altman, *The American Film Musical,* 85.

50. M. Wood, 147.

51. J. Feuer, "Spectators and Spectacle," *The Hollywood Musical* (Bloomington: Indiana University Press, 1993), 47.

52. R. Altman, *The American Film Musical,* 63.

53. Ibid., 3.

54. P. Aufderheide, "The Look of the Sound." In T. Gitlen, editor, *Watching Television: A Pantheon Guide to Popular Culture* (New York: Pantheon Books, 1986), 118.

55. Rick Altman notes that the post synchronisation of the musical soundtrack removes any real world sounds and imperfections creating "an eerie, far-off effect, an injection of the ideal world into the real." R. Altman, *The American Film Musical,* 64.

56. Ibid., 61.

57. T. Schatz, *Old Hollywood/ New Hollywood,* 90.

58. Schatz notes that a fundamental component of the musical is the narrative's build up to the finale. T. Schatz, 90–91.

59. P. Braunstein, "Disco," *American Heritage,* 50.7 (1999), 43.
60. J. Feuer, "Spectators and Spectacle," 27.
61. R. Altman, *The American Film Musical,* 51.
62. Ibid., 50–51.
63. T. Schatz, *Old Hollywood/ New Hollywood,* 123.

Works Cited

Abercrombie, N. *Television and Society.* Oxford and Cambridge: Polarity Press, 1996. 7–73.

Altman, R. *The American Film Musical.* Bloomington and Indianapolis: Indiana University Press, 1987. 16–89.

Aufderheide, P. "The Look of The Sound," in *Watching Television: A Pantheon Guide to Popular Culture.* Edited by T. Gitlen. New York: Pantheon Books, 1986. 111–135.

Bordwell, D. et al., *The Classical Hollywood Cinema: Film Styles and Mode of Production to 1960.* London, Melbourne and Henley: Routledge and Kegan Paul, 1985

Braudy, L. *The World in a Frame: What We See in Films.* Garden City, NY: Anchor/Doubleday, 1976. 140.

Braunstein, P. "Disco." *American Heritage* 50.7 (1999) 43.

Collins, J. "Towards Defining a Matrix of the Musical Comedy: The Place of the Spectator Within the Textual Mechanism," in *Genre: The Musical, a Reader.* Edited by R. Altman. London, Boston and Henley: Routledge and Kegan Paul, 1981. 134–146.

Ellis, J. "Broadcast TV Narration." In *Television: The Critical View.* Edited by H. Newcomb. New York and Oxford: Oxford University Press, 1987. 553–565.

Feuer, J. "Spectators and Spectacle." In *The Hollywood Musical.* Bloomington: Indiana University Press, 1993. 23–66.

_____. "Yuppie Envy and Yuppie Guilt: *L.A. Law* and *Thirtysomething.*" In *Seeing Through the Eighties: Television and Reaganism.* Durham, NC: Duke University Press, 1995. 60–81.

_____. "Narrative Form in American Network Television." In *High Theory/Low Culture.* Edited by C. McCabe. New York: St Martin's Press, 1986. 101–4.

Fischer, L. *Shot/Countershot: Film Tradition and Women's Cinema.* Princeton: Princeton University Press, 1989. 132–171.

Frith, S. *Music For Pleasure: Essays in the Sociology of Pop.* Cambridge: Polity Press, 1988. 154–168.

Glascock, J. "Gender Roles On Prime-Time Network Television: Demographics and Behaviours," *Journal of Broadcasting and Electronic Media.* 45.4 (2001) 656–670.

McKissack, F. F. "Ally Gets Jiggy." *The Progressive,* 63.11 (Nov 1999) 38.

Mordden, E. *The Hollywood Musical.* Newton Abbot and London: David & Charles, 1982. 17–108.

Nochimson, M. P. "*Ally McBeal* Brightness Falls from the Air." *Film Quarterly,* 53.3 (2000) 25–30.

Porter, M. J., et al. "Redefining Narrative Events: Examining Television Narrative Structure." *Journal of Popular Film and Television* 30.1 (2002) 1–6.

Ray, R. *A Certain Tendency of the Hollywood Cinema, 1930–1980.* Princeton: Princeton University Press, 1985. 132–171.

Schatz, T. *Hollywood Genres: Formula, Filmmaking and the Studio,* New York: Random House, 1981. 186:221.

_____. *Old Hollywood/ New Hollywood: Ritual, Art and Industry.* Michigan: UMI Research Press, 1986. 88–95,120–125, 154–158.

Willis, N. "110 Per Cent Woman': The Crotch Shot in the Hollywood Musical." *Screen* 42:2 (Summer 2001) 121–141.

Wood, M. *America in the Movies.* New York: Basic Books, 1975. 146–164.

Wyatt, J. "Construction of the Image and the High Concept Style." In *High Concept: Movies and Marketing in Hollywood:* Austin: Texas University Press, 1994. 65–108.

Filmography

The Music Man.   Morton Da Costa, 1962.

Television Programs

"The Promise." *Ally McBeal.* Fox, October 27, 1997.

"Forbidden Fruits." *Ally McBeal.* Fox, March 2, 1998.

"The Theme of Life" *Ally McBeal.* Fox, March 9, 1998.

"You Never Can Tell." *Ally McBeal.* Fox, November 23, 1998.

"Sex, Lies and Politics." *Ally McBeal.* Fox, March 1, 1999.

"Those Lips That Hand." *Ally McBeal.* Fox, April 19, 1999.

"Let's Dance." *Ally McBeal.* Fox, April 26, 1999.

"The Green Monster." *Ally McBeal.* Fox, May 10, 1999.

"Love's Illusions." *Ally McBeal.* Fox, May 17, 1999.

11

Segments in an Endless Flow: Narrative Gaps and Partial Closure in *Ally McBeal*

Thomas Christen and *Ursula Ganz-Blaettler*[1]

Once upon a time there was a Boston lawyer who was sexually harassed by a colleague who claimed he had obsessive compulsive disorder. When she threatened to sue, she was fired. The rest is television history: Ally McBeal started work at Cage & Fish, a newly established law firm soon to be notorious for its domestic cases, beautiful babes in charge as well as its— uhm — harassment suits. While Ally's professional career soared (most of Cage & Fish's cases were to be sure winners) her emotional life suffered considerably from being (too) close to her all-time significant other, Billy Thomas, as well as his then-wife, Georgia. When Billy died from a brain tumor, in the courtroom in the midst of a closing argument, she was heartbroken. Billy's death left marks on Ally's further romantic engagements which would either be extremely short lived or extremely complicated.

Just when Ally McBeal was ready to settle down with either Brian (lawyer, British and dull), Michael (a widower, laid back and suave) or Jonathan (lawyer, young and handsome; also Michael's son) another significant other stepped into her life: Larry Paul — lawyer, divorced, and the father of a little boy in Detroit. And Larry proved to be the ideal match, by all standards ... except maybe for the fact that he would move to Detroit, eventually, to be closer to his son, Sam. There she was, alone again, and this time ready to assume the burden of adulthood. Over the following months she not only bought a house and became the temporary mentor of a younger "alter ego," Jenny, she also developed her business sense and found herself, rather unexpectedly, to be the biological mother of a street-wise teenage girl — Maddie. And she learned to accept the fact that love would never, ever come easy, not in families nor in couples.

As Ally started to enjoy her new professional status as senior partner at Cage, Fish & McBeal, Maddie's doctors and principals alerted her to the fact that her daughter suffered from severe emotional distress and was in need to go back to New York *immediately.* Ally decided to follow her there, leaving her booming law career as well as heartbroken friends and colleagues behind. And she lived happily ever after — or so at least we hope.

Seriality versus Episodicity — Ally McBeal *as* Segmented Ongoing Narrative

As with every serial narrative, there are two ways how to tell the story of *Ally McBeal.* There is the ongoing story of a heroine, or hero, who did this or that during such many seasons of a specific series' runtime. Hence the story of Ally loving and leaving, being loved and being left until a series of newly assumed responsibilities made her grow up and eventually move away.

On the other hand there was the story of a law firm, which may be told more or less in terms as to what actually happened at Cage & Fish: There was this tight-knitted group of highly ambitious lawyers getting together in morning staff meetings, in order to discuss the pending lawsuits which were introduced by senior partner Richard Fish. They would later meet with clients, develop their respective strategies for court and go about their daily routines. Once their case was scheduled for court, they would attend hearings, negotiate with lawyers on the opponents' side, work on their closing argument, give the best of their rhetoric skills and finally wait, more or less patiently, for the verdict to be announced. After their case was ruled and over, they would either reflect on unexpected outcomes or celebrate their victory down at "the Bar," set in the same building as Cage & Fish. And they would, eventually, go back to a late night work shift, or go straight home, or wander through the streets of Boston, alone or in twos. Because *Ally McBeal* was — of course — not so much about brainy lawyers and their daily routines, but more about love at the workplace, about broken hearts and unbreakable friendship, about personal theme songs, unisex toilet meetings and (other) therapy sessions, about lust and envy, hopeful dates and the looming prospect of loneliness at the end of a busy workday. All of which would come up more or less regularly and conventionally on *Ally McBeal.*

And with each segment irrevocably fading to black there would be at least one person contemplating his or her current relational state, while the

Bar singer (Vonda Shepard) would resume the segment's main (musical) theme, on-screen or off.

Predictable Patterns ...

While the syntagmatic overview on *Ally McBeal*— or any other serial narrative — was oriented toward the evolving patterns of change over time, the paradigmatic perspective points to recurring events and repetition as such: What did *usually* happen in an episode, at such or such point? What was to be expected at any given moment in time, rather than any other event? And to what extent did exceptions occur, for whatever reason and to what possible purpose?

Some series are more structured toward the paradigmatic order and thus most easily recognizable in their repetitiveness. Most police and detective series used to work that way, be it *The Untouchables* or *Starsky & Hutch* or *Murder, She Wrote*. A series like *Magnum, P.I.* (1980–1988) will forever be about this moustached private detective hunk driving a red Ferrari and hanging out with his Vietnam veteran buddies, while only few devoted fans will remember the same Thomas Magnum as a married man searching for his long-lost wife and becoming a little girl's father, at the end of an eight-year series' run. Other episodic series— which then tend to be labelled as "serials"— are more clearly structured toward the syntagmatic order of continuity and change.

Take *The X-Files*, for example: While Fox Mulder and Dana Scully were always on the run chasing mutants and freaks and explaining the unexplained, they would be appreciated most for their ongoing search for "the Truth" and their share of a mutual trust, which was or was not to become loving affection, in the end. It was the ongoing "mythology arch" that marked the series' run over nine seasons (1993–2002), not so much the episodic, or momentaneous "monster of the week" exploits.[2]

On *Buffy the Vampire Slayer* (1997–2003), on the other hand, episodes from different seasons would constantly be cross-referenced, thus producing not less than four different story types over this series' run of seven seasons (for details see Turnbull and Stranieri, 2003): There were *seasonal story arcs* and considerably wider-reaching *cross-seasonal story arcs* besides the one-time *episodic storylines* (or "monsters of the week," to quote the *X-Files* terminology) and finally the more complex, typically on-and-off *relationship arcs* which would define the series' serial narrative structure over the long run.

As these examples show there are usually two things at work within a one-hour drama series' framework, at least since the mid-eighties (see Newcomb, 1985): distinct patterns of repetitiveness that inscribe themselves in our memory after only a few and maybe irregular viewing or reading sessions, as well as a distinct sense for continuity, which is rooted in events that are accumulated over time and will therefore reflect in our long-term viewing habits only.[3]

As has been stated by Hagedorn (1995) and others, the serial narrative as such did not so much evolve from some talented writer's yearning for artistic expression than from corporate interests in diminishing production risks in a highly cost-intensive industrial sector such as mass-distributed popular culture. The basic idea was—and is—to accumulate profits from accumulated story segments over time, be it through selling and renting out of respective copies or through use of the textual units as vehicles for paid-for messages which are either incorporated or otherwise brought along. The respective constraints do, not surprisingly, define a series' content just as much as its narrative structure.

Any series' segment—be it told in sequence with others, put down on paper and read individually, screened in movie theatres or tuned in at specific moments in time, is *formatted*, since it has to fit more or less precisely into a recurring program place or slot. In the case of commercial broadcast television serial episodes have to correspond not only to hour- or half-hour slots, but also to the official sponsors' need for advertisement (commercial or act breaks) to be inserted. In order to be easily recognized by large segments of viewers, the same segment is *formulaic*, or based on a set of narrative conventions, which follow pre-existing molds such as genre structures or other, more media-specific, text types. And finally, each series' segment comes fully equipped with a distinctive *corporate identity*, or *canon of recognizable traits*, including licensed material such as a recurring theme song, catchy opening credits, some regularly offered bonus material (such as the outtakes at the end of each segment of *Home Improvement*), etc., but also diegetic devices such as a recurring voice-over, a standardized timeframe per episode,[4] an uncommon protagonist's dress-code, or mannerism, or maybe a cinematic visual style (see Caldwell, 1995, for examples).

While *formats* (a program's prescribed length and formal structure) do guarantee an easy implementation in program schedules (be it cinema, television, or any kind of editorial program), a *formula,* with its conventional developments and foreseeable outcomes, works as a mediating agent between producers and audiences. What is told and shown reverberates with cultural patterns that are already more or less well known. It is here where ideologies and popular myths come into play, either to reconfirm dominant social norms and values, or to undermine them to a certain degree. While commercially organized media systems tend to follow whatever public opinion is safe enough to be considered mainstream (Gitlin, 1983, and in Newcomb, 2000), they may also reflect different world views and thus provide a "forum" for a more pluralistic public debate on such norms and practices (see Newcomb and Hirsch in Newcomb, 2000).

As John Cawelti, and later John Fiske and others, have stated, formulaic patterns and conventions do not define popular culture texts on their own. Just as important is narrative invention, or innovation, which does account for newness and freshness. It is the right balance between surplus and surprise, routine and special event, between the well known and the unknown, which lures established audience members into coming back, week after week, while newcomers may jump in eventually, due to a well-marketed narrative turn or perhaps a singular stunt. Surprises undermine our expectations, work against the established canon and do eventually break molds (in order to evaluate and develop new ones). As for the right mixture between convention and invention there is no established recipe to follow.

That is why a serial narrative can, at basically any stage of its eventual run, be looked at in terms of paradigms (on accounting for what is always there, episode for episode) but also in terms of syntagma: There is necessary development and growth, and even if protagonists come back, week after week, they do indeed go somewhere, over their respective series' overall run.

... and Unpredictable Outcomes

When speaking of serial narrative, we usually speak of ongoing stories that "never end." What does not end — or is not supposed to end, rather — is

a. the actual output of episodes, or segments (since the series' success is defined by its "long legs" — here translating into a long-term stay on the airwaves). And
b. the narrative flow, which is more or less continuous, but not foreseeable — at least, again, not in the long run. Nobody does know beforehand where all those recounted acts and events, dilemmas and conflicts, relationships and (un)lucky streaks may eventually lead.

In other words: While any mini-series' ending is pre-written, a police or detective or court series' ending is not. There is no one to definitely know where and why the narrative will stop and rest; not the contractually hired players nor the crew members or studio employees— not even the showrunners, executive producers or network officials. As for the highly expensive prime time program slots, it all depends on whether a prolonged output of even more episodes is considered lucrative enough at some decisive stage. A series, just like any other social institution, lives by public interest: Once ratings drop and sponsors start to look elsewhere, the run of a series is seriously endangered.

Since nobody is clairvoyant enough to tell what one series' run may eventually lead up to, literally anything can happen. As long as a serial narrative is actually peopled (and not animated or run by synthespians), that fact alone guarantees unpredictability. Protagonists may walk away or die, or be fired for reasons which may or may not be made public. Female protagonists may become pregnant, and the question is if the pregnancy will be built in or not. Similarly crew members may quit and walk away, or suddenly die, or be fired and replaced by persons whose vision is radically different from the original one. What distinguishes the *cumulative narrative* from the earlier paradigmatic model is the fact that such developments inevitably show. And need to be explained further in the realm of the fiction.

As for *Ally McBeal,* once Gil Bellows (alias Billy Thomas) decided to leave the production of the ongoing series, his character was almost certainly doomed to die an untimely death. But he would not be forgotten. The same applied when Robert Downey Jr. ran into legal troubles of his own: His playing of Ally's new love interest, Larry Paul, was not simply cut short, but relegated to a somewhat less obligating on-and-off-appearance — with the snowman as a temporary stand-in, and the embodiment of a *freeze frame,* eventually. Larry was not necessarily to come back, at some stage or another, but shared memories would set standards for things to come.

It is because of such continuities (and more to be played upon in the series' fifth and last season) that even drastic changes in cast or a character's function have not been sufficient enough to alter the show's original vision, which has been kept upright by the series' creator and head writer, David E. Kelley.

In the following three sections of this essay we shall develop the specific *cumulative* structure of *Ally McBeal* by a systematic close reading of each segment's beginnings and endings. We shall first concentrate on the paradigmatic, or recurring elements of each segment in order to establish the main plot, or *master plot* structure of the series. We will then go on to investigate what has been changed over time, or was unruly enough to be considered a one-time exception. By reconstructing the ongoing story of Ally McBeal and her friends and colleagues, finally, we shall ask ourselves how much *Ally McBeal* had indeed moved away from its initial narrative concept when Ally McBeal did say goodbye to Cage & Fish to pursue another life in yet some other (and still unknown) diegetic universe.

Ally McBeal *as Plot and Accumulated Story*

In-between September 11, 1997, and May 20, 2002, 112 episodes of *Ally McBeal* aired on the Fox network, on regular Monday nights at 9 p.m.[5] Season breaks were conventionally provided every summer, with repeats of episodes broadcast either between May and mid–September or May and mid–October. With the show set entirely in Boston (except for two episodes, which took some of the cast and crew to Los Angeles), it was no wonder that wintertimes— and especially Christmas seasons— would reflect heavily on the events portrayed. One season counted 21 to 23 episodes, with frequent "preemption" times (when delayed production schedules collided with broadcast schedules) mainly

a. during October (if the respective season started in mid–September),
b. somewhere around Christmas and New Year and
c. around Easter, with either a longer midseason break or a series of minor gaps to be filled with *Ally McBeal* reruns.

As may not be surprising, *Ally McBeal* did work as a hybrid television program in several ways— not only as a peculiarly moody mix between two well-established series formats (the half-hour comedy turned into a four-act dramedy running a full 45 to 52 minutes) but also as a narrative mix between series and serial. As a series, *Ally McBeal* did represent the classical courtroom drama just as much as its more life-and-death-oriented, gritty sibling *The Practice* (also created by David E. Kelley), with which it interacted occasionally.[6] As a prime time (and clearly soap opera-inspired) serial, however, *Ally McBeal* established — on more than one diegetic level — an ongoing discourse on the fragility of human relationships, by investigating guiding principles of courtship and couple-making in an urban setting and with regards to a clearly privileged, young and hip upper class segment just as well as the "impossible" dreams and ideals haunting and sabotaging any serious attempt at settling. Both the cases and the lawyers' private lives commented on the same subjects and were interwoven to some degree. But while the cases were all to be "closed," literally, in act three or four, the private struggles would go on. And on. From episode to episode, and from season to season. And from the beginning straight to the end.

As for the cumulative aspects of *Ally McBeal*, there is a distinct continuity of ongoing narrative threads (or arcs) to be observed, as well as a constant, albeit highly selective sense of memory.[7] Continuity referred to what *was to be* in episodes yet to come just as much as to what *had just happened* in one of the earlier segments. Narrative gaps were often to be filled in later, to an extent where the ongoing events in the series would directly reflect the time-structure of the "real world" — in terms of broadcast schedule, that is. That goes for explicit links between weekly episodes (with protagonists commenting on what happened *last week*) as much as for links made between seasons (Brian reminding Ally of the fact that they met *six months ago*) or for the series' run as such (Ally's entry into Cage & Fish remembered by some colleagues as happening *four years earlier*). What the cumulative structure did and did not for the series, in terms of conventional and inventive story resolution, will be re-evaluated at the very end of this essay.

The Paradigmatic Plot Structure of Ally McBeal

In order to establish the specific (and as such conventional) narrative structure of *Ally McBeal*, we elaborated an ideal — or paradigmatic — model episode as *master plot,* based on systematic scans of the series' 112 episodes. In doing this, we focused

a. on recurring plot points and their usual place in a segment's four-act-structure. And
b. on recurring formal and narrative elements with regards to segments' beginnings and endings, such as summarizing moments ("Previously on *Ally McBeal*" or "Last season on *Ally McBeal*"), opening and closing credits, and specific prologue or epilogue characteristics.

As for the latter the typical program "flow" of broadcast television (see Williams, 1992, his observations dating back to 1974) proved to be quite ambiguous: While the beginning of any feature film in a cinema can be defined as the one crucial moment "when there is *nothing* before, but (usually) *something* after," with the ending mirroring the beginning inasmuch as "there is (usually) *something* before and *nothing* after" (Christen 2002, 17) television programs pretty much resemble the Volkswagen car in an early printed ad: They go on ... and on ... and on. That is why we defined the beginning of an *Ally* episode as moment "when there was (usually) *another program* before and *Ally McBeal* after," while endings would be situated where "there was *Ally McBeal* before and (usually) *another program* after." (And commercial breaks did not count as another program, but as inserts, rather.)

As for recurring plot points they were easily identified with those legal affairs brought to Cage & Fish. The clients' individual stories did indeed structure any individual episode to the extent where stages of the juridical process were confined to specific narrative acts. The morning staff meeting would usually be staged in act 1, if not in the prologue leading up to act 1. Case meetings would happen anytime at Cage & Fish, as would spontaneous meetings in the court building and official court hearings. Two decisive stages, however, were located firmly in the second half of an episode: the closing arguments of both parties (either in act 3 or 4) and the judge's or jury's verdict, which would be made known earlier only when some more important event (such as a wedding or a funeral) came up and took most of act 4. Otherwise it was to be the verdict that literally "closed" a juridical argument as well as this week's argumentative roundup. Right after a verdict clients would either thank their lawyers and leave (forever) or get to be invited "downstairs" at Cage & Fish to dance and celebrate. This always happened at "the Bar"—a somewhat transitional, or liminal[8] place where Vonda Shepard and guests would sing and comment on (or cover) the outcome of trials as well as those storylines to be followed further, while the solo players of this week's episode would either sit in a pensive mood in their office, late at night, or walk home, alone.

As for the "Bar" and its usual host and performer, Vonda Shepard, there was more to it than a simple place for after work parties and fun and dance. Not every episode would end with people dancing and cheering at the "Bar." Sometimes a segment was to start right there, only to lead over to a morning banter between Renée and Ally, before the latter left for the regular morning meeting at Cage & Fish. However, most episodes did indeed announce an imminent ending by having everybody gather at Vonda's place. And more than once the songs performed would bear the episode's title, or at least refer to a main storyline and its eventual outcome, yet to become true.[9]

Following Victor Turner, the "Bar" served as a classical liminal stage — it was set between the firm and the street (in a rather mythical setting, which by day or by night would look completely different!), between day and night, and the stage itself worked as a strictly confined territory where only some actions were legitimate — singing, playing an instrument, announcing a recurring guest's birthday, or maybe the occasional telling of a dirty joke. Otherwise the lawyer protagonists (that just happened to command their own professional stage earlier on, at the courthouse) were bound to stay down on the dance floor, and either sit and talk or join in dancing. While songs' lyrics might explicitly act as a comment made on this week's episode's events (taking on the episode's title song, for instance), Vonda Shepard would never intervene as a diegetic bard. While being part of the same diegetic world as the lawyers, she nevertheless stayed distant and would never leave the stage — with the only exception of one of Ally's birthdays, which was celebrated back home at Ally's place in "All of Me" (5–20). And even if Vonda wouldn't make sense as a performer, for different reasons (see 4–16: "The Getaway," with most of the action transferred to Los Angeles) the "Bar"— or "a" bar, as in any bar — would still work as final closing and commenting stage for that episode's story events, with Anastacia replacing Vonda, for once.[10]

In more than one sense, then, Vonda Shepard belonged to the same musical universe as the protagonists' various "theme songs," and notably Barry White, or various crooners stalking protagonists at unexpected moments in time. As with those vocal and visual renderings of Al Green, Barry Manilow, or the "Dancing Baby" and other musically enhanced special effects in *Ally McBeal*, Vonda's role defied traditional definitions of diegesis. While she would always be visible to all visitors at the Bar and definitely "real" in this her realm, her voice would also carry on into other stages of an episode's narrative, most notably at the very end, when the narrative action would slow down and come to a halt, while the music would linger on over (usually) some "fade to black." Some episodes would even close in on one or two protagonists privately performing a song at home (see 2–21 "The Green Monster," or 4–10 "The Ex-Files"), with Vonda Shepard taking over and finishing the song either nondiegetically, in voice-over, or diegetically, at the Bar.

Absolute Beginnings: Establishing
Shots and Summarizing Sections

With regard to the visual style of *Ally McBeal* (and also its specific musicality) its extended establishing shots proved to be highly significant. They would usually introduce a new episode right after the opening credits. Later into the episode, they would introduce a new act after a commercial break, or sometimes announce a new thematic subject. Only occasionally, however, would they indeed introduce (establish) a specific place, such as the firm, the courthouse or Ally's respective homestead (first the apartment shared with Renee Raddick, and later the brownstone building shared with Maddie and Victor). This is true also for the lengthy aerial shots of Boston, which were taken either by day or by night and enhanced by musical intros, or Vonda Shepard singing. More an illuminating (and clearly "televisual," to quote Caldwell, 1995) trademark than an orienting device they did not so much establish a place as indicate a change in mood, or a narrative ellipsis evoking "later" that day, that evening, or that night. From the fourth and fifth season onward, however, aerial views would extend to the courthouse

(4–10: "The Ex-Files") and the brick building of Cage & Fish (4–12: "Hats Off to Larry"), thus establishing those two main buildings as somewhat "real" and "authentic."[11] And at least once in the series' run would the camera zoom in from an overview establishing shot directly onto the firm's characteristic high windows, as an apt illustration of John Cage storming into Richard Fish's office, mad as hell about his friend's use (or misuse, rather) of his, John's, secret "Hole" (see 5–06: "Lost and Found").

As for the actual episode beginning (in terms of having *other programs* before and the scheduled program *from now on*) there was often an introductory "previously" section, looking back on former episodes and establishing narrative links over quite some time. These sections would not follow any pre-defined rule, neither in terms of occurrence (yes or no) or length (30 to 80 seconds) nor with regard to formal structure and narrative function. Some were quick summaries resuming an ongoing narrative thread over two or three episodes up to here (see 4–05: "The Last Virgin," or 4–06: "'Tis the Season"). Others would present several threads as an interwoven puzzle, reflecting on a multitude of storylines yet to be resolved (examples: 4–13: "Reach Out and Touch," 4–14: "Boys Town," 4–15: "Falling Up," and 4–16: "The Getaway"). While the first season of *Ally McBeal* did not seem too much in need of such summarizing visual cues, only five out of the 23 episodes of season four did without. However, the female voice announcing this section would never so much remind us of what simply "happened before" on *Ally McBeal* as give us a highly selective and privileged insight into some specific conflict situation(s) which was or were yet to go on and evolve right before our very eyes.

In terms of the "selective" memory the "previously" sections would sometimes refer to episodes spread over several seasons, such as in "Cloudy Skies, Chance of Parade" (4–20, with a gallery of Ally's most memorable birthday shots taken from 2–18: "Those Lips, That Hand" and 3–18: "Turning Thirty") or "Queen Bee" (4–21; the comeback of a church reverend and his jealous chorus leader introduced by recycling of footage previously seen on 2–03: "Fools' Night Out"). At any rate they would, like the establishing aerial shots of Boston, work much more as visual markers than as informative, orienting devices— be it by referring to singular events or specific subjects, or maybe to a complete "Last season on *Ally McBeal*" chain of events.

While any regular prologue would open "in medias res," with either Ally stumbling onto some rather embarrassing situation or her telling us in voice over what was going to happen on that specific day, maybe, some segments' openings would be completely different. If indeed "in dreams begins responsibility" (as has been claimed by the Irish poet William Butler Yeats) then Ally began growing up in her dreams ... at least a little bit.

About a dozen times have episodes been introduced by Ally's (wet) dreams and nightmares: She found her ideal match — but only in her sleep. She was to die in an airplane crash (or falling out of one), kissed John Cage with true passion (or Glenn, or Victor, or others), and she underwent heart surgery only to find that broken hearts never mend. The dreams as such had several narrative functions: they worked as summaries of past events, presented an upcoming segment's main subject, gave away precious information as to Ally's mental state, and they definitely made us, the audience, jump. In dreams even more than in regular sequences literally anything was prone to happen, and any episode's opening as a dream would open up new perspectives — for us, the audience, just as well as for Ally, the dreamer.

Final Endings and Beyond

As has been stated before, any regular *Ally McBeal* episode consisted of several open-ended, and mostly private, storylines as well as one or several "closed" legal affairs. And it was, with a few notable exceptions, the protagonists' private lives which would be taken beyond an actual segment's ending in order to be "faded to black."

Most of the end sequences began right after either a verdict was spoken or a settlement achieved. While the morning staff meeting would introduce a segment's legal affair(s), the nightly Bar meeting put them at rest, so to speak. In-between the court ruling and after work party, however, there was usually some important narrative twist or turn to be expected. Couples would eventually split up or maybe question their relationship, or an unassuming bystander might find his or her match. If the outcome of a legal case was to reflect on the lawyers' own standards and practices, this was usually the moment of truth. Later, at the Bar, there would be meaningful glances as well as commenting remarks (on and off stage), but no (more) decisions taken, that day. Only consequences shown and displayed, as with couples happily dancing (or kissing and making out, back home), while some solitary souls would once more stay single, and accordingly be "singled out" in the closing images of the respective segment.

Two distinct "senses of an ending" (to quote Frank Kermode, 1967) need to be differentiated here, with regard to the series' double narrative structure as a text carrying one protagonist's name in the title all while being identified just as easily as an ensemble story. Consequently there were endings which would correspond to Ally McBeal's status as the quintessential "lonely hero," while other endings placed her alongside her friends and colleagues and their respective whereabouts. Solitude was to be found in both types of ending, eventually — in final images following one person into some unspectacular *digressive* activity, or situation, as much as in those *state-of-the-art* endings, where several persons were shown in parallel montage. In a typical *digression* ending Ally would be left playing with strangers in the streets of Boston (2–16: "Sex, Lies and Politics") or holding on to one of these forever faithful (and inflatable) companions (2–17: "Civil War"). Or both Renee and Ally would poke fun at their hopeless state as hopeless singles, by dancing and singing to the Everly Brothers' "Bye Bye Love" (2–21: "The Green Monster"). Typical examples for a state-of-the-art-ending, however, are to be found in "Once in a Lifetime" (1–15), "Fools Night Out" (2–03), "World's Without Love" (2–06), "Happy Trails" (2–07, with a very happy John Cage singled out in the end), "Making Spirits Bright" (2–10) or "Love Unlimited" (2–12, with no less than three solitary persons paralleled in one and the same split screen shot).[12]

Based on such recurring elements the *master plot* of *Ally McBeal* can be conceived as following: There would — in nearly each or at least in very many of the 112 episodes — be

1. some "previously" shots, as a resuming narrative actualizing specific thematic subjects over a shorter or longer period of time
2. a prologue, leading up to a hilarious or shocking moment, or to an unexpected self-revelation
3. the opening credits (mirroring current staff changes at Cage & Fish, mostly)
4. recurring establishing shots which took viewers on a round trip through Boston while introducing a specific mood, or sometimes a song which would be assigned a commenting function later on. Here, consistent with the series in itself, seasons were closely monitored and represented according to airdates
5. Staff meetings at the firm were held every morning, as the most regular event occurring in act 1 (since 1–6: "The Promise"). The meeting was sometimes introduced before the opening credits in the prologue (as in 1–20: "The Inmates," or 3–20: "Buried Pleasures"). Toward the end of the episode the meeting would be mirrored in the regular gathering at the "Bar" where Vonda Shepard and guests sang and entertained their respective guests
6. There were one to a maximum of three legal affairs, which were or were not tied in with the life and trials of the lawyers involved, and later to be closed by the
7. court's ruling, followed by
8. other closing events and decisions taken. Then there was
9. the afterwork party at the Bar, with songs referring to an episode's title, probably, or having other summarizing functions

10. The ending sequence would gather some or all protagonists of this episode in their respective place and mood, while the action would slow down to an eventual stop and only then fade to black, with the end credits starting to roll.

Significant Paradigm Shifts on Ally McBeal

While the fourth season of *Ally McBeal* promised significant changes already in the very first opening credits (with Larry Paul and other recent cast additions established once and for all) the series' fate proved to turn in circles over the following weeks and months to come. At the end of season four Ally was bound to be lonelier than ever before, with Larry Paul gone for good and no other steady relationship in sight. The fifth season than opened with a literal "bang," deliberately reflecting on the series' earlier beginning in 1–01: When Ally met Jenny (by nearly running her over with her motorized city scooter) the series did start over as well — only this time it was Jenny recently being fired, mourning a lost love and being hired by impulse, only to discover that her former lover did actually work at Cage & Fish.

This "cloning" of Ally as a much younger "alter ego" went as far as having the former — Ally — dream up the latter — Jenny's — nightmares, complete with Jenny waking up, screaming, within Ally's dream (in 5–03: "Neutral Corners"). And yet the extraordinary move of doubling Ally's main character didn't lead anywhere, in terms of the ongoing narrative: With Jenny as well as Glenn gone and erased from the opening credits after only a few episodes, Ally could not simply go back and become her old and somewhat childish self *again*. Instead she followed the "serious" narrative path originally established alongside Larry Paul, bought a house and settled down, all while assuming professional as well as private responsibility. Following in Larry's footsteps, then, made Ally McBeal grow up, eventually.

In direct consequence, however, these significant character developments affected the narrative structure of *Ally McBeal:* As a responsible senior partner — and as a single mother raising a daughter — Ally would not necessarily spend any more time down at the Bar. As for endings, then, they would find this series' protagonist over and over back home, dealing with domestic affairs rather than with legal outcomes, or loneliness. The decisive, "pirouetting" moment for all these changes is to be found at the end of "Playing With Matches" (5–08), in a highly symbolical ice-skating scene which had Ally finding her inner balance, somehow. In this ending, she spread her wings on the ice, and she did not seem to be in need of a helping hand anytime soon.

Cumulative Overview, or: The Multiple Endings of Ally McBeal

The series began with Ally's entry into Cage & Fish and consequently ended with her exit from the said law firm. While season one found her struggling with her private and professional demons, she also developed to be a reliable team player (alongside Billy Thomas, his wife, Georgia Thomas, and others, reflected also on the series' credits), and she started to work on her inner demons by attending therapy sessions. Season two saw her developing several serious relationships before she fell back into her old affection for Billy (see the kiss in 2–14: "Pyramids on the Nile"), which lead to more "fighting the demons" therapy sessions and a very exceptional segment's ending (2–15: "Sideshow": Ally closing the door of the psychiatrist's apartment behind her, having found out the truth about Billy's mixed feelings toward her). The overall tendency was to put other firm members into the spotlight as well, such as Nelle and Ling, whose respective love affairs with the two senior partners of Cage & Fish would become quite dominant.

Season three began with the infamous *Car Wash scene,* with Ally living out a sexual fantasy and promptly ruining a marriage. More important were Georgia's and Billy's eventual split-up and his cancer-induced death (in 3–16: "Boy Next Door"). The remaining episodes found Ally mourning Billy and eventually finding a new love interest, Brian (in the nearly all-sung 3–21: "The Musical — Almost"). After he, and other candidates for a cosy ménage-à-deux, were dumped in season four, events concentrated fully on the growing affection between Ally and Larry Paul, which was mirrored by other quite long-running love affairs (such as John Cage's with a kindergarten teacher, Melanie).

It is interesting to note that Ally's first encounter with Larry happened exactly where her love for Billy died two seasons earlier — in Tracey's (the psychiatrist's) apartment, on the very day of Larry Paul moving in there (as a lawyer, not a shrink). Also noteworthy is the fact that Larry's definite leaving of town (in 4–22: "Home Again") was announced earlier on, with "Cloudy Skies, Chance of Parade" (4–20) being literally riddled with hints pointing towards an upcoming separation. And finally, whatever attempts at love there were "after Larry," they would resemble Ally's rather ineffective moves "after Billy": Nobody would come close to the perfect partner once (or, rather, again) found and lost, not even "the boy" (Glenn, established as Jenny's "Billy" earlier on) or someone as caring and understanding and patient and ... uhmm, perfect as Victor, Ally's own personal handyman-carpenter-plumber (see 5–09: "Blowin' in the Wind" up to 5–18: "Another One Bites the Dust"). It was quite obvious that no one would — ever — come close to Larry Paul, and more than one episode did close in on that recurring statement (see, for an example, 5–06: "Lost and Found").

Apart from these occasional lust or love objects which would all be dumped again, at one stage or another, things did change dramatically in season five. There was a literal new start (Ally bumping into her alter ego, Jenny) and — after this narrative strategy backfired — a consequent development of the "new" and wiser Ally into a woman fully assuming her responsibilities. Only that those responsibilities made her eventually leave the workplace, leave town, and leave her own series for good.

In hindsight Ally's (and Maddie's) move away from Boston to New York doesn't appear so much as a cheap "emergency exit" (due to poor ratings, for instance) but rather as a consequent final decision — after all Cage & Fish was never to work without the McBeal attached to it, and on the other hand there would never, ever, be an *Ally McBeal* in any other place than the quintessential lawyers' hometown Boston. Ally's move also clearly mirrored Larry's earlier move away from town, after Sam's eventual attempt to sue him for emotional distress. As for family responsibilities, then, parents would move wherever their needy offspring was headed. And that was that ... end of story.

Looking back on the series as such, its diegetic overall arch definitely marks it as "a" narrative, not as a series of — more or less interrelated — individual anecdotes. The paradigmatic structure of each segment notwithstanding (a weekly case or several individual cases, with legal work extending from morning meetings to late after work parties at the "Bar"), it was the lawyers' personal and ongoing storylines that kept *Ally McBeal* on track, providing for the series' specific humour as well as its distinct cumulative aspects. In order to follow Ally's temptations and tribulations, week after week, you needed at least some basic knowledge of the title character's sentimental whereabouts, and you probably needed to *like* her and her not less eccentric colleagues at Cage & Fish, before you allowed yourself such a long-term investment.

As for any segment's ending (or multiple endings) they would always be partial — more a consequent slow-down than an actual stop, and a lingering moment used to reflect and look back rather than a transgressive move forward. After all Ally herself seemed to be quite caught up in her past, fearing nothing so much as her own annual birthdays and mourning any lost love for a long time to come. Until, at the end of five long and turbulent years (on- as well as off-screen), there was no other way to go anymore but forward: right out of the picture, into an unforeseeable as well as forever unforeseen future.

Notes

1. We would like to thank various *Ally McBeal* experts for providing helpful suggestions and thoughtful comments, especially Anna Maria Krajewska and Caroline Schmidt.

2. The terms have been borrowed from fan discussions on *alt.tv.x-files* and other Internet platforms concerning *The X-Files.* According to the series' "Frequently Asked Questions" (see www. televisionwithoutpity.com/faq.cgi?show=5, last consulted 05/06/02) the Monster-of-the-Week or *MotW* episodes were the ones that stood independent of each other while the mythology arch or *mytharch* segments would refer to any "seemingly unending and progressively more confusing story line involving aliens (...) but also Krycek, the bees, the clones, CSM, the alien ships, the black oil, Billy Miles" or other ongoing narrative threads.

3. For details see Turnbull and Stranieri, and especially Newcomb (1985). Horace Newcomb analyzed *Magnum, P.I.* as well as other examples of series "with a memory" and suggested to label them as *cumulative narrative.* Thompson (1996) ranks the memory aspect amid those properties that dignify a series as *quality television.* Quality TV, then, is 1) not "regular" TV, has 2) a quality pedigree, attracts 3) a well-educated audience, is 4) daring, and thus "usually the result of fights with the airing network," tends 5) to have a large ensemble cast, has 6) *a memory,* creates 7) a new genre by mixing old ones, tends 8) to be literary and writer-based, with a writing that is "usually more complex than in other types of programming," is 9) self-conscious, with a subject matter that tends 10) toward the controversial and is, "in the best of senses, liberal TV," aspires 11) toward realism, and is 12) "usually enthusiastically showered with awards and critical acclaim."

4. *Ally McBeal*'s morning staff meetings may well have been inspired by *Hill Street Blues* whose every segment would be introduced by the obligatory morning call and Sgt. Phil Esterhaus' fatherly advice: "Let's roll. And hey — let's be careful out there."

5. The episode numbers used in this essay (5–02, for instance) do not refer to actual production numbers but to seasons and individual segments as they were initially broadcast.

6. "The Inmates" (1–20) was conceived as a crossover episode with *The Practice*'s "The Axe Murderer." Bobby Donnell would come back for a specific case (and a passionate kiss with Ally) in the first season's final episode, "These Are the Days" (1–23). And there were other members of the same Boston-based law firm to drop by in court or at the Bar, such as Helen Gamble in "Making Spirits Bright" (2–10) or Jimmy Berluti in "I Know Him by Heart" (2–23).

7. For the selective memory of series' protagonists (or their writers) see Kozloff in Allen (1992[2]).

8. The term of the *liminal stage* borrowed from Victor Turner (see Turner, 1982, and Ashley, 1990, and also Fiske, 1989).

9. Episode titles taken from songs actually sung in the said episode were (according to *http://www.geocities.com/merrystar3/allylist.htm*) in 1–03: "The Kiss" (It's in His Kiss"), in 1–05: "One Hundred Tears Away," in 1–21: "Being There" (I'll Be There"), in 1–22: "Alone Again" ("Alone Again — Naturally"), in 2–01: "The Real World" ("In the Real World"), in 2–03: "Fools Night Out ("Fools Fall in Love"), in 2–09: "You Never Can Tell," in 2–11: "In Dreams," in 2–23: "I Know Him By Heart," in 3–11: "Over the Rainbow" (from *The Wizard of Oz*), in 3–17: "I Will Survive," in 3–19: "Do You Wanna Dance," in 4–09: "Reasons to Believe" ("Reason to Believe"), in 4–11: "Mr. Bo ("Mr. Bojangles"), in 4–22: Home Again," in 5–05: "I Want Love," in 5–08: "Playing with Matches" ("Matchmaker," from *Fiddler on the Roof*), in 5–09: "Blowin' in the Wind," in 5–10: "One Hundred Tears" ("One Hundred Tears Away"), in 5–11: "A Kick in the Head" ("Ain't That a Kick in the Head"), in 5–13: "Woman" ("I'm a Woman"), in 5–18: "Tom Dooley" and in 5–20: "What I'll Never Do for Love Again" ("What I Did for Love," from *A Chorus Line*).

10. Anastacia also joined Vonda Shepard some episodes later, when Jane came over from the West Coast to visit Richard Fish in Boston — see the end of 4–22: "Home Again."

11. It is interesting to note that the outside world in the series was usually portrayed as highly realistic, from urban street life right up to views seemingly taken from the firm's characteristic high windows. All while the actual indoor concept of Cage & Fish, as well as the respective arrangements of rooms at court, would remain a mystery.

12. Very rarely would episodes end with a bang instead: Episode 5–12 ("The New Day") did end with the court's ruling instead of any more private thread evolving further. And two double episodes (4–03 and 4–04 as well as 5–16 and 5–17) used the classical cliffhanger ending to suspend the ongoing action in mid-air, literally.

Bibliography

FAN WEBSITES CONSULTED:

http://allymcbeal.tktv.net/ (extensive plot summaries done by Dana Hagerty and others)
http://www.geocities.com/merrystar3/allylist.htm (all lyrics to songs sung on *Ally McBeal*, compiled by merrystar@yahoo.com)

ACADEMIC AND OTHER WORKS CONSULTED:

Allen, Robert C., ed. *To Be Continued ... Soap Operas Around the World.* London and New York: Routledge, 1995.

Anderson, Christopher. "Reflections on *Magnum, P.I.*" In: Horace M. Newcomb, ed., *Television, The Critical View.* New York: Oxford, 1987, pp. 112–125.

Appelo, Tim. *Ally McBeal: The Official Guide.* New York and London: HarperCollins, 1999.

Ashley, K., ed. *Victor Turner and the Construction of Cultural Criticism. Between Literature and Anthropology.* Bloomington: Indiana University Press, 1990.

Caldwell, John Thornton. *Televisuality: Style, Crisis and Authority in American Television.* New Brunswick: Rutgers University Press, 1995.

Cantor, Muriel G., and Joel M. Cantor. *Prime-Time Television: Content and Control.* London: Sage, 1992.

Cawelti, John G. *Adventure, Mystery, and Romance: Formula Stories as Art and Popular Culture.* Chicago and London: University Press of Chicago, 1976.

_____. *The Six-Gun Mystique.* Bowling Green, KY: Bowling Green State University Popular Press, 1970.

_____. *The Six-Gun Mystique Sequel.* Bowling Green, KY: Bowling Green State University Popular Press, 1999.

Christen, Thomas. *Das Ende im Spielfilm: Vom klassischen Hollywood zu Antonionis offenen Formen.* Marburg: Schueren, 2001.

Eco, Umberto. "Innovation and Repetition. Between Modern and Post-Modern Aesthetics." In *Daedalus* 114 (1985) 4, S. 161–184.

Fiske, John. "Reading the Beach." In *Reading the Popular.* Boston: Unwin Hyman, 1989, pp. 43–76.

_____. *Television Culture: Popular Pleasures and Politics.* London and New York: Methuen, 1987, and Routledge, 1999.

Gitlin, Todd. *Inside Prime Time.* New York: Routledge, 1983, 1985.

Hagedorn, Roger. "Doubtless to Be Continued. A Brief History of Serial Narrative." In Robert C. Allen, *To Be Continued ... Soap Operas Around the World.* London and New York: Routledge, 1995, pp. 27–48.

Hayward, Jennifer Poole. *Consuming Pleasures: Active Audiences and Serial Fiction from Dickens to Soap Opera.* Lexington: University Press of Kentucky, 1997.

Kermode, Frank. *The Sense of an Ending.* New York: Oxford University Press, 1967.

Kozloff, Sarah Ruth. "Narrative Theory and Television." In Robert C. Allen, ed., *Channels of Discourse, Reassembled: Television and Contemporary Criticism.* Chapel Hill: University of North Carolina Press, 1992, pp. 67–100.

Lavery, David, ed. *Full of Secrets: Critical Approaches to Twin Peaks.* Detroit: Wayne State University Press, 1995.

McLuhan, Marshall. "Horse Opera and Soap Opera." In *The Mechanical Bride: Folklore of Industrial Man.* New York: Vanguard Press, 1951. Also Corte Madera: Gingko Press 2001, pp. 155–158.

Newcomb, Horace M. "*Magnum*. The Champagne of TV?" In *Channels of Communication*, May/June, 1985, pp. 23–26.

_____, and Paul M. Hirsch. "Television as a Cultural Forum: Implications for Research." In Horace Newcomb, ed., *Television, The Critical View*. New York: Oxford, 2000, pp. 561–573.

Nochimson, Martha P. *No End to Her: Soap Operas and the Female Subject*. Berkeley: University of California Press, 1992.

_____. "*Ally McBeal*. Brightness Falls From the Sky." In *Film Quarterly* 53 (2000) 3, pp. 25–32.

O'Donnell, Hugh. *Good Times, Bad Times: Soap Operas and Society in Western Europe*. London and New York: Leicester University Press, 2000.

Oltean, Tudor. "Series and Seriality in Media Culture." In *European Journal of Communication* 8 (1993) 1, pp. 5–31.

Scherer, Brigitte, Ursula Ganz-Blaettler, Monika Grobkopf, and Ute Wahl. *Morde im Paradies: Amerikanische Detektiv- und Abenteuerserien der 80er Jahre*. Munich: Oelschlaeger 1994 and 1995.

Thompson, Kristin. *Storytelling in Film and Television*. Cambridge: Harvard University Press, 2003.

Thompson, Robert J. *From Hill Street Blues to ER: Television's Second Golden Age*. New York: Continuum, 1996.

Turnbull, Sue, and Vyvyan Stranieri. *Bite Me: Narrative Structures and Buffy the Vampire Slayer*. Melbourne: Australian Center for the Moving Image (ACMI), 2003.

Turner, Victor. "From Liminal to Liminoid, in Play, Flow and Ritual. An Essay in Comparative Symbiology." In *From Ritual to Theatre: The Human Seriousness of Play*. New York: Performing Arts Journal Publications, 1982, pp. 20–60.

Williams, Raymond. *Television: Technology and Cultural Form*. Hanover and London: Wesleyan, 1992.

About the Contributors

Thomas Christen is a professor of film studies at the Cinema Studies Institute at the University of Zurich.

Ursula Ganz-Blaettler is an associate professor at the Media and Journalism Institute at the University of Lugano. She is the author and co-author of several articles on memory and identity.

Twyla Gibson is an assistant professor in the McLuhan Program in culture and technology and the Department of Information Studies at the University of Toronto. Her research focuses on problems at the intersection of philosophy, religion, education, and communications technology. She has worked as a researcher and writer for Canadian Broadcasting Corporation National Television, among others.

Kristyn Gorton is a senior lecturer in the School of Cultural Studies, Leeds Metropolitan University. She has published articles on feminism, desire and television and is currently writing a monograph entitled *Theorizing Desire: From Freud to Feminism to Film* (forthcoming, Palgrave Macmillan).

Michele Hammers is an assistant professor at Loyola Marymount University. She is a former lawyer whose graduate studies focused on rhetorical criticism, critical media studies, and social movement and public sphere studies. Dr. Hammers utilizes field research and interviews in her ongoing study of the ways in which the female body is perceived in various public and professional arenas. Her current research interests involve *The Vagina Monologues, Buffy the Vampire Slayer,* and the construction of identity in online role-playing games.

Jennifer Harris is an assistant professor in the Department of English at Mount Allison University. Since 2001, she has been managing editor of the Alphabet City book series, including the subtitles *On the Foreignness of Film* (edited by Atom Egoyan and Ian Balfour), and *Suspect* (edited by John

Knetchtel). She is also the co-editor with Elwood D. Watson of an anthology tentatively titled *The Phenomenon of Oprah* (forthcoming, University of Kentucky Press).

Patricia Leavy is an assistant professor of sociology and director of gender studies at Stonehill College in Easton, Massachusetts. She is co-editor of *Approaches to Qualitative Research: A Reader on Theory and Practice* (Oxford University Press, 2004) and co-author of *The Practice of Qualitative Research* (forthcoming, Sage Publications), *A Feminist Research Primer* (forthcoming, Sage Publications) and *Handbook of Emergent Methods* (forthcoming, Guilford Publications). She has published in the areas of body image, collective memory, mass media, popular culture and qualitative research methods.

Amanda D. Lotz is an assistant professor in the Department of Communication Studies at the University of Michigan at Ann Arbor. She earned a Ph.D. in radio-television-film and certificate in women's studies from the University of Texas at Austin in 2000. She has published articles in *Critical Studies in Media Communication, Feminist Media Studies, Communication Theory, Journal of Broadcasting and Electronic Media, Television & New Media, Screen,* and *Women and Language.* She recently completed a book, *Redesigning Women: Female Centered Television After the Network Era* (forthcoming, University of Illinois Press).

Susan E. McKenna is the director of the Research Literacy Center at Commonwealth College at the University of Massachusetts at Amherst. She has a master's in fine arts in photography and is completing a doctorate in communication. Her research interests focus on the connections among popular cultural forms, social identities, and daily life experiences with a specific focus on the ethics of representing cultural difference. Her photographic installations have been exhibited nationally and explore the interactions of language and the body.

Laurie Ouellette is an associate professor of media studies at Queens College, City University of New York. She is the author of several articles that discuss post-feminist theory and gender politics.

David Payson is an associate professor and chair of the Department of Communication at Keene State College in Keene, New Hampshire. His scholarly interests include television criticism and television production, particularly images of racial identity in television. He is the author of *Racial Minorities in Television* (forthcoming, Greenwood Press) and produces documentary and promotional videotapes for arts and educational institutions.

Diana Sandars is an assistant professor in the Cinema and Cultural Studies program at the University of Melbourne, Australia, where she currently coordinates the undergraduate courses on the film musical and television cultures. She also lectures at the Australian Center for the Moving Image Film in the Text Teacher Seminar Program. Diana was the guest editor for the "What Lies Beneath" edition of the online multimedia journal *Refractory* and has contributed to the academic journals *Australian Screen Education, Idiom, Metro, Screening The Past,* and *Sensesofcinema.* She has co-written a chapter with Rhonda Wilcox in the forthcoming anthology *Sounds of the Slayer: Music and Silence in* Buffy *and* Angel, edited by Paul Attinello and Vanessa Knights.

Jessica Lyn Van Slooten is an assistant professor in the Department of Writing, Rhetoric and American Culture at Michigan State University. Her other publications include articles on *The House of Mirth* and *Sister Carrie,* and Sophie Kinsella's *Shopaholic* trilogy. Still a devoted romance genre fan, Jessica is writing her own chick lit novel.

Elwood Watson, editor of this essay collection, is an associate professor in the Department of History at East Tennessee State University and currently the interim director of its Africana Studies Program. His work has appeared in *The Journal of Religious Thought, The Journal of Black Studies, The Journal of African American History, Endarch, Maine History, USA Magazine* and other publications. He is the co-author with Darcy Martin of *There She Is, Miss America: The Politics of Sex, Beauty and Race in America's Most Famous Pageant* (Palgrave Macmillan, 2004), the author of *Nothing but a Woman: African American Women in the Legal Academy Since Brown* (forthcoming, Rowman and Littlefield), and co-author with Jennifer Harris of *The Phenomenon of Oprah* (forthcoming, University of Kentucky Press). His co-authored article "The Miss America Pageant: Pluralism, Femininity and Cinderella All in One" received the Russel B. Nye award for the best article of 2001 in the *Journal of Popular Culture.*

Index

243